Self-Esteem Therapy

SELF-ESTEEM THERAPY

R. A. Steffenhagen

PRAEGER

New York
Westport, Connecticut
London

Copyright Acknowledgment

Figure 1.1 is reprinted with the publisher's permission from R. A. Steffenhagen and Ruben Fournier, "Self-esteem: A Model" in *Hypnotic Techniques for Increasing Self-esteem* (New York: Irvington, 1983).

Library of Congress Cataloging-in-Publication Data

Steffenhagen, R. A.
    Self-esteem therapy / R.A. Steffenhagen.
        p.   cm.
    Includes bibliographical references.
    ISBN 0–275–93193–5 (alk. paper)
    1. Self-respect—Therapeutic use. 2. Psychotherapy.   1. Title.
RC489.S43S73   1990
616.89'14—dc20   89–49159

Library of Congress Catalog Card Number: 89–49159
ISBN: 0–275–93193–5

First published in 1990

Praeger Publishers, One Madison Avenue, New York, NY 10010
An imprint of Greenwood Publishing Group, Inc.

Printed in the United States of America

The paper used in this book complies with the Permanent Paper Standard issued by the National Information Standards Organization (Z39.48–1984).

10 9 8 7 6 5 4 3 2 1

In memory of my wife Shirley
and
To my daugher Lori Ann Witham

Contents

Table and Figures

Preface

The present volume is intended to show the utility of self-esteem theory to therapy, from the empirical (quantitative research on drug abuse) to the theoretical (self-esteem theory of deviance), to its practical application as a therapeutic modality.

The book, although it focuses on therapy, will be of interest to social and psychological theoreticians as well. It is the third in a series of books on self-esteem, the first being *Hypnotic Techniques for Increasing Self-Esteem*, edited by the author; the second, *The Social Dynamics of Self-Esteem: Theory to Therapy*, by the author and Jeff D. Burns; and now the present volume, *Self-Esteem Therapy*. The first in the series was primarily a book dealing with the development of the self-esteem theory of deviance. This work is the result of the author's interest in drug use and abuse, especially among middle- and upper middle-class college youth. Most structural theories of deviance are concerned with lower-class deviants, whereas this not only deals with the middle- and upper-middle class but adds a strong psychological dynamic to such theories. This work is a synthesis of the author's philosophical background. The theory draws largely from the dialectic of Karl Marx and Hegel, as seen in Chapter 5, from the phenomenology of Edmund Husserl, the Social Conflict Theory of Georg Simmel, and the Individual Psychology of Alfred Adler.

The author's work on self-esteem is the result of his association with the noted Adlerian Dr. Heinz Ansbacher. It was Heinz who suggested that I write a paper explaining drug abuse (among college youth) in the framework of Adlerian theory instead of other traditional theories and it was his dynamic personality that sparked my interest in the

work of Adler. My background in social psychiatry under the care of
Dr. Marvin K. Opler provided the diverse background necessary for
the development of the present theory. It has been my good fortune to
have found many scholars interested in my theory. Such noted scholars as N. Danigelis, J. Harry, H. G. McCann, G. G. Milgram, W. O.
O'Connell contributed chapters on self-esteem and deviance to the first
book. This led to the proposition that self-esteem is the basic psychodynamic mechanism underlying deviance. Deviance (to deviate from
the norm) is both social and individual. The social deviances are generally the most obvious: rape, economic crimes, homicide, alcoholism,
and drug abuse. The individual deviances may be less obvious: including the subtle (minor neuroses) to grossly obvious (e.g., catatonic
schizophrenic), however, all social deviates are individuals and have
self-esteem problems. From my work as a therapist I began to see that
every client I had had a self-esteem problem. I have found that when
the client's self-esteem increased, the problem abated. It is my contention that if, as a therapist, you focus on helping the client build self-
esteem you will not have to, nor should you, focus on the problem. I
believe that one can help a client without ever knowing what the problem is if one helps him/her build his/her self-esteem. From my association with students I have found this to be true.

Chapters 1 and 2 are largely a condensation of *The Social Dynamics of
Self-Esteem*. For those who have read that work, this material will provide a quick review of the salient ideas presented there by the author.
For those who have not read it, the chapters will provide the ideas
necessary to understand the foundation of self-esteem theory for its
application in therapy.

Chapter 3 looks at current psychotherapies with an attempt to show
how self-esteem therapy provides a more simplified theory and to show
fundamentally that any therapy that is successful helps the client build
self-esteem regardless of the complexity of its conceptual development.
This chapter is not meant to disparage the other therapies but rather
to provide a simpler and more usable conceptual framework.

Chapter 4 provides the theory underlying the therapy.

Chapter 5 is designed to provide a number of modalities that can be
used to build self-esteem.

It is hoped that this work will be of value to our educators. Alfred
Adler promoted child mental health centers in Austria to help prevent
delinquency later on. Our teachers today can use the theory presented
here to help our children to build strong, healthy self-esteem and in so
doing help them to lead happier lives.

Self-Esteem Therapy

1

What Is Self-Esteem?

What is *self-esteem*? Before discussing self-esteem therapy (SET) we need to define self-esteem, nominally, operationally, and in terms of a real definition. It is imperative to distinguish between the nominal and the real definition in order to clarify the concept so that it can be used meaningfully within the therapeutic modality. Nominal definitions are a declaration of an intention to use a word as a substitute for another phrase or word. Adlerian psychology, the individual psychology of Alfred Adler, is a humanistic psychology, a psychology of self-esteem. Self-esteem is the very core of the personality and consequently the basis of all behavior, normal or pathological. Personality itself is an expression of self-esteem.

This emphasis upon clarity of definition is not an exercise in pedantry or an exercise in intellectualization, but has the goal of clarifying the most important concept in the therapeutic process so that the therapist as well as the client can gain a better understanding of the machinations that provide the underpinnings for observable behavior. William James (1890) formulated the simple equation: Success over pretensions equals self-esteem. This particular definition has been considered in greater depth in an article by Steffenhagen (1983). We need to look at the term's pretensions in order to gain an understanding of what was meant by James during that time period. By "pretensions," we mean here: intention, purpose or goal. Success with one's goals equaling self-esteem is inherent in Adler's work on the striving for superiority. Within the Adlerian framework an individual tends to evaluate himself in relationship to his goals, with the goals providing the basic motivational force for the individual. Goal setting formulates the basis for action. Adler's striving for superiority, then, is the movement toward goal attainment. Returning to James' formula, self-esteem then would be dependent upon the individual's success or failure in achieving the goals that he has set for himself. As we progress with our analysis we will find that the actual attainment of the goal is not the most important element in the perception of self-esteem, but rather the individual's cognitive process, his internal evaluation of the importance of· the goal, the means utilized for attaining the goal which is also a function of a time/place orientation. The following example will help to clarify this process: A student takes a course and sets a goal for himself of achieving an A. First, we will look at an individual who takes the course because he likes the subject matter, goes to class regularly, studies, puts in an adequate amount of effort and achieves an A. He/she feels proud of the A and, in essence, we may call this an ego boost or, in terms of our paradigm, the achievement of the goal enhances his/her self-esteem. A second individual has set a similar goal but is not particularly interested in the course, goes rarely, pulls an all-nighter, and also gets an A. In the case of the second individual, we have someone who has a very high IQ but also has set a godlike goal for him- or herself. This godlike goal is the result of the socialization process where he/she had been pushed toward success in an upper-middle-class family in which he/she had been presented with role models of people who had become very successful from rather meager beginnings and who had internalized the need to excel. In this instance the individual, as we said, achieves his/her A, but this does not guarantee self-esteem. When delving into the cognitive processes involved we find that he/she (1) did not particularly find the course interesting; (2) rarely went to class as stated; (3) used speed, pulled a few all-nighters, and was easily able to achieve the A. But there is no sense of accomplishment, "the course was too easy, I didn't really enjoy it, I rarely went to class, I didn't read much of the material"; he/she was relying upon his/her native innate intelligence and a crash study program to net him/her the A. Therefore, although his/her goal was to excel academically, there was not the sense of accomplishment that is necessary for the development of self-esteem. For a third example, we have a student who comes from an upper-middle-class family and who has been socialized to believe that good academic success is essential for later economic success. The parents have put emphasis on getting good grades and he/she has internalized these values. This individual, however, is not as innately intelligent as the students in the first two examples and although he/she worked hard, went to class, and put in a lot of effort, all he/she could achieve was a C. In this instance we find that the individual is working to capacity but again, because of emphasis placed by a broader society, he/she feels thwarted and self-esteem is lowered by the grade. In yet a fourth instance we have a student who is similar to the third paradigm, but who worked hard and performed in the C–B range. This student, however, had been taught to believe that the important thing is to put forth effort and to work to one's capacity. Here the individual's self-esteem is actually raised by getting a C because he/she sees the C as a satisfactory grade that he/she earned and was content with. Finally, we have a fifth student who again aspires to success but is inherently lazy. This individual, although desiring good grades, will not put forth the effort but is willing to cheat to get a better grade. In this instance he/she copies from a friend who sits next to him/her and also gets an A, which is accepted without qualification. The fact that the grade was not earned does not bother him/her as a different value system was developed in which the end justifies the means. His/her self-esteem is good because the performance is good, which satisfies both the academic requirement and the parents' desire for good performance. In all these instances we see that performance, achieving an A or not achieving an A, is not the issue which is involved in the development or the maintenance of self-esteem but the basic cognitive processes which are evolved in the evaluation of the performance. The development of self-esteem is not a simple mechanistic/behavioristic stimulus response process but is the result of an interpretive process that is highly involved.

According to Robinson and Shaver (1973), self-esteem is defined: "simply as liking and respect for oneself which has some realistic basis." Here self-esteem stands for a feeling or affectional state of consciousness—'I feel good about myself therefore my self-esteem is good'—thus self-esteem equals one's assessment and evaluation of oneself at any particular time. We will refer to this as a *nominal* definition; the difficulty with this definition in part is that it is time bound, meaning that it is a liking, a respect for oneself, that has a realistic basis but would have to have a reference point in time—further, any condition that would effect our emotional condition would also be effecting our self-esteem. Self-esteem would be extremely variable and would depend largely on the immediate environment and those factors in the environment that impinge upon us in a certain way. If a friend of ours compliments us on our performance in the weight room we feel good about ourself, we like ourself and we have respect for our performance. But let us suppose as we walk home from the weight room that we meet a friend who informs us that he/she has just read the grade list for our exam in the last class and proceeds to tell us that we received an F in an important chemistry exam. This knowledge of an F (failure) would have an immediate effect upon our evaluation of ourself. It would make it difficult to like and respect ourself in view of the failing performance.

It is important to develop nominal definitions in the beginning phase of theory development because we need to define words in such a way that they have meaning for us and can be used by others in a similar context. Thus far we have examined two definitions, Robinson and Shaver's and William James'. In both instances we have clearly shown that self-esteem is variable and subject to fluctuation based upon performance. In the case of William James' "success over pretensions equal self-esteem," we can see from our examples that we can be successful and have good self-esteem or we can be successful and have low self-esteem. In the case of Robinson and Shaver, liking and respecting oneself, even though rooted in reality, can vary tremendously because of the interpretation we place upon the performance. If we work and get an A and feel good about it, this helps the liking and respect we feel for ourselves. If we get the A and do not feel good about it, it does absolutely nothing to help us to like and respect ourself, in fact the A may actually work in a contradictory sense by increasing our feelings of inadequacy based upon our goal orientation.

We would suggest that in general, definitions of self-esteem are fundamentally nominal definitions and as a result of these nominal definitions the field of self-esteem research has been greatly curtailed by a lack of precision, that is, until we can define our key words more precisely, in terms of real and/or operational definitions, the effectiveness of our research is limited. Robinson and Shaver speak to this issue by stating that "no standard theoretical or operational definition exists." We concur with this observation and would contend that self-esteem research and self-esteem theory have progressed little since the formulations of William James and Alfred Adler. Further, we suggest that although William James is certainly one of the great humanist psychologists, his definition is influenced by a mechanistic or behavioristic interpretation. It is constructed as a proposition and as such is based upon the contention that when we achieve our goals we have good self-esteem or that when we fail in achieving our goals, we have poor self-esteem. But as we shall show, self-esteem is far more complex than a simple S-R (stimulus-response) proposition would contend. Nathaniel Branden (1969:110, 144), in his book *The Psychology of Self-Esteem*, says: "If and to what extent that men lack self-esteem . . . " and further speaks of pseudo-self-esteem. Can one live without self-esteem? No, all men have self-esteem, but vary in degree, high in the healthy personality to low in the mentally–emotionally ill personality. In Adlerian psychology one might suggest that all life is a function of building, preserving, and maintaining self-esteem, with suicide as the ultimate self-esteem–protecting mechanism. One cannot be alive without a sense of self; albeit, when one's self-esteem reaches a dangerously low level, the risk of suicide becomes imminent and personality aberrations are but a function of the preservation of self-esteem. Alfred Adler's work is the foundation of self-esteem psychology. Life is a process of striving after goals, all action is goal oriented, and the actor pursues goals that are consciously or unconsciously defined and are culturally inculcated through the socialization process. Life is action in which no action is the choice of action in itself. The motivation toward social action is the striving toward superiority (self-esteem). Robinson and Shaver point out that self-esteem and self-acceptance have been conceptually separated but that the actual correlation between the two is unusually high. To further emphasize the confusion in the field we would like to quote the names of some of the prevailing self-esteem tests cited by Robinson and Shaver: the Tennessee Self-Concept Test, Janus Field Feelings of Inadequacy Scale, Self-Esteem Scale, Index of Adjustment and Values, Jackson Personality Inventory, California Psychological Inventory, Adjective Checklist, Burgler Acceptance Scale, Phillips Self-Acceptance Scale, Self-Activity Inventory, Self-Description Inventory, Regression Sensitization Scale, Barron Ego Strength Scale, Brownfain Self-Concept Stability Measure, and Measure of Self-Consistency. These names in and of themselves indicate the degree of confusion that prevails in the field. We can show empirically that at least one of these proposed self-esteem tests does not measure self-esteem but measures a different construct. It is clear from the names of these tests that self-esteem has been largely seen as unidimensional or as containing one underlying component. Is it self-concept? Is it self-acceptance? Is it social concept? Is it self-actualization? We shall show developmentally that self-esteem is a vastly complex, multifaceted construct and only when the individual components are clearly understood and brought together in a unified measure will self-esteem research and/or therapy become productive. As indicated in our enumeration of self-esteem tests, Barron's Ego Strength Scale (1953) (a subscale of the MMPI) is considered to be a test of self-esteem. In *The Social Dynamics of Self-Esteem: Theory to Therapy* (Steffenhagen and Burns 1987), we draw out in detail the differentiation between self-esteem and ego strength and show empirically that these two terms are not synonymous. Robinson and Shaver further point out that self-esteem and self-acceptance have been empirically related but that in actuality self-acceptance, although necessary for good self-esteem, is not sufficient in and of itself to produce self-esteem. We would like to emphasize the same contention in regard to ego strength and we also would contend that although ego strength is a necessary component for good self-esteem, it is certainly not sufficient and definitely not concurrent or synonymous with self-esteem. We list 12 cases in which Barron's Ego Strength Scale and the Brownfain Stability of Self-Concept scores were looked at concurrently, and we were able to show that while it is possible to have good ego strength and low self-esteem, it is less probable that one have low ego strength and good self-esteem. In our development of these concepts we will show as we progress that ego strength is an entirely different concept from self-esteem although it is an important component of self-esteem. Generally speaking we will consider ego strength to be a measure of our reality orientation, in other words, an individual with good ego strength will have a good grasp of current reality, whereas an individual with low ego strength will have a poor perception of current reality.

Further, Barron's Ego Strength Scale is a good prognosticator of success in therapy. Individuals in mental hospitals with good ego strength have a good prognosis for success whereas individuals with low ego strength have a poor prognosis for success in therapy. We will further contend that ego strength itself is not a clearly understood measure and that a need for clarification of ego strength is also essential for a better comprehension of the more conclusive concept of self-esteem.

Ego strength as stated is an important underpinning of self-esteem. However, ego strength alone is not sufficient for the development of good self-esteem but is a necessary component of good self-esteem. We cannot feel good about ourselves or have good self-acceptance if our contact with reality is so tenuous that we cannot differentiate between our objective and our subjective reality.

In the *Social Dynamics of Self-Esteem: Theory to Therapy* (1987), Steffenhagen and Burns stated that our development of self-esteem is built upon the Adlerian tradition and is infused with the philosophies of Marx, Husserl, and Simmel. We depart from the mechanistic, behavioristic tradition in psychology. Mechanism and behaviorism in an attempt to become scientific became too narrow in their focus. Interestingly some of the new material coming out of the neurosciences is becoming increasingly supportive of the older humanistic tradition. Within the framework of a nominal definition, we would suggest that to possess self-esteem entails having respect for oneself and liking oneself as well. When we consider the word *liking*, we see that it includes such elements as being pleased with, having a fondness for, and enjoying. In conclusion, we might simply define self-esteem as "a favorable affectual state of consciousness." This suggests that to have self-esteem is largely to enjoy a positive emotional state of being. Low self-esteem would then embody many of the characteristics of a negative emotion, such as hate and resentment. It is not unusual to find an individual saying that he hates himself. Certainly this is a verbal manifestation of a strong negative emotion and extremely low self-esteem. A number of years ago when working with a student who had low self-esteem I had reached a point where his self-esteem had immeasurably increased and at that point his verbalization was "I used to think

Figure 1.1
Dynamic Model of Personality

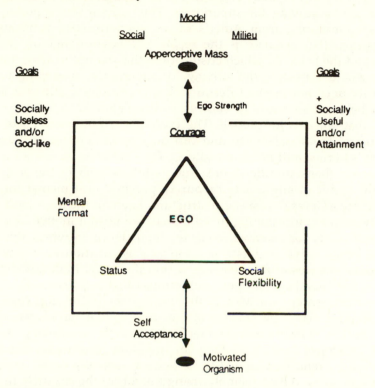

Source: Steffenhagen, R. A., *Hypnotic Techniques for Increasing Self-Esteem* (New York: Irvington, 1983), Chapter 5, "Self-Esteem: a model" (Figure 1) by R. A. Steffenhagan & Ruben Fournier, p. 50. (Reprinted with Permission.)

good self-esteem meant feeling oneself better than anyone else. Now I realize that self-esteem does not concern evaluating and comparing oneself with others but accepting oneself in a comfortable way." When he acknowledged liking himself and feeling better than others, we began to see that "to feel better" implies an affectual state. At this point suffice it to say we are suggesting that self-esteem, as traditionally seen, contains the components of emotion, a characteristic that has not been carefully analyzed.

Steffenhagen (1983) presented a model of self-esteem (see Figure 1.1) with Ruben Fournier. This model contains our earliest charting of self-esteem and contains the basics upon which our first attempt to operationalize self-esteem was developed. In discussing the format systematically, we begin with the first circle at the bottom, the motivated organism. Behavior is the function of motivation. Motivation is not the most clearly understood construct in psychology but for our purposes we will basically suggest that motivation is the result of what Adler calls a striving for superiority. This striving for superiority, a concept emanating from Adler's organ inferiority paper, posits the proposition that behavior is the result of a goal orientation. We set goals and the behavior which ensues from the attempt to achieve those goals would constitute the striving for superiority. A striving for superiority does not imply a desire to become superior but to evaluate one's behavior in terms of success and/or failure in achieving those goals that one sets for oneself. The goals that an individual sets are a product of the social milieu and can only be understood in terms of society's norms, attitudes, and values. The goal of becoming a successful banker (bank president) or a successful member of the Mafia are not the result of any innate or purely psychological mental function but accrue as a result of a social structure. Even on the most basic level of physiological functioning (need deficit) we posit a motive as a goal-directed drive: for example, consider fluid deficit in which the basic physiological drive is thirst, and the goal is satiation or a return to normalcy in terms of fluid balance within the body. In discussing self-esteem we must begin a priori with a motivated organism.

The next concept we wish to discuss in detail is the top circle, the apperceptive mass. The concept of the apperceptive mass is one of Adler's most important contributions to humanistic psychology. Adler's work developed out of the Freudian tradition historically, but as he broke with Freud he changed the Freudian unconscious to the apperceptive mass as well as deemphasizing the role of the sex drive in favor of the striving for superiority. The apperceptive mass, although similar to the Freudian unconscious, is a much broader concept than the unconscious. The Freudian unconscious has a certain etherial quality in that it cannot be grounded empirically and thus must be taken on faith. Many neo-Freudians postulate that 50 to 80 percent of one's behavior is due to or the result of unconscious motivation, that is, experiences that have been suppressed and repressed into the unconscious from where they then merge into the conscious in disguised form; for example, a student works hard, strives for good grades, but is flunking out of school. He says that his goal is to become a good photographer, that he wants to get good grades, yet he is unable to achieve this goal. Through analysis we find that he is a very bright young man, capable of A–B performance; he goes to class regularly and studies more than necessary for someone of his intellectual ability. During analysis we find that this student has had a major conflict with his father from the time he was very young. This conflict became submerged and much of it was buried in the unconscious. How does one explain the lack of performance when the behavior content suggests that this student should be doing very well. We find that this conflict, between wanting to do well and the submerged desire of wanting to punish the father, has created a barrier to performance. The student, through analysis, is able to realize that he is getting low grades to punish the father. This case is somewhat unique in that the father is a university professor well renowned in his field. The father, because of his own values and his desire for his son to do well, has constantly placed undue pressure upon the son to perform well. This constant nagging ultimately eventuated into a conflict, the conflict largely becoming buried, and thus we find that we have two opposing goals: (1) to do well in school, (2) to fail. The desire to fail is due to the conflict with the father, the desire to punish the father; since the father values education so highly, the best and possibly the only way to really punish the father is to fail academically, which would be a real blow to the father. When this particular conflict was brought into the open and the student realized that his lack of performance had nothing to do with his ability, his performance immediately improved and he began to get Bs and As. This is an excellent example of the unconscious and the role of the unconscious in determining the behavior of the individual. The analyst would say that examples like this prove and support the role of the unconscious. But the unconscious is still an etherial construct we cannot empirically define nor can we study the unconscious. Only through such examples can we support existence of the unconscious. However, could it be due to something else?

The importance of apperception is paramount to the Adlerian framework. We basically perceive through the senses and the sensory input is then interpreted in the brain, in the prosencephalon or the forebrain. The work on the split brain by Roger Sperry is beginning to shed light upon the role and function of perception in relationship to the differentiation within the hemispheres. We shall elaborate on this later.

We feel something and then the sensation of touch is then transmitted to the brain by nerve impulses, which then are interpreted. We feel something round and suppose it is a ball. But why a ball? It could be a small globe, it could be a ball or it could be a fruit. Why would one call a fruit a ball or a ball a fruit? With other cues this error would not be made, sensory input has its limitations. If we posit that it is an oblong ball and squeeze it, and it crushes in our hands so that we feel the sticky contents, we realize that it was not an oblong ball but an egg. However, if we were to add a visual cue, this error would not be committed. We need to emphasize that interpretation, even reduced to the naming of an object, is a function of past experience. We could not call a round object a ball if we had never seen a ball or learned the word. Knowledge is the function of experience and cognition. In this book we demonstrate the importance of subjective experiences in behavior. In phenomenology we learn that existence is by nature subjective and the basis of subjectivity is intentionality. Second, every intentional act itself relates to what is presented—our reality. Cognition refers to knowing or experiencing; existence itself is an individual thing where cognition apprehends the existence or the reality. The physical reality of an existence is relatively unimportant. The tree that exists in the forest that is one hundred miles away is totally meaningless to us. At this distance we can neither prove nor disprove its existence and furthermore the fact that it does exist and grows in the forest is totally irrelevant to us in terms of our own cognition. The tree that stands in front of our house takes on a totally different dimension: (1) We see it as an object; (2) we attribute a certain beauty to it; (3) we enjoy its shade; and (4) we have to deal with the leaves that fall during the autumn. That tree is not important to us objectively but only subjectively. If the tree is a magnolia, we may desire to cut it down because we get tired of constantly having to clean up the debris that falls from the tree. Yet one could not contest that the magnolia is especially beautiful during the flowering period. The subjectivity itself is the function of interpretation, and interpretation is the function of past learning, and past learning is the function of past action of the individual within the physical social environments. Further interpretation also becomes intricately related to the milieu interior and the milieu exterior, further compounding the simple act of seeing an object and defining, describing, or interpreting the object. Our interpretive process comes largely limited by our past experience and our natural social environment.

Thus far we have discussed apperception largely in relationship to our natural environment and to physical objects within the natural environment. Next we briefly need to examine the role of social interaction. Man is a social animal who can only exist within the framework of a social environment. He is not capable of surviving alone and therefore is dependent upon the group. A group is defined as simply two or more individuals interacting meaningfully with each other. It is this interaction which provides the basis for social knowledge; man learns as a result of social interaction. In this context, the work of Cooley (1909) and Mead (1934) is important but it will suffice for our purposes to say that interpretation is influenced by the group, especially our significant others, the peer group. What this leads to is the underpinnings of the concept of the apperceptive mass. The apperceptive mass is not an unconscious process, per se, but is the sum of all of one's past learning. The apperceptive mass includes everything that happens to us from the time we were born and it is probable that it contains information that we gleaned from the intrauterine environment. Data seem to indicate that the child, during the gestation period, has learned to respond to the tonal qualities of the mother's voice and also that stress and other bodily chemicals/hormones affect the child as well as the mother.

Without some knowledge of technology, a primitive individual is unable to think in terms of machines. These structures must be interpreted in the framework of a natural environment. Primitive individuals seeing a Cadillac in their native environment would have to relate to an animal since it has a certain structure and moves. The distinction is made between an animate and an inanimate object and anything that moves is then in the framework of an animate object, therefore a 1956 Cadillac with its big bullet shaped structures on the front bumper might well be viewed as a grotesque form of rhinoceros with its two horns and its lumbering charging movement. We also find that modern urban dwellers tend to think more in terms of right angles since so much of our environment is made up of perpendicular structures. The American Indian tends to think in terms of curves and smooth lines in which objects blend into nature; rivers bending slowly, trees moving and bending in the wind, birds flying in circular patterns, and so on.

The importance of the apperceptive mass cannot be overstressed. The differentiation between the apperceptive mass and the Freudian unconscious is, then, the fact that the apperceptive mass includes all past learning, not just repressed traumatic material. It is interesting to note that through hypnotic age regression, we can bring back incredible recall, seemingly going back to the point of birth and having the individual relate and describe his own birth process. While this may be a bit speculative, it is certainly accepted that age regression is legitimate and that an individual can bring back an incredible amount of material; seemingly nothing is lost, materials are merely buried in the memory of the neural structure of the brain.

Next, we wish to discuss the function and the formation of the mental format. Within the mental format we find a triangle the center of which is the ego. This ego is relatively similar to the Freudian ego which we will discuss in great detail as we progress with our development of self-esteem. The points of the triangle are made up of status, courage, and flexibility and we need to consider each of these concepts in order to explain the importance of the mental format in the development of self-esteem. First, we will look at status, one of the most important concepts in the development of self-esteem. Status may simply be defined as the position assigned to you by society and is grounded in the biology of man. The two most important differentiations in status positions are male and female—then come age differentiations, and others. Upon these biological structures culture is superimposed; we then take on by accretion innumerable elements related to the culture in which we live. Hunting and gathering cultures have status positions that differ from agrarian cultures, which in turn differ from industrial cultures. As man moves from the more primitive to the highly complex, the number and differentiation in status positions increase dramatically in relationship to the complexity of the culture. Status provides the basis for order within a culture. It is because of the expectations we have of one another that we are able to function in an orderly fashion. We speak of norms and values as providing the prescription for behavior but these norms and values are rooted in the status positions created within and by the culture.

We emphasize the importance of goals and that the striving for superiority emanates from the inferior position that man is born into and is constantly striving to reduce this inferiority. The extent to which he/she is able to achieve his/her goals enables one to attain a feeling of satisfaction, with that satisfaction providing the basis for the development of self-esteem. Goals are not created in a vacuum but become intricately related with culture and status positions. In primitive society we have ascribed status positions, meaning the culture determines and ascribes these positions for each individual and then the individual's role performance becomes the basis for the development of good self-esteem. In modern society we also have the phenomenon of achieved status positions which are accomplished through role performance. An individual may set a goal for which he has no formal education. He may observe individuals within the status positions, and through the successful performance of these behaviors he may then be awarded that status. A friend of the author's many years ago quit high school to become an errand boy at one of the local banks. This individual was very intelligent and highly motivated. He performed his role of office boy so successfully that he was promoted to a higher position and ultimately, through successful role performance in the bank and through additional evening education, he became one of the vice-presidents of the bank. College and the college degree offer a status position. The status of a college graduate can only be attained through the successful performance of being a student within the established institution. High status positions are achieved through successful role performance and accord an individual a measure of esteem. We suggest that it is impossible to have good self-esteem in modern industrial society without holding or achieving success in the framework of status positions. It is difficult to have good self-esteem when you are accorded the status of a failure, an incompetent, a weakling, and so on. How does the adolescent male feel when in the high school gym class he is always the last to be chosen for the various sport activities that are required by the gym teacher? It may be that he is uncoordinated, has no real interest in sports, but—whatever the reason—to have his friends all chastise him for being responsible for losing the game is not productive of good self-esteem. We suggest that competition as a social process is one of the most important modern social processes responsible for the development of good or poor self-esteem in relationship to success as a goal orientation. The high school jock or the team captain is in a very enviable position. High school jocks look up to the team captain and, as a result of this particular status position, he is also in a very enviable position in terms of the dating situation. Athletics is highly regarded within our culture, as evidenced by the salaries of our professional athletes. The athlete is seen as someone special by both the male and the female and consequently is accorded a very high status position. This emphasis upon athletics and athletic ability further becomes interwoven in the culture in relationship to the macho image. We place great emphasis in our culture upon the body and "the body beautiful." Without question the increasing emphasis upon being handsome or beautiful and having an excellent body provides the basis for the dramatic increase in anorexia nervosa among females and males. Obesity itself becomes an albatross around an individual's neck. The incredible number of fad diets, the volume of written material about dieting and weight control further attest to the importance of a lean, trim, athletic body. A myth has been created that overweight people tend to be jolly but this outward behavior is not necessarily what the individual feels. When all your male friends and companions use such derogatory remarks as lard butt, fatso, and so on, an individual has the option of becoming angry and retaliate (an exercise in futility) or outwardly laughing, or going along with the derision. We would further suggest that overweight people, male or female, generally have low self-esteem and that this low self-esteem is the result of a negative status position, a special position of being seen as obese within our culture. How far have we come from the primitive animal kingdom where the most beautiful, powerful, and graceful male bird or animal was most successful among the females? As long as our culture emphasizes materiality over spirituality we will find it increasingly difficult to ignore the role of the physique as extremely important in the development of self-esteem. The success of health clubs and spas further attests to the importance of physical appearance. In summary, we wish to emphasize that within the Western culture it is impossible to develop good self-esteem while lacking status.

The next concept we wish to consider is that of courage. Courage again is a concept that varies in its importance between primitive and complex societies. In hunting and gathering cultures courage often is in direct relationship to the status position of warrior and an individual is accorded a high status position in relationship to his prowess and success in both the hunt and in war. Courage is particularly related to the individual's behavior in relationship to the physical activities, that is, success in hunting and bravery in warfare. One cannot be brave unless one has courage; thus we see courage itself as intricately related to status and very important in the development of good self-esteem. In modern society courage takes on a somewhat muted but still important position. We speak of an individual as having the courage of his own convictions. What does this mean? When we believe in something strongly and someone ridicules or derides the particular value evidenced, do we have the courage to stick up for what we believe? Courage is not unrelated to physical activity in our culture but is probably more important in relationship to its mental component. We still have to have courage to engage in most physical contact sports, although such important sports as golf and tennis probably require less physical courage than do wrestling, boxing, football, and even basketball. Courage itself is intertwined with status positions in relationship to physical activities and mental activities in terms of belief systems. We suggest that good self-esteem can only occur when an individual has at least the necessary courage to stand by his or her convictions.

Our final concept that we wish to discuss in relationship to the triangle in the mental format is that of flexibility. Flexibility is far more important in modern society than it was in primitive society. In primitive society, because of the static nature of the culture and the rigid status positions assigned by the culture, flexibility was relatively unimportant. The society required strict adherence to the values and standards inherent in the fixed status positions. However, in modern society we find that the increased complexity requires increased flexibility. When we set our goals we may find that because of some impediment—physical, mental, or social—we may need to change or modify our goal if we are going to succeed. For example, let us say that we aspire to become a musical virtuoso but are tone deaf. In a situation like this it is impossible to become good, let alone excellent, at playing a musical instrument; we may be well grounded in technique, but there is no way that we an develop musicality of a sufficiently high order to contemplate a concert career. Further, we are not going to become a good pianist if we have lost a finger or have stiff arthritic joints. Self-esteem is built upon a striving for superiority, an achievement of goals. We are constantly called upon to moderate our goals or otherwise to alter them if we are to achieve success. Without flexibility it is going to be increasingly difficult to develop good self-esteem. As stated, flexibility becomes more and more important as society becomes more complex. I have often suggested to my students that they create a foundation for more than one economic pursuit. We constantly are being bombarded with such concepts as burnout, mid-life crisis, and so on. What we find is that when an individual locks him- or herself into a single pursuit and then for one reason or another that pursuit no longer provides the satisfaction or the individual finds that there are certain impediments preventing him/her from really succeeding within that chosen profession, he/she becomes increasingly unhappy. Although we all tend to internalize society's goals, success (central to the American credo) is not achievable by everyone. Not everyone is provided with the means whereby goals leading to success may be met. The concepts of democracy and equality have blurred the picture and in many instances provided the very basis for the development of poor self-esteem. Films, television, and the mass media in general extol the concept of equality, which suggests that anyone can become president, but it is not the case. Using this particular example we see that women thus far have not been accorded this particular opportunity, nor have Jews, American Indians, Blacks, Chicanos, or American Orientals—in short, that these people do not enjoy equal opportunity. Further, anyone under the age of 35 is by law prevented from becoming president; thus the opportunity to become president is considerably more limited than one might think. Financial backing is becoming a prerequisite for a successful political career. People growing up in the slums are not accorded the same opportunities as those of the middle and upper class. Even the quality of the school system is not the same in the inner city as it is in the more elite upper-middle-class suburbs.

This provides the basis for Merton's Theory of Anomie, a major theory of deviance which demonstrates the disparity or the disjunction between the means and the ends. This in itself provides a basis for low self-esteem. Good self-esteem is developed within a fertile social milieu. In a recent brochure on teenage sex I read a statement to the following effect, "Good self-esteem and a healthy self-concept are of ultimate importance in developing a healthy sexual orientation towards life." Good self-esteem and a healthy self-concept—are these two distinct entities? Certainly, as this statement implies, they are seen as two separate variables. We will show through our development of self-esteem that self-esteem and self-concept are not the same but that self-concept is an inherent part of self-esteem.

The next concern to be discussed is ego strength, the distance between the top point of the triangle and the apperceptive mass. Ego strength is a somewhat elusive concept at best. It refers to the effectiveness with which the ego discharges its basic functions. These functions are largely in relationship to the mediation between the id, the superego, and reality. It is further dependent upon flexibility, so that energy will remain for higher creative intellectual functions. Rigid and flexible personalities may both have strong egos, the difference being in how the ego discharges its function in relationship to conflict. Ego strength manifests itself strikingly in the area of conflict. The rigid personality maintains its ego strength at the impoverishment of the personality, whereas the flexible individual is able to maintain the mediation between the id, the super ego, and reality, allowing for energy to be used for other needs.

We have labeled the heart of the triangle the ego—the Freudian ego. Freud dotes upon the ego and presents a theory of personality built around a theory of ego development. Personality aberrations in his model are related to the function of ego defense mechanisms. In the Freudian model it is ego defense mechanisms, while in the Adlerian model they are self-esteem–protecting mechanisms. Laughlin (1970), in his book *The Ego and Its Defenses*, lists 22 major and 26 minor ego defenses. We will not discuss the ego at this point since the Freudian ego ultimately is not the ego that we will be working with in SET.

We have placed our goals to the right in Figure 1.1. Goals as stated, become the focus of the striving for superiority, the basic motivating force of human behavior. It is well known that Adler broke with Freud over Freud's insistence on the all-pervading existence of the libido or sex drive. In the Freudian model we can interpret all behavior in relationship to the fundamental drive, a drive paramount to the existence of all complex organisms, plant or animal. It is not the sex drive, but the sexual differentiation, the dialectic that is of primary importance. In our model, the striving for superiority becomes the basic source of human motivation. To the left (in Figure 1.1) we have placed Adler's godlike goals or unrealistic goals. These as stated are goals that are set so high that they are outside the realm of the individual's attainment. Not infrequently we find a neurotic disposition as the aftermath of the function of the godlike goal. If we are unable to attain the goals we set, we then are prone to self-degradation, self-criticism, or a lack of a feeling of self-worth.

The final component of the mental format is movement. Movement itself is a dynamic force in nature. Movement is change and change is movement. Statics, that branch of mechanical science dealing with bodies at rest, is a statistical concept at best. We can distinguish movement from nonmovement only in its most relative perspective. Solid bodies themselves are a product of movement in that all known material in the universe is composed of atoms and atoms are in essence miniature solar systems made up of "the sun" (the proton) and "the planets" (the electrons). It is not movement that is of importance in behavior but the degree and the kind that should be the focus of the therapist. A depressed person manifests what we might consider to be static behavior as distinguished from that which is dynamic. At the same time it must be acknowledged that all behavior is dynamic; even the decomposition of life is dynamic.

The development of the concept of the mental format (see Figure 1.1) is our first attempt to operationalize the concept of self-esteem. The points of the triangle presented in the mental format are status, cour-

Figure 1.2
Material/Situational Model of Self-Esteem

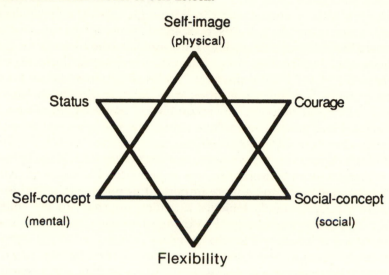

Self-image
(physical)

Status

Courage

Self-concept
(mental)

Social-concept
(social)

Flexibility

age, and social flexibility. In Figure 1.2 we see superimposed over this triangle another triangle comprised of self-concept, self-image, and social-concept. These latter three concepts derive from the material in Robinson and Shaver and the work of Brownfain (1952). The Brownfain Test of Self-Esteem is developed within the Adlerian tradition and is subdivided into self-concept and social-concept. Self-image is another very important concept in the self-esteem literature. From the author's work in counseling it has become increasingly evident that self-image is extremely important in the development of self-esteem. Self-image also relates to self-acceptance in that, as we have stressed, our culture places tremendous emphasis on the body beautiful, therefore, one's perception of his/her body image is inherently important in that overall development of self-esteem. Our second point in the triangle is self-concept, the mental or cognitive aspect of self-esteem and the third point, the social-concept, the cultural or interpersonal aspect of self-esteem. When we place the one triangle over the other we create a Star of David providing our first functional model for evaluating self-esteem quantitatively.

Our first self-esteem test (see Appendix B) first appeared in the appendix of *Hypnotic Techniques for Increasing Self-Esteem* (Steffenhagen, 1983). It is comprised of 27 questions and these questions are based on the model (the Star of David); self-concept is broken down into three questions on flexibility, three on status, three on courage. Self-image has three questions on flexibility, status, and courage, as does social concept. We evaluate self-esteem in terms of the total score and break it down into three main areas: mental, physical, and social. This test has high reliability and is found to have high validity as evidenced in experimental work done by psychology students at the University of Vermont. In two studies dealing with athletics they found that male athletes have higher self-esteem than nonathletes and that their highest subscore is self-image, physical. This makes perfect sense because athletes place great emphasis upon their bodies, the development of coordination, and muscles. The second set of students followed a similar pattern but controlled for sex, and they also found that women athletes, like men, had higher self-esteem than nonathletes. However, in this study women athletes were not higher on self-image, physical but rather on social-concept, the area of interpersonal relations. Athletics, for women, tend to be more important in relationship to interpersonal relations. Certainly athletics provide a mechanism not only for male camaraderie but also tend to develop an ease of communication on the interpersonal level for the female.

From the mental format we then developed the first Star of David, the first self-esteem test of 27 questions for measuring self-esteem. Robinson and Shaver (1973) have listed 33 tests of self-esteem and, as stated, we find these basically inadequate as they do not measure self-esteem in toto, but merely one or two components of self-esteem. The literature presented clearly indicates that self-acceptance is connected to self-esteem and thus these researchers have developed their tests around a particular concept that they see as fundamental or equivalent to self-esteem. We would contend that these scales are basically in the framework of nominal definitions in that they actually create a verbal definition or a declaration of intention to use self-concept in lieu of self-esteem, self-acceptance in lieu of self-esteem, ego strength in lieu of self-esteem, and so on. Current research has lost sight of the early work of William James with respect to his emphasis upon success over pretensions as equaling self-esteem and striving after goals. We need to define self-esteem nominally, in practical terms ("really") and operationally. It would seem from the current literature that we do have nominal definitions and through the creation of tests we are moving toward the operational but find a lack of meaningful propositional form in the creation of a practical or real definition. Bierstedt (1959, 127) suggests that "real" definitions are propositions affirming a given meaning of the subject and have three properties: (1) two symbols having independent meaning are equivalent, (2) they are true as are any propositions, and (3) they therefore serve as a premise for further deductions. From our mental format we have developed our first *real* definition: "Self-Esteem is the totality of the individual's perceptions of self, his self-concept mental, his self-image physical, and social-concept

Figure 1.3
Transcendental/Construct Model of Self-Esteem

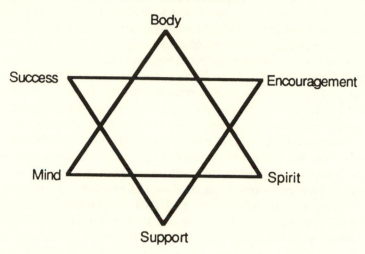

cultural" (Steffenhagen 1983, 69). These constructs have been borrowed from the literature in that they are terms which frequently are used as synonymous for self-esteem. We suggest that self-esteem is not a unidimensional concept but rather is a very complex, interrelated system of constructs and elements. Thus far, we have suggested that self-esteem is composed of three constructs and three elements, that is, six facets, and that this level of self-esteem is material-situational.

Borrowing from *The Foundation of Phenomenology* by Marvin Farber (1943), we find that there are three egos: (1) the world-emersed ego (material/situational), (2) the transcendental ego, and (3) the epoché performing ego. This approach removes the ego from the simplicity of the Freudian model. In the Freudian model the ego is concomitant with or equal to the self or the I. In this framework the ego is considered to have the function of the administrator of the personality and largely develops as a result of the id and the superego, the two conflicting components of the personality. From the mental format we have created our first ego, the world-emersed ego or what we call the material-situational ego (see Figure 1.2). Without question, in Western culture the world-emersed ego is the most visible and frequently is equated with the totality of the self-esteem.

In Figure 1.3 the transcendental ego, the components are body, mind, and spirit and the elements are success, encouragement, and support. Body, mind, and spirit are similar to the constructs in Figure 1.2 but are on a somewhat higher level of abstraction. As stated, the ego in Figure 1.2 is grounded in the lowest level and is most important in the

Western culture. Historians have commented that the mentality of the East and West shall never meet, at present the ego model of Figure 1.2 is of primary importance in the West and that of Figure 1.3 of primary importance in the East. We would suggest that the West has been caught in the Cartesian dualism of mind and body. Psychology in the West, in the experimental-behaviorist tradition, is largely concerned with this duality. We would suggest that India has created a similar duality, which is mind and spirit, giving little attention to the body. How often we find Indian swamis and gurus paying no attention to the physical body, even to the point of degrading it by their lack of attention. In Figure 1.3, the transcendental ego is on the higher level of abstraction, closer to the Indian tradition. The elements success, encouragement, and support comprise the second triangle. In educational literature we find that these three elements are considered of primary importance in the development of high self-esteem and they can be used by teachers to help develop self-esteem. They suggest that success is the most important element in building self-esteem in that when children succeed they begin to feel good about themselves. It is further emphasized that they should be encouraged and supported in their endeavors. These three elements can be used by teachers in the classroom situation and they can be used equally by parents in the home environment. Although important, they do not comprise self-esteem but are elements thereof. A number of years ago I had a student who was extremely successful in the college milieu. He graduated with a 3.9 and was an excellent student. In terms of his goals of doing well in college, he certainly had succeeded. His father had died and his mother provided all the encouragement and support that one could ask for. Further, he had received encouragement and support from his brothers and, on campus as a fraternity member, received encouragement and support from his fraternity brothers. At that point when I encountered him in therapy, he had zero self-esteem and was becoming so anxious that he could not have continued his college career. He would study for an exam with such intensity that he would spend 20 to 40 hours preparing for individual quizzes and ultimately agreed that this pace could not be maintained for the four years.

Figure 1.4 shows the epoché performing ego or the reductionist ego. We have labeled the epoché performing ego *ego strength*. Ego strength has been equated with self-esteem. It is possible to have very low self-esteem while having good ego strength. In Figure 1.4 the components are comprised of the three most important concepts of the Adlerian model: social interest [*Gemeinschaftsgefühl*], goal orientation, and degree of activity. The integrative elements are perception, creativity, and adaption, which will be discussed in detail below. First, social interest is conceived by Adler to be one of the most important components in

Figure 1.4
Ego Strength Awareness/Integration Model of Self-Esteem

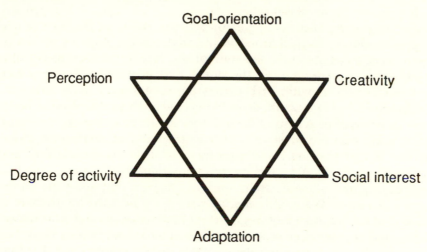

the development of good self-esteem. Adler suggests that it is impossible to have good self-esteem without good social interest and that it is only in the context of a cooperative social environment that man can develop to his fullest, and Adler further suggests that the degree of social interest is the barometer of the normalcy of the individual. Man is a social animal or, according to Freud, he has a herd instinct (the need to be with his own kind). It is only in the social context and within the social environment that man can survive. He is not a solitary animal, has neither the physical adaptability to live in a solitary environment nor the inclination to remain alone. Beyond physical health, man's problems are social and the function of society is to provide a rich social milieu within which the individual can operate. Adler suggests that there are four types of individuals in relationship to social interest. The ruling, the getting, the avoiding, and those who solve problems in a way that is useful to others. The first three are in the category of the socially useless and are in conflict with a life-style and a social milieu that demands social interest. Therefore, we consider social interest one of the most important Adlerian concepts in the development of self-esteem.

Next, goal orientation is of primary importance in the striving for superiority. From Adler's work on organ inferiority we contend that self-esteem can only be achieved through the striving for superiority or a reduction in inferiority. The concepts of inferiority complex and superiority complex are fictional, or functions of ideal type analysis. One can neither be totally inferior nor superior but, in order to attain a feeling of worth to meet the social demands of society, the individual sets goals as the basis for motivation. The striving for superiority provides motivation for social action.

Our final component is degree of activity. Adler maintains that the degree of activity is established very early in life and becomes a constant throughout life in the life-style of the individual. Degree of activity is extremely important in the development of self-esteem and has an interconnection with, or becomes an integral part of, motivation. An individual who lacks motivation becomes lethargic and expresses a very low degree of activity. Within educational circles one is constantly bombarded with the question of how instructors can motivate their students. Should teachers become motivators? This question lends itself to much debate. Should we motivate our students to do better or should we provide the means whereby they can learn if they have the necessary motivation. We might suggest that the concept of motivation is related to the transcendental ego—the elements of success, encouragement, and support. Certainly success, encouragement, and support can motivate the child. In the college milieu should we function as motivators or disseminators of information? We will not pursue this debate but merely point out that we believe the degree of activity is intimately related to motivation and that individuals who become motivated begin to manifest a higher degree of activity. Second, from a client-therapist relationship we are all aware that depression reduces activity to its lowest ebb. When an individual is depressed he or she manifests extremely low activity levels, even to the point of not wanting to get out of bed. Degree of activity is important in the development of good self-esteem and individuals who manifest a low degree of activity cannot have good self-esteem.

The integration elements are perception, creativity, and adaption. The role of the apperceptive mass is extremely important in the development of good self-esteem. Perception should not be equated with the stimulus but is the function of the interpretation of the stimulus object. It isn't what we perceive that is important but rather our interpretation of the stimulus object, and it is our interpretation, then, that becomes the basis for our subsequent behavior. Perception is a function of the apperceptive mass and is related to self-esteem. Self-esteem is a totality of these perceptions of our mental, physical, and social selves. Further, our perceptions can closely approximate reality or can be far removed from reality. An individual who is sensitive and introverted may perceive a remark made by another person out of context as negative, where an outgoing, extroverted, jolly individual may accept it as, for example, a pun. The stimulus object is the same but the interpretation of the object varies dramatically. Creativity is an interesting element of self-esteem. We stated that creativity in our culture is basically not allowed to flourish. Looking at historic anthropological data we see that most or all cultures, in creating the normative structure within which the individual operates, prevent the true development of creativity since creativity in itself is unique, different, and provides a basis for change. How much unique individualized behavior can a group or society tolerate before it becomes anomic? The balance between demanding an element of conformity of our youth and allowing them to develop creativity is a crucial one. Although one cannot allow total individualization of behavior, the prevention of creativity is a deterrent to the development of self-esteem and also deters cultural advancement. The important thing is not creativity or noncreativity but rather to set the boundaries and allow the individual to become creative within the framework of those social boundaries.

Our final element is adaption. By adaption we mean the ability to conform to the normative standards of behavior in society. How we adapt or don't adapt, per se, is of primary importance. S-R (stimulus-response) implies rote behavior that smacks of automatism. Certainly much of our behavior is the result of operant and respondent conditioning and we do not suggest that conditioning theory is invalid but rather that we become aware of why we do things, not just do them without thinking about the consequences of the behavior. The consequences may relate to our behavior's effects on others or to ourselves.

The first attempt to make self-esteem operational was to develop a self-esteem test based upon the model Marx (1964, ch. 1) provides. His theories in contemporary psychology offer three basic elements of scientific theory construction as observation that goes from everyday observation to experimental control. In experimental psychology, experimental design is the foundation for building a theory of behavior. In clinical psychology, the experimental design is not as applicable since each patient is unique; Alfred Adler called his theory Individual Psychology, as differentiated from Freudian theory which attempts to categorize and generalize. Adler emphasizes that we see each patient as individual and unique.

Constructs, which are the second element, are crucial to theory development. Cassirer (1944, 10) in his *Essay on Man*, lays the basis for a theory of behavior in a humanistic tradition when he defines man as a symbolic not a rational animal. Man is differentiated from the other animals in that man uses symbols whereas other animals use signs: Words are symbols and are used to express ideas; signs bear a one-to-one relationship with their referents, whereas symbols are open to an infinity of interpretation. A picture of a triangle can be taught to a rat so that it can learn to see the sign as a stimulus for food or pain (approach-avoidance) motivation, but it cannot learn to see a triangle as a symbol expressing the idea of triangularity. Behaviorism relies too much on sign theory. Earlier, we discussed apperception of which symbols are the key to interpretation.

A symbol may have many different meanings to many different people. A construct may be considered a high order symbol in that it contains a number of symbols—ideas within itself. Emotion is a word; it is a symbol standing not for one general idea but for a broad spectrum of things; it is a feeling state, a state of consciousness, a type of awareness, instinctive reaction and has elicited a number of theoretical formulations, for example, James-Lange theory, Cannon's hypothalamic theory, Papez theory (and its role in Freudian theory), and so on. Constructs have broad cultural meaning for the layman and have explicit empirical referents for the scientist. This further supports our contention that we need precise definitions if we are to advance scientifically. Self-esteem is a construct, is vital to Adler's Psychology, is paramount in the work of William James, and is undergoing a revitalization but still holds the distinction of being faddish and the brunt of satirical jokes. The comic strip Doonesbury lumps self-esteem and reincarnation regression together in the belief system of the airhead Boopsie. Here, Boopsie is on the committee of the California Task Force on Self-Esteem and is into channeling voices from beyond. Self-esteem is important in modern psychology as attested by the proliferation of tests purporting to measure it, but lacking clarity and precision (see Robinson and Shaver 1973). Our goal has been twofold, to develop a coherent theory of self-esteem and an effective therapy based upon the theory. In order to bring this to its proper conclusion we need precise definitions and a functional model that will provide the empirical referents.

Hypothesis, Marx's third element, is the final basic element to theory construction. He suggests that theories need to be sufficiently precise so that not all outcomes can be incorporated within a single theory—this is a major failing of the psychoanalytic model. Hypotheses are propositions stated in testable form and which provide the foundation for theory.

The first attempt to operationalize the concept of self-esteem was presented in *Hypnotic Techniques for Increasing Self-esteem* (1983, see p. 66). The mental format provided the paradigm from which the various components received a value.

Our first definition of self-esteem as stated was "self-esteem involves a totality of the individual's perceptions of himself; consequently it includes self-image (physical), self-concept (mental), and social concept (cultural)." Victor Barnouw presents five contrasting definitions of personality, and refers to three contrasting views of personality as the conflict model, the fulfillment model, and the consistency model and says that theorists may be grouped according to their conceptions. We suggest that self-esteem is the core of the personality and that it provides for conflict, fulfillment, and consistency.

Our theory derives from the work of Adler, Simmel, Karl Marx, and Husserl. Simmel's conflict theory of society carries over onto the individual level which then incorporates into our theory of self-esteem. The dialectic of Karl Marx is fundamental to our theory, all life is a dialectic process; a yin/yang, a movement between opposites, eros/thanatos, and so on. In Steffenhagen and Burns (1987, ch. 9) we discuss the role of contradictory tendencies in the development of personality. Our theory rests upon the self-as-object view of personality and rests upon consciousness of self resulting from social participation becoming the core of self-esteem, and integration of the three levels of ego.

The self-esteem–protecting mechanisms are similar to the Freudian ego defense mechanisms. Our contradictory tendencies provide the guidelines for behavior. These contradictory tendencies can become debilitating if out of phase. Conflict, fulfillment, and consistency are incorporated within the self-esteem theory of personality. Conflict is a motivating force; all life is conflict and conflict is normal, the goal of therapy being to get the patient to accept this conflict and use it in a healthy fashion. We discussed 15 conflicting tendencies and we pose this as the beginning model not a completed model. We have attempted to incorporate the three models within our self-esteem theory of personality.

The balance within the contradictory tendencies provide for the unique adjustment of the individual. They are dialectic processes and we see life as a composite of opposing forces. The fundamental dualism is physical and mental, while mind, body and spirit and the dialectic exist among these components. From our original definition of self-esteem in Steffenhagen (1983) to a model made up of three Stars of David, which we call Egos 1, 2, and 3. These derive from the work of Marvin Farber; the world immersed ego, transcendental ego and ego strength, self-awareness and integration. Our definition would now say that self-esteem is the totality of the individual's perceptions as portrayed by Egos 1, 2, and 3 and that personality is the integration of these egos. Within this framework one cannot simply refer to a normal or abnormal personality but to an integration special to each individual.

The author's original work concerned drug use and abuse among college students and was fundamentally quantitative in nature. The goal was to describe the social behavior and not theorize. The author then moved from a Freudian interpretation to an Adlerian perspective and attempted to explain drug use and abuse in terms of self-esteem, which became a self-esteem theory of deviance. The self-esteem theory of deviance was followed by an application of the theory to a therapeutic approach.

2
Self-Esteem and Deviance

Sociology as a social science is concerned with social action; in the words of Weber (see Parsons 1947, 88), it "is a science which attempts the interpretive understanding of social action in order thereby to arrive at a causal explanation of its cause and effect." Sociologists are concerned with deviance and have developed major theories of deviance to explain social action that deviates from society's norms. The six most important theoretical positions that have been advanced are : (1) the anomie theory of Durkheim, as developed by Merton (1938); (2) the differential association theory of Sutherland (1947); (3) the subcultural theory of Cohen (1955); (4) the labeling theory of Becker (1963) and others; (5) conflict theory, general and random, Sellin (1938) and others and (6) the classic Marxian position, set forth by Kennedy (1970), Chambliss and Seidman (1971), and others. These will be discussed briefly.

The focus, in sociology, is upon society and the group. In psychology it is upon the individual. The self-esteem theory is an attempt to meld the major sociological theories with self-esteem as developed from the Adlerian tradition. Steffenhagen presented his first paper on this theme, "An Adlerian Approach Toward a Self-Esteem Theory of Deviance" (1978). Steffenhagen (1983, ch. 4) presents an expanded version with an emphasis on drug abuse. H. Gilman McCann (1983, ch. 9) states: "In sum, self-esteem theory adds a psychological dynamic to social structural theories of deviance that helps account both for deviance on a large scale or by groups and for deviant individuals who seem to violate the norms of their associates as well as those of the dominant class." In the late 1960s, I devoted my time and energies to the empirical study of drug use on the college campus. Because of my specialty in social psychiatry, a part of that effort was devoted to individual and group therapy of student drug abusers. This dual interest in empirical research and applied therapy have provided the basis for the work presented by Steffenhagen and Burns in *The Social Dynamics of Self-Esteem: Theory to Therapy* (1987). The basic information will be presented again to provide the theoretical basis for an understanding of the development of SET.

In the initial stages of the research, the emphasis focused upon the sociodemographic characteristics of student drug use in an attempt to help understand the dynamics of use and abuse. Coupled with the sociodemographic information, the Minnesota Multiphasic Personality Inventory (MMPI), was used to provide an understanding of the personality characteristics of the college drug user. The focus was traditional and much of the information was explained in relationship to current psychiatric models. At this time the author became acquainted with Dr. Heinz Ansbacher and, as a result of this association, he reinterpreted the early research in light of the Adlerian model. This eventuated in the aforementioned article "An Adlerian Approach toward a Self-Esteem Theory of Deviance: A Drug Abuse Model," which attempted to provide a theoretical model.

The self-esteem theory of deviance emanated from the upper-middle-class college environment and was then expanded to cover a broad range of deviance. We suggest that a cursory review of the literature almost inevitably indicates self-esteem as a problem in the development of deviance. In *Youth and Suicide* (1977), Klagsbrun makes reference to self-esteem as a crucial factor in youthful suicide. In dealing with deviance, most authors will cite low self-esteem as a major factor in the development of the deviance.

The study of deviance is largely within the purview of the field of sociology. Deviance or deviation refers to conduct that departs significantly from societal norms that have been set as standards of behavior for positions in society. Deviance then refers to conduct outside these norms and includes such broad social categories as crime, delinquency, suicide, rape, promiscuity, family violence including child, husband, and wife abuse, drug abuse, alcoholism, and so on. These behaviors are then largely quantified and rates are then assigned to a specific deviance so comparisons can be made between groups (e.g., ethnic and or geographical) and over time periods. The major difficulty in assessing rates for these social deviances is the inability to assess accurately or determine the frequency of response. It has been suggested by a number of social scientists that most, if not all, of the rates assigned to these social deviances are portrayed as nothing but the tip of the iceberg. For example, with rape we see that the behavior itself is very poorly defined. The generally accepted definition considers imposing oneself sexually without consent on another person as rape. The category of date rape further muddies the waters. This gets particularly fuzzy if friends of the defendant have witnessed behavior by the woman which can be interpreted as provocative, suggesting that she would have been willing to participate in the sex act. If a woman openly solicits, she is by definition a prostitute and of course the client has not committed rape, even if he forces himself upon her. If, on the other hand, a wife makes it adamantly clear that she is not interested in participating in the sex act with her husband, we now refer to this as husband rape. Are the parameters clear? Of course not, and, furthermore, a woman runs a risk of becoming publicly censured when she brings charges.

Along similar lines, another deviance that we have not mentioned is that of incest, which is biologically, legally, and socially undesirable. Incest again is another behavior largely conducted within the confines of the home and most unlikely to come to the knowledge of the authorities. Doctors in an emergency room setting may become aware of such behavior. Many forms of deviance are largely hidden, therefore in essence the rates portray nothing more than the tip of the iceberg.

In reference to crime and delinquency, the incidence figures portray only the actual number of delinquents and criminals who are caught by the authorities and whose behavior has been defined legally as such. It is an established fact that the vast majority of all criminals and delinquents are not caught and that many crimes are not reported. This is proven by the fact that insurance companies pay out far more claims for burglary and theft than cases are actually reported by the city for that year. We could provide many more examples of the various forms of deviance to indicate that the vast majority of these deviant behaviors are neither detected nor reported.

Deviance can be compared over periods of time to indicate whether there is an increase or decrease and the extent of the change. In the area of crime and delinquency these changes are more likely to represent legitimate change, since the actual effectiveness of the law enforcement authorities is not likely to vary much over periods of time. Some inaccuracy may be the result of internal, political manipulations where the number reported is reduced to show effective law enforcement. It is frequently stated that child, wife, and husband abuse and rape are deviant behaviors that may not actually be increasing but appear to be only because of an increased consciousness of the phenomena and because more cases are being noticed and reported than were in the past. We suggest that, when dramatic increases are presented, the real situation is worse than that reported. It has been shown, in terms of sociodemographic data, that a child who is abused is likely to become a child abuser. If this is a legitimate assumption, then the actual data—number of cases per hundred thousand—should remain relatively stable. The actual rates should remain consistent. However, rape is occurring increasingly in our culture and the actual numbers are staggering. We also find that husband and wife abuse are both increasing. In the past it was largely in the lower class that we found high incidence of wife abuse, child abuse, and rape. Today, it is clear that family abuse seems to run the entire gamut of the social classes and that no social class is now free of this phenomenon. The rate of child abuse may have increased due to the fact that the category is now broken down into physical, emotional, and sexual. It would seem that emotional child abuse may be more prevalent in one social class and physical in another; nevertheless, these phenomena are increasing dramatically.

Within the field of drug abuse Dan J. Lettieri et al. (1980) present 43 essays on drug abuse, each presenting a separate theoretical perspective. This work is an excellent treatise on drug abuse in that it covers all the main theoretical perspectives in terms of initiation, continuation, transition of use to abuse, cessation, and relapse. The authors further break drug abuse down into theories that are derived from the various sciences, such as psychiatry, general psychology, psychology of learning, social psychology, developmental psychology, sociology, criminology, anthropology, biology, genetics, the biosciences, and the neurosciences. If this does nothing else, it indicates that there is a great deal of confusion regarding the causes of drug abuse. The present work developed out of a theory of drug abuse and then expanded to cover other areas of deviance. Initially, I found from my individual therapy that the only consistent element I was able to see underlying drug abuse was low self-esteem. One day while pursuing my student records I found I had two students with almost identical MMPI profiles but one was a drug abuser and the other showed no major deviation. The drug abuser had an I.Q. higher than 140, graduated with a 3.7 and went on to graduate school, however he was killing himself on drugs. The other was an undergraduate, had a 135 I.Q., was flunking out of school, but was not abusing drugs and showed no other forms of major deviation. As stated, the MMPI profiles were almost identical; further, each student had an identical ego strength score; the drug abuser had very low self-esteem whereas the student who was flunking out had functional self-esteem. The self-esteem measure that was utilized was the Brownfain Self-Concept Test. This accidental discovery serendipitously provided the insight for the development of the self-esteem theory of drug abuse. After going through many more profiles and case histories the author concluded that low self-esteem was always the basic psychodynamic mechanisms underlying drug abuse as deviance. Through his counseling practice, he began to see that all his clients who manifested major emotional difficulties had underlying low self-esteem. The self-esteem theory of drug abuse was expanded to a self-esteem theory of deviance.

Deviance from a sociological perspective is seen as being largely social since the sociologist does not work in that area of individual deviance. It is our suggestion that the form of deviance an individual will pursue will be the result of his or her social milieu, family, peer group, subculture, and so on. We suggest that, in the college setting, when we encounter deviance, it frequently takes the form of drug abuse and/or cult membership. In the lower classes, we would suggest, deviance follows a somewhat similar pattern regarding drug abuse, but instead of the occult we find delinquency. The choice of deviance is not accidental but rather the result of influences on the individual during the socialization process. Garth Wood (1986), in his book *The Myth of Neurosis*, suggests that society has perpetrated a conspiracy to expand the boundaries of mental illness and that the medical profession—the experts—have suggested that people suffering from an excess of life's problems need expert attention. His position is that if we are not ill, we are well, although we may be unhappy. We would not disagree with this particular assumption but would contend that an individual who becomes sufficiently unhappy to commit suicide is in need of medical attention and that we need to be careful not to overgeneralize. We take the position, in developing the theory of deviance, that all behavior that deviates from the norm is deviance, a self-evident statement, but that deviance is a societal form of behavior that is utilized by an individual for a special purpose. When an individual is reasonably well socialized into society's norms and finds that he or she can obtain gratification through behaviors that approximate the norms and that allow for the development of good self-respect, he/she has no impetus to develop deviant behavior. On the other hand, when an individual does not have high self-esteem he/she resorts to behaviors that may be inappropriate or self-defeating, but provide him/her with excuses for failure. The self-esteem theory of deviance will provide the basic explanation for all major forms of deviance, with rare exception. An exception could exist in the area of crime and delinquency and would be the result of a unique subcultural socialization process. The individual who grows up in a delinquent subculture and has internalized those values and norms might well engage in behavior espoused by the subculture and, to the extent that he/she has integrated such behavior into the personality, he/she could have high self-esteem. In *Hypnotic Techniques for Increasing Self-Esteem* (1983, ch. 9), H. Gilman McCann shows how self-esteem theory is able to explain deviances or exceptions that other major sociological theories are unable to deal with. As he indicates, most sociologists study the lower class and therefore most of the theories emanating from the field of study tend to explain only a limited number of deviances and rarely deal with neuroses or psychoses except to view them in terms of rates and the social structure.

The self-esteem theory of deviance is a social theory encompassing both sociological and psychological focuses. At this point, we wish to review briefly some of the more important current sociological theories of deviance and again briefly to indicate how self-esteem theory complements these current theories. One of the most important sociological theories of deviance is the anomie theory originally developed by Durkheim and expanded and elaborated upon by Merton (1938). Although the Mertonian version of anomie theory has been criticized extensively, especially by such researchers as Taylor et al. (1973, 105–109; 1965) it still exists as one of the important theories of deviance.

The basic proposition inherent in the Mertonian model is that deviance is a result of a disjunction between culturally determined goals and the institutional means for attaining these goals. Merton's theory, although structural, focuses upon the individual and his or her behavioral adaptation resulting from being blocked from obtaining culturally prescribed goals. The paradigm consists of conformity—accepting the goals and the means; innovations—accepting the goals but rejecting the culturally prescribed means; ritualism—a rejection of the goals but an acceptance of the means; retreatism—rejection of goals and means; and rebellion—rejection of goals and means and substituting new goals and means. Although anomie theory should be universalistic, Merton's discussion and focus deal with American society and its incredible emphasis on the achievement of material success. Without question, this paradigm does not apply to more primitive sacred cultures but only to more secular ones. We would suggest that Merton's paradigm is most applicable to the social deviances, crime and delinquency in particular. Retreatism does not serve as an adequate explanation of opiate or alcohol use. Lindesmith and Gagnon (1964), in reference to opiate addiction, and Snyder (1964), in reference to alcohol, suggest that anomie theory does not explain these two forms of deviant behavior—that anomie may result from the use of the drug rather than drug use resulting from the anomie. However, the use of drugs is a totally different phenomenon from drug abuse in our culture. The use of drugs, legitimate and illegitimate, is part of the very fabric of the social structure and their use does not imply deviance, other than normatively. In the case of alcohol, our society accepts and generally condones its use; in the case of marijuana, many young people on college campuses are users and in their subculture do not see the use of marijuana as deviance—certainly in no way is its use related to anomie. Within the self-esteem theory, we basically contend that the difference between use and abuse is a function of the amount of self-esteem the individual has. Being largely a structural theory, Merton's speculation only vaguely indicates the type of deviance that someone might express. Certainly the lower class is more likely to operate in the framework of delinquency or crime than the middle class. A retreatist might be a bureaucrat, as much as a lower-class person. Within self-esteem theory we maintain that the form of deviance chosen is not only related to the social structure but equally to the psychodynamics expressed within the family milieu. We further maintain that deviance cuts across all social class lines. Anomie theory considers the actor as a passive recipient and the form of deviance as the outcome of the disjunction between the means and the ends, whereas self-esteem theory is based on the process, the milieu-actor interrelationship.

The next theory we wish to discuss briefly is Sutherland's differential association theory which postulates, basically, that deviance is a learned behavior and as such is related to the individual's associations within his/her peer group or subculture. It suggests that the amount of time spent with the various groups would form the basis for the value system to be accepted by the individual and the behavior then would result from the acceptance of the value system. Sutherland postulates that these associations vary in frequency, duration, intensity, and priority. Within this framework, it is possible to be a normal deviant— normal in the psychopathological sense—or an emotionally disturbed deviant. Self-esteem theory suggests it is possible to be deviant in a nondeviant group, particularly in terms of the social deviance of drug abuse and of course the interpersonal categories of neuroses and psychoses, where the individual may be deviant although holding to the norm and values, the deviance serving as a compensatory mechanism. It is also possible for an individual to be functionally a part of a deviant subculture and yet, because of some unusual circumstance, have adopted the broader cultural norms and have good self-esteem and not be deviant. One's values and attitudes do not always reflect those of the group one associates with since in modern society, especially in response to the mass media, one is exposed to myriad values and attitudes complicating an otherwise simplistic picture. We suggest that self-esteem theory helps explain many of the deviations not explained within differential association.

In many ways, Albert Cohen's subcultural theory comes close to our self-esteem theory, implying that problems of lower-class youth may well stem from their standing in the classroom setting in which they are forced to compete with middle-class youth, whereby competition may well produce low self-esteem. We shall consider this in greater detail later in the chapter. A major weakness of the subcultural theory is that it tends to explain deviance only relative to certain subcultural groups and certainly does not adequately explain middle- and upper-middle-class deviance, especially the personal deviances.

Labeling theory is a much more comprehensive theory than the more structural theories and tends to imply that deviance is a function of the labeling process. Labeling itself may have a beneficial or a deleterious effect upon the development of self-esteem. Within self-esteem theory we stated that it is a function of one's evaluation of goal attainment.

Labels have the quality of stereotyping, stigmatizing, and generalizing. Self-esteem would effect the individual's response to the label probably more than the label would effect the development of self-esteem, although it is a reciprocal process. Certainly an individual with high self-esteem is more resistant to the effects of the label while an individual with low self-esteem would be more responsive to the effect of the label. Steffenhagen (1983) presents a self-esteem theory of homosexuality in the male. He illustrates the theory on the basis of two case histories. In the first instance we find a youth with low self-esteem who feels threatened by his sexuality. It is not unusual for male youth in our culture to feel threatened by the question: "Will I function adequately the first time with a female?" This individual then found it was much easier to allow himself to be picked up and initiated into sexuality by another male where he became the pursued rather than having to play the part of the pursuer. Self-esteem is a major factor in the development of a gay life-style. In the second instance we have a client who did not have low self-esteem, who became sexually active heterosexually at a young age, there being no indications of a gay orientation. In college he broke up with a young woman with whom he was sexually active. As a result of the breakup, of course, there was a brief diminution of self-esteem at the situational/material level. At this particular time, an advance was made by a gay male and he allowed himself to submit as a way of handling his sex needs. We then found that he went from a heterosexual to a homosexual orientation. The advent of his gay life-style promoted low self-esteem because of society's pressures which demean gay people. Within our culture one of the most cutting insults one can hurl at another male is to call him a fag. As a result of an improving self-esteem in both these cases we find that the first male moved toward a heterosexual life-style while the second adopted a bisexual life-style. We find that, according to labeling theory, being labeled gay can be detrimental to an individual's self-esteem.

Conflict theory as espoused by Marx sees conflict emerging from the capitalist society where profit comes from the labor of workers used to produce goods. In this instance we see labor in conflict with capital. A Marxist takes seriously the observations of the labeling theorists; they agree with anomie and subcultural theories which identify disjunction as a motivating force in the development of deviance. The roles of status, goal orientation, and the social milieu to self-esteem are all important to the Marxist as well as to the self-esteem theorist. In developing our concept of self-esteem we are particularly sensitive to the Marxist view. In *The Social Dynamics of Self-Esteem: Theory to Therapy* (Steffenhagen and Burns, 1987), we have indicated that our theoretical development of the Adlerian model includes Marx, Simmel, and Husserl. We are particularly cognizant of the importance of conflict in the development of (or deterring) good self-esteem. We strongly agree with Marx that the alienation of the worker from the means of production is particularly crucial to the development of self-esteem. Marx's dialectic is of eminent importance in the development of an adequate therapeutic model, whereas Simmel's work on conflict is crucial to our development of self-esteem theory.

The various sociological theories have been developed for the purpose of explaining deviance in culture. Psychology on the other hand does not concern itself with a broad cultural perspective but rather psychologists developing theoretical perspectives pertaining to individual deviances. The self-esteem theory of drug abuse presented by Steffenhagen was categorized under developmental psychology. It generally can be seen that within the two fields of sociology and psychology, sociology has developed broader theoretical perspectives for explaining a host of deviances, whereas psychology presents individual or limited theoretical perspectives in relationship to individual deviances. Psychologists explain alcoholism in the framework of learning theory, behavioristic theories, and so on, not conflict theory. Self-esteem theory in and of itself is a social theory. It emanates from the Adlerian tradition and attempts to pull together the disciplines of sociology and psychology in presenting a broad-based philosophical perspective.

Adler's theory of compensation on the physical level is similar to Cannon's theory of homeostasis. It would appear that overcompensation is most often beneficial in correcting a basic deficiency, whereas compensation may or may not be beneficial. The direction of the compensation is the key factor in determining its benefit or pathology. Compensation that takes into account social interest becomes beneficial, whereas compensation that is engaged in irrespective of social interest is detrimental. On this issue Ansbacher (1956) says, "Self-Boundedness [*Ichgebundenheit*] differentiates the individual lacking social interest, from the individual with social interest. The self-bound individual is unaware that the self would be better safeguarded in the preparation for the betterment of mankind." Social interest is a primary construct in individual psychology. In relationship to compensation it is evident that overcompensation that accounts for social interest is beneficial, whereas compensation or overcompensation that is engaged in irrespective of societies' best interests is detrimental to individual development of good self-esteem.

We have labeled compensation from the Freudian perspective as an ego defense mechanism to the Adlerian perspective of an organ inferiority correcting mechanism and now would develop our own position in regard to our intended use of the concept of compensation. Compensation in our paradigm will be viewed, not as a defence mechanism, not as an organ inferiority–correcting mechanism, but as a self-esteem–safeguarding or –protecting mechanism. In this framework all our social and individual deviations will be referred to as compensatory mechanisms. We use the term *compensatory mechanism* to distinguish our usage from the Freudian and the Adlerian, allowing for Adler's use of compensation in reference to inferiority. We use the term in the negative context. As a safeguarding or protective mechanism it is used to protect the self-esteem but with resulting negative consequences thus, while rape may be an extreme form of a compensatory mechanism, a mechanism to safeguard a fragile self-esteem with no redeeming qualities. Compensatory mechanisms safeguard; they do not help to develop, achieve, or maintain good self-esteem. Self-esteem therapy utilizes the concept of the compensatory mechanism as a foundation for understanding the modus operandi that will be used for a productive therapy. We are not concerned with the conscious or unconscious value of compensation but concentrate on its expression as a manifestation of weak self-esteem. Whenever we see compensation we know that self-esteem is low. As stated, we categorize compensatory mechanisms in terms of the social and the individual. This dichotomy is not precise in that there are compensatory mechanisms that bridge the gap between the individual and the social although ultimately all compensatory mechanisms have an individual component as well as a social. The classification of social compensatory mechanisms is on the basis of the behavior that is viewed as a deviation in society and seen in a negative context. Crime, delinquency, promiscuity, family violence, rape, alcoholism, and so on, are all viewed as social in that they have social consequences for society. Individual deviances such as neuroses and psychoses may or may not be seen as deviance by society. Psychoses that become debilitating take on the function and aspect of a social deviance. Schizoid personality characteristics that allow the individual to maintain a functional balance, albeit precarious, in society are not seen as deviance in the social context, although they may be marginally debilitating and painful for the individual. Neuroses are more often than not individual and may or may not have social consequences. It would be ridiculous to assume that we participate in our social deviances irrespective of personal pathology. One could not say that the criminal, the delinquent, the rapist, or the sexual deviant is individually normal or nonneurotic but is the expression of the behavior of a value system. Adler would contend that crime is an expression of low self-esteem in that it lacks social interest and that it is impossible to have good self-esteem without social interest. This allows for the classificatory scheme. The need for the development of good self-esteem is a basic condition of man. We have previously looked at various definitions of self-esteem and have postulated our own definition in which we see self-esteem as providing a foundation for the development of personality. Let's use an analogy: Think of personality as an architectural structure. When self-esteem is good, the architectural structure is sound and solid; when self-esteem is poor the structure is similar to that of a building where the outside shell or fabric is attached to a weak substructure. In such a case, self-esteem is always tenuous and easily shattered by any adverse external condition. In developing our theory of deviance we have postulated that all deviance is a result of low self-esteem and that deviance is a compensatory mechanism. We suggest the reader consult Ansbacher's *Individual Psychology of Alfred Adler* (1956, 108–110). Herein, we find the neurotic purpose as stated: the enhancement of self-esteem, originating in the masculine protest, the macho guiding fiction. This can only be understood in relationship to the particular cultural context out of which it emerges. The masculine protest is a culture-bound concept and we would suggest that it does not exist in various primitive cultures at all and, further, that our current mass media provide the maximum foundation for the development of this fiction. Adler, moreover, suggests that the basic sex drive, normal or perverse, becomes subordinate to this fiction. We would postulate that modern heterosexual pornography blocks the development of healthy sexual attitudes and values. It places the woman in the most degrading and inferior position where she becomes but a receptacle for male sexual input, she is a recipient for the most basic and lustful aspect of sexuality in the male. How then does the adolescent male distinguish between the physical lustful aspects of sexual satiation and satisfying, meaningful relationships. Further, modern pornography seems to imply that what might have been considered sexual perversions are now normal and to be enjoyed and experienced by the young male.

Adler says that humiliation that emerges from inferiority provides the basis for aggression and aggression is then viewed as a means to enhance self-esteem or goal superiority. Adler further states that pathological fear is always a fear of loss—we will say it is a fear of being unable to achieve the goal of superiority, the attainment of which is essential in the development of good self-esteem. Striving for superiority is the basic motivating force in life and the desire to develop, enhance, and protect self-esteem is the superstructure of all behavior.

Self-esteem can only be viewed in relationship to the function of homeostasis, an attempt to maintain the psychic balance.

Ansbacher (1956) characterizes safeguarding tendencies as the essential character traits of those neuroses which we have called compensatory mechanisms. Feelings of inadequacy and fear of loss provide the very foundation for the development of pathology. The compensatory mechanism is aimed at getting rid of the feeling of inferiority in order to enhance self-esteem which must be viewed in relationship to the masculine protest. Adler says, "The greater and stronger men and their size are made into the fictional final goal . . . " which brings us to the Freudian ego defense mechanism, upon which we wish to concentrate.

Fantasy is seen both in its positive aspect, as providing an avenue for planning and goal setting, and in its more insidious pathologic aspect of regressive unrealistic behavior, and may provide an unconscious component in motivation. In the Adlerian sense, fantasy is a crucial part of one's personality. Fantasy addresses the future since potentiality is a part of our striving for superiority; if it were not for the striving for superiority, fantasy would have no positive value. Fantasy can be an essential, normal, and productive part of life. Fantasy gives us a respite from reality. We then move to fictionalism, the 'as if' world which, though unreal, is as important as the one we call real or the actual world of the mechanists. In our theoretical work we discussed the importance of a phenomenological foundation for an understanding of behavior. The subjective world of the actor is the real world in that psychical phenomena exist both actually and intentionally, whereas physical phenomena are regarded as existing merely phenomenally and intentionally. Desires exist actually whereas sense sensations exist only phenomenally and intentionally. It is only the perceived content of the real world that we react to. In the study of society we come to realize that all social laws are enacted for the control of human behavior; they are society's purchase of social effects. Without getting into an in-depth discussion of emotions, it is obvious that our emotions largely result from our interpretations of the actions of others. We frequently classify emotion into two broad categories—positive and negative or pleasant and unpleasant. While pleasant emotions are generally considered beneficial to the mental health of the organism, unpleasant emotions are seen as detrimental. When an individual overreacts to a positive stimulus, he or she is creating an undue stress within the body; the effects of adrenaline are just as prevalent as in the case of the fight/flight reaction. In therapy it is essential to focus on the subjective component of the individual in relationship to the milieu exterior. Ellis's rational motive therapy would contend that neuroses are basically functions of the client's irrational beliefs and the goal of therapy is to get the client to see the basis of his/her neuroses and irrational beliefs, and to begin to develop a rational approach to behavior. We would contend that while this is a realistic and effective approach to therapy, it has certain inherent weaknesses in that irrational beliefs may well reside within the fantasies or the fictions of the individual and that certain irrational beliefs may be as productive and beneficial to good mental health as other negative irrational beliefs are destructive. The difficulty lies not in the construct of irrational beliefs but in the interpretation of the construct. The physical scientist, the social scientist, and "the esoteric scientist" may all differ on their interpretation of the nature of reality. The mechanist is objective-teleological within science and nomothetic, whereas the idealist is subjective-teleological within man and idiographic. This is an oversimplification of the differences between humanism and mechanism but clearly points out that each sees behavior as resulting from different factors and forces operating in the social environment. If a fantasy or a fiction is beneficial, then there is no reason to assume the client needs to change his or her reality organization to become better adjusted. On the other hand, it may be that the reality organization is of no major consequence and we need to focus on the subjective aspect of behavior.

As stated, we are not concerned with Freud's ego defense mechanisms, per se, as we have replaced the need to protect the ego with the need to safeguard self-esteem. However, there are certain Freudian defense mechanisms that are important in understanding the development of self-esteem. Compensation is a defense mechanism in the Freudian sense, and is, in our development, the key to our understanding deviance, since all deviance is compensation, a mechanism for protecting a fragile self-esteem. The mechanism we need to look at is denial. Denial is negation. If we do not wish to deal with something we can deny it or we can disown it, pretending that it does not exist. Denial itself is a primitive process, infantile in its development—normal in the infant but definitely pathological in the adult. As we grow, we realize we cannot deny the existence of reality and in this respect denial is intricately related to ego strength. In our paradigm, denial as a mechanism is an indication not only of pathology but of low ego strength. As ego functions become stronger, denial becomes less appropriate as a defense mechanism. Denial on an unconscious level is often imperfect and incomplete but on the conscious level denial is used to resolve emotional conflict and to reduce conscious anxiety. As will become increasingly evident in our therapy, conflict is normal and realistically should be used for the enhancement of life's satisfactions and not be resolved or minimized in its importance for emotional development. There are various forms of denial: denial for confidence in which the individual denies the existence of a perception in order to bolster his or her self-confidence (self-confidence being closely related to self-esteem). There is national or public denial in which we deny an event in order to enhance our feeling of mastery. This is particularly crucial in the culture today in the sense that we are living in a volatile world in which a nuclear holocaust is not merely a possibility but rather an impending reality. We would suggest that in many respects denial is a national defense mechanism utilized by all age groups in order to minimize a fear of impending doom. We tend to go blithely on our way as though this did not exist as a reality. Denial also is intricately related to suppression, by which means we put things out of our mind, and ultimately repression, whereby we displace memories to the Freudian unconscious. We will discuss denial in detail in our chapters dealing with therapy.

The next ego defense mechanism we shall discuss is disassociation, limiting our concern to its function as an ego defense mechanism, for it is a dynamic mechanism operating outside conscious awareness. In part, to disassociate is to remove oneself, or separate or detach oneself from a social milieu, situation, relationship, or idea. It is sometimes referred to as a fugue state, a flight from reality, a type of amnesia, and also as a type of depersonalization. We are particularly interested in that aspect of the fugue state dealing with depersonalization. To a degree, all defense mechanisms have a disassociative or disjunctive effect upon the personality. It is interesting that in breaking disassociative reactions down into their various components, we find hypnosis listed as one form of disassociation but without clinical symptomatology. We are not interested in the various aspects of the disassociative process but rather in understanding its effect upon self-esteem. We are interested in the aspect of disassociation as depersonalization, in which we detach ourselves. Originally dehumanization, was thought of as taking place in insane persons, especially in chronic maniacs and in melancholics. However, we find that dehumanization, as a process, is becoming increasingly prevalent and is a major element in the development of low self-esteem.

The final ego defense mechanism we must look at is identification, which we define as a mechanism operating on the level of the unconscious in which the individual tends to make him- or herself like someone else with whom she identifies. Early in life the child identifies with love objects and this is essential for normal healthy development. The media in modern times, especially television, have not always created the most ideal character images for identification. Many television programs are centered around violence. Often the particular hero is on the side of good and helps the underdog but we are still witness to brutality and killing. This identification is not only detrimental but often unrealistic in that television people are not real but actors whose scripts have been carefully edited so that we do not see these people performing the normal faux pas of life. Identification may well become the cause for the development of low self-esteem as well as the development of good self-esteem.

Next, we will focus upon the cultural factors that are responsible for the curtailment of the development of good self-esteem. If our culture were 'ideal' then each individual would develop good self-esteem and there would be no manifestations of social or personal deviance, no need for therapy. We have postulated that modern Western society has become so complex and so secularly oriented that it does not provide the basis for the development of good self-esteem. If this statement is true, then one might question the therapeutic value of intervention since it would be impossible to develop good self-esteem. We contend that good self-esteem can develop if we understand the mechanisms and processes that operate, a need to make the covert content overt. In understanding the deterrents to the development of good self-esteem we are provided with techniques we can use to help the client raise his or her self-esteem.

First we present a model utilizing the theory of Freud, Adler, and Becker in showing why modern children have difficulty developing good self-esteem. The Freudian concept we wish to concentrate on is the superego. The superego is comprised of the conscience and the ego ideal. The conscience is frequently defined simply as one's parents speaking the negative component through you; the ego ideal, on the other hand, is the positive component and should become the source of emulation. Christ might well be seen as the ultimate ego ideal for those of the Christian faith, representing a behavior that one should emulate. Becker has postulated the theory that modern society has lost its culture heroes or that through science, modern technology, and secularization we have given up our culture heroes. Culture heroes comprise the very fabric of our culture and are evidenced in all the myths and legends that we find in our European heritage. The culture heroes provide the material for the development of the value and normative systems of society. Society cannot exist without norms. As we have seen, Durkheim's concept of anomie or normlessness is a state of anarchy and chaos. In order for people to survive, they must create patterned norms—the guideposts for action. It is only through these expectations that human beings can create order. It is not uncommon in the psychiatric literature to find authors espousing the position that the neurotic and psychotic are only deviant by virtue of labeling and definition, in other words, deviance means to deviate from the norm. We further see, from a historic and crosscultural perspective, that in different periods of time the Volkgeist and the Zeitgeist will label behavior as abnormal, then normal, then abnormal again, or what is normal in one culture may be abnormal in another. A serious social problem in

Victorian England and even into the early to mid 1900s was masturbation. It was thought that masturbation would cause physical and mental problems. Today, it is considered normal; thus by definition, by label, that which was abnormal became normal and no longer a problem for the physician or psychiatrist. Further, the great anxiety about homosexuality in American culture is largely a function of a label. If we look at other cultures and different historic periods, we find that homosexuality has actually been the norm. Certainly in Greece it was accepted as a normal part of culture. We find, in somewhat similar fashion, the sodomy laws being upheld by the Supreme Court (July 1986) are an example of what is deviant by definition. Apparently the sodomy law of Georgia does not restrict sodomy to anal intercourse between males but also refers to the practice on the heterosexual level. There are also state laws that consider oral sex abnormal or deviant. If our culture heroes are polygamous, then polygamy is the standard as can well be seen in the history of the Mormons.

Culture heroes provide unifying paradigms in the culture. As we have stated above with the sodomy laws in Georgia and other states, the approved standards of behavior may vary by virtue of state statutes. By dispensing with culture heroes, we give up a foundation for the development of unifying normative themes or values. In the socialization process we have two main options in terms of child rearing: punishment and reward, and of course their myriad variations. As stated, the superego is made up of the conscience and the ego ideal, and the ego ideal is equated with the cultural hero. When we lose culture heroes, we lose our most important ideals in the socialization process. We have an option of saying you should do something because it is the right (ideal) thing to do or because it is not the wrong thing to do. What are we saying? We are saying that much of behavior today centers around not what is ideal, not "You're going to feel good because you have done something that your ego ideal would approve of," but rather that we either do something or don't do it because we're afraid of feeling shame, blame, and guilt if we do or don't do it. Do we help someone because we really want to help them, because, for example, this is what Christ stated as one of the most important propositions in his teachings, or because we merely would feel bad if we didn't do it? Even when we do the right thing, we can't feel good because we did it out of coercion, not because we wanted to. How do we develop good self-esteem? The superego no longer functions to our benefit. Following this line of reasoning, we would posit that many of our youth have low self-esteem and this contributes to their feelings of loneliness and despair, which are evident in youthful suicide. Further, we have failed to instill a (religious) value system in our youth. Most religions frown upon suicide. There are a few cultures in which suicide is considered acceptable but always under highly structured circumstances, such as among the Kamikaze in Japan and in terms of "saving face." Religion provides us with important cultural heroes that can provide a 'leitlinie' (the Adlerian guiding line) for social action.

When we give up culture heroes and instead use the conscience as the baseline for the socialization of our youth, we are achieving obedience from a negative perspective and cannot build self-esteem from the negative. In many ways the role of supportive therapies, therapies focusing on attempting to make the client feel good, are dealing with the negative aspect of socialization. This will become important in our therapeutic model later.

In our theoretical framework we discuss some of the major social factors that contribute to the development of low self-esteem. We cannot develop an effective therapy unless we understand what in our culture contributes to the development of good self-esteem or hinders its development. What we tend to know about child rearing or the development of a normal personality is largely due to pathology studies. What do we know about the functions of various parts of the brain? Again, it's basically through pathology that we are able to determine many of the brain's component functions. When we have a human being who, due to an accident, has a certain area of the brain injured or destroyed and find that certain behaviors are then eliminated or altered, we then can link that area of the brain to a specific behavior. The work on the right and left hemisphere is also a result of the cutting of certain pathways and the observation of behavior. In our theoretical development we are looking at institutionalization and social processes as they relate to the development of good self-esteem.

Two concepts we should consider are status and role, for these are fundamental to the very structure of society. In every society, from the most primitive to the most complex, a status system develops that basically delineates the position assigned to you by society. The most basic status positions relate to age and sex. These positions become increasingly complex as the nature of the society expands. Technology and industrialization have made the nature of status positions even more complex. All vocational and recreational activities imply a status position.

Role is simply defined as the dynamic aspect of status and consequently for each individual status one has a role that is required of that status. Social scientists have concentrated on role conflict as one of the important areas leading to emotional conflict in our society. When status is clearly defined the role is likewise clearly understood. However, not all status positions are equally clearly defined and consequently certain roles may be ambiguous. Furthermore, because of the complexity and number of status positions, roles may actually be in conflict with each other. We may play a superior and inferior role simultaneously in the course of one hour. It is essential that we keep these roles clearly defined or we run into conflict. Ascribed and achieved statuses further complicate the picture. In simple societies the statuses are ascribed by the society whereas in modern society, many of our higher status positions are earned through our individual efforts or, in essence, are achieved by us. When we play the role of a higher status position successfully, we add strain—perhaps we achieve that status or perhaps we do not. Sometimes this is permissible and sometimes it is not. Many examples might be cited, but consider the case of the man some years ago who, without medical training, pretended (successfully) to be a surgeon.

Abraham Kardiner (1939) distinguishes between two types of social institutions—primary and secondary. Under primary institutions he would place the basic survival functions, sustenance techniques, family organization, and the sexual prescriptions designed to regulate sexual behavior. The primary institutions are directly concerned with the survival of the species and are seen as natural by the individual and are especially important in shaping the personality. Secondary institutions are those that include religion, beliefs, and fashion, with our beliefs about God being modeled after the child-parent relationships. The idea that basic personalities are shaped by the primary institutions, and that these then form the secondary institutions of the cultures make up the foundation for Kardiner's work on basic personality structure. The concept of basic personality structure implies that every society produces a core personality structure which is inherent in its members. This idea was particularly prevalent during World War II when anthropologists were concerned and dealt with the basic personality structures of the Japanese and the Germans in an attempt to understand how to produce counterpropaganda. This idea of the secondary institutions is consistent with Becker's idea of culture heroes who can take on the aspect of deification and be treated as gods. The idea of a culture hero is important in understanding the development of the secondary institutions and in the development of a consistent basic personality structure. If we are going to develop a functional effective therapy we must be extremely cognizant of the importance of culture as it provides for the development of good self-esteem or hinders the development of good self-esteem.

Competition as a social process was discussed in great detail by Steffenhagen and Burns (1987). We shall briefly look at the various social processes and concentrated on competition as the key social process of modern Western society. Competition is effective in increasing productivity but on an individual level can be extremely destructive of an individual's self-esteem. Within each and every group, on each and every level, there is a number one on top and everyone else is somewhere between that person and the bottom. In athletic competition, in grammar school or high school, the boy or girl lacking coordination is always on the bottom and only the best athlete is the number one. Yet number one is only number one for an individual school, so that in rivalry with other schools there is a challenge to number one. Instead of the emphasis being on developing skills and enjoying athletic and calisthenic activities, competitive sports are used for exercise, thus creating a basis for the development of low self-esteem, at least in one area of one's activities. We hold many diverse statuses: In high school or college we hold a status in terms of academics, athletics, social activity, and so on. Competition can lead to feeling good about oneself, helping to develop good self-esteem, or feeling bad about oneself, lowering one's self-esteem. Our self-esteem tests were used by several psychology majors doing research on self-esteem to test the hypothesis that jocks on campus would have higher self-esteem than the nonjocks. This hypothesis proved true, with the jocks having higher self-esteem in the area of self-image (body concept), and female athletes in the area of social-concept or interpersonal relations. The social process operating in athletics is competition; consequently the competition can be used to foster or weaken self-esteem. One might further hypothesize that the nonjocks are probably those who are not as skilled athletically as those who go out for athletic activities.

Alienation is a relatively important modern condition that is destructive to self-esteem. Seeman, in his article "On the Meaning of Alienation" (1958), posits five types of alienation that are prevalent in modern society. These five types are: (1) powerlessness emanating from the Marxian view—the worker being alienated from the means of production; (2) meaninglessness—examples being found in the works of Adorno and Mannheim—creates a decline in the capacity to react intelligently; (3) normlessness—deriving from Durkheim's anomie, implies a condition where basic norms to guide behavior are weakened or destroyed. Such a situation can exist after a war or certainly in a state of revolution. In modern society, due to the tremendous changes in technology, transportation, mass media, standards in education, and so on, it is sometimes difficult to know what norms exist to guide behavior. Certainly the sexual revolution and its consequences might well be deemed the result of a condition of anomie or normlessness resulting from rapid changes in cultural standards; (4) isolation—another type of alienation which seems to closely approximate rebellion; (5) self-estrangement—the final type, in which one becomes estranged from oneself, and is unable to find self-rewarding activities. Self-estrangement is similar to Kierkegaard's "sickness unto death," or, in essence, the inability to die.

Dehumanization results from alienation and includes such ego defense mechanisms as denial, repression, and disassociation in that it contains elements of isolation of affect. If we isolate ourself from close emotional relationships, then we cannot be hurt when they terminate. Pre-World War II, the majority of people in our culture (as well as in European cultures—there, even more so) tended to be born, work, marry, raise their family, and die, within the same city and very often in the same general locale. Back in the 1940s, it was estimated that the working class in our culture generally tended to find a spouse within a five-block radius of where they lived. Although this may generally have been true for the working class, the middle class (especially those college educated) are now horizontally mobile and, because of this mobility, make and break relationships frequently. It is difficult for youth who grow up in the same city where they were born and went to college to understand the fragility of relationships. In the army and in college we meet new people, make close friendships, and then in a short time go off in different directions. We continue a correspondence for a short period of time, and then tend to become more distant. In order to deal with this mobility, dehumanization becomes the safeguarding mechanism by which we protect ourselves from emotional loss. When we become emotionally isolated we are protected. Dehumanization was extremely common in the army and it protected us from the sorrow of seeing our friends—close friends—being killed in battle or even just getting transferred. In order to discourage this feeling of loss, the army moved people frequently and kept them from developing close friendships; thus seeing a comrade killed, the pain was lessened. Dehumanization gave the loss more of a material nature, as when an object or thing is destroyed. Certainly the process of dehumanization is most destructive for the development of self-esteem.

The concept of personal freedom is destructive to the development of good self-esteem. We suggest that the concept of freedom as understood in our society in reference to political freedom, religious freedom, academic freedom, and vocational freedom, are all delusions; that there really is no freedom and that to postulate a society based on freedom is to hinder the development of self-esteem where the ideal and the real clash. We suggest in SET that the only true freedom that exists for man is a transcendental freedom, that which transcends a cultural reality. Freedom is a relative concept and of course the American has greater freedom than the Russian; but is this true? Eric Fromm in his *Escape from Freedom* (1941) creates the analogy whereby freedom may well be viewed as a freedom from choice. However, when we create a freedom from choice we do so by virtue of an authoritarian, totalitarian approach. Freedom itself means responsibility and consequently is contradictory. The greater the freedom, the greater the responsibility. Freedom and responsibility are both crucial in self-esteem therapy.

Time as a cultural concept is also important in the development and understanding of self-esteem. Modern society is built on time: Time means money; money means status; status means success. Time and space are two intricately related concepts: Space can be translated into time and time can be translated into space; for example, it takes one-half hour to go from point A to point B in a car traveling 60 miles an hour. The space between A and B is 30 miles or the distance between is one-half hour. Time itself conflicts with freedom in our culture. We are literally automatons controlled by a minute little machine worn on our wrist referred to as a watch. We allow ourself to become extremely upset and experience intense emotion, when we look at the watch and realize we are one-half hour late for an appointment. This is largely cultural bound, in that Spain and Latin American countries deal with the concept of *mañana* or tomorrow more cavalierly: What we don't do today we can do tomorrow.

Noise is a condition in modern society, the properties of which can have an extremely detrimental effect upon the human organism. Noise creates tension and increasingly more and more studies are proving the negative effect of noise upon production and the mental health of the individual. Noise has a detrimental effect on sleep; we learn not to wake up from the frequent roar of the subway train passing our apartment, but it does not allow for a quiet and restful sleep. We will not belabor this point but merely point out the fact that, since it has such an adverse effect on the individual, it is a condition in modern society that must of itself ultimately affect self-esteem.

Capitalism and industrialization are two concepts which we feel adversely affect the development of good self-esteem. In the framework of capitalism and industrialization we would briefly review our social class system and point out the inequities that exist that can provide an economic foundation that can hinder the development of good self-esteem. We need to look at the social class structure—upper, middle, and lower—to realize that 10 percent of the population in the United States controls about 90 percent of the wealth and also to realize that the members of the lower class do not have the same opportunities to develop their abilities within the competitive system (see Merton's work on anomie [1938]).

The mass media feed into a differential social class structure; they portray an imaginary social structure that then becomes accepted by the average American. In a chapter on anorexia and self-esteem (Steffenhagen and Flynn 1983, ch. 7) we pointed out the importance of the mass media in creating an illusion of the body image that has come to affect our youth adversely. Anorexia nervosa differentially affects the sexes; previously thought to be largely a late adolescence disturbance, it now occurs in 20- and 30-year-old women, as well as affecting more men. Anorexia nervosa centers around the idea of physical desirability; we would hesitate to call it an ideal. We have created an image of the body beautiful for the female (as a sex object) and the handsome male as a sexual aggressor. For women, unless they have sex appeal, they feel inferior. The male, unless he exercises his sexual prowess, feels inferior, so much so that physical communication—the sex act itself— has become a major means of communication among modern youth. In a case history (1983, 140) I indicated the importance of sexual prowess as a compensatory mechanism in maintaining a fragile self-esteem. The actual conquest, while promoting the male macho image and serving as a form of physical communication, was nonetheless far from adequate for the development of self-esteem, serving only to maintain a fragile self-esteem, a safeguarding mechanism.

We discussed earlier the importance of advertising both overtly and subliminally and its relationship to self-esteem. Advertising fosters sexism in our culture and again extols the "body beautiful" while helping to embed the basic values of the capitalist society and their acceptance. Subliminal advertising is inherently built around two themes, sex and death or *eros* and *thanatos*. We further suggest that advertising fosters superficial values, preventing the development of good self-esteem. These are but a few of the more important conditions of our culture which are detrimental to the development of good self-esteem as seen by the authors. Understanding the social factors that impinge upon the individual can help one negate the negative effects of these factors upon the development of self-esteem. We can protect ourselves and negate the effects when these conditions are understood. This is important in therapy, since the individual is a functioning unit in this culture and must deal with the conditions that prevail. Man is not an island unto himself. He must of necessity deal with adversity but, in relationship to the dialectic, we maintain that negative conditions can become a source of motivation and can be used positively for the development of good self-esteem. Freudian psychology, in which the unconscious is the underlying dynamic force of behavior, is both deterministic and dynamic. Within the Freudian model of id, ego and superego, we find in the development of personality that the id is frequently in conflict with the superego. This conflict results in *Unlust*, ego pain or displeasure. Anxiety plays a major role in psychoanalytic theory and when anxiety becomes too severe it becomes debilitating. In similar fashion, Karen Horney makes basic anxiety a central concept in her theory. However she feels that this basic conflict emerges from environmental sources rather than having the biological motives of Freud. Both psychiatrists would contend that environmental obstacles frequently block the individual's attainment of his or her goals. This blocking results in frustration, producing anxiety. Horney suggests that basic anxiety in the child results from any social condition that produces fear in the child and then needs to be solved. Horney further suggests that the child then learns to process this anxiety, eventuating in neurotic needs. Thus Horney, like Freud and most theorists, emphasized the role of conflict in developing neuroses and in the therapeutic process. In an Adlerian framework we would suggest that a major form of conflict arises from the individual's inability to attain goals that he has set for himself. Adler stresses the role of the more than lifelike goals, in other words, goals that are framed in a context that makes it impossible for the individual to attain them. Obstacles that frustrate our attainment of our goals are sources of frustration.

CONCLUSION

SET is a unique psychotherapy which has roots in sociology and psychology. As stated at the beginning of this chapter, my early specialty area was empirical drug research. Sociodemographic, quantitative research formed the basis for the development of my self-esteem theory of deviance. SET evolves out of the theoretical works of Alfred Adler, Karl Marx, Edmund Husserl, and George Simmel, plus a general grounding in sociological and psychological theory. At first the sociodemographic and quantitative approaches seemed somewhat disparate in that the research was fundamentally empiric and the therapy was grounded in traditional psychological theory. As time progressed, however, we began to find that all my clients showed the effects of low self-esteem.

Psychotherapies merge from the traditional grounding in psychology and psychiatry, and as such deal with deviance mostly on an individual level. If and when psychiatrists and psychologists attempt to deal with deviance, they do so in the framework of individual cases. An example of this would be the tremendous psychiatric and psychological literature developed around Hitler and the Nazi movement. In each case the individual was the focus of the theory. SET theory on the other hand is grounded in the sociological literature and originally was an attempt to develop a specific theory of deviance, a theory of drug abuse, and then began to include all deviances, individual and personal. It is our belief that as a theory of deviance, the self-esteem theory has a greater universality than the existing theories of Sutherland, Merton, Cohen, Marx, and others, and further that with this broad beginning it will have a greater applicability. We will attempt to show in our chapters on therapy how an understanding of the social structure is important in effective therapy on an individual level. We further believe that our theory will have applicability to educators and that SET will provide a rich source of material for the development of pedagogical techniques which we believe will provide the basis for the development of a new area of concern within the field of primary prevention in psychopathology.

As we stated, psychotherapies tend to merge from a theoretical basis, as was the case with Freud's psychoanalytic theory, Jung's analytic psychotherapy, Roger's client-centered therapy, among others, or are process-oriented and built around a technique devoid of theory. SET is a sociopsychological theory—a theory of deviance and a psychological theory, therapy based upon theory. It is our contention that most therapies, if effective, are so in that they inadvertently build self-esteem. Many therapists devote time and effort to helping their clients resolve their conflicts. We contend that this is an exercise in futility in that a conflict resolved is unique and that new conflicts will arise for which the knowledge of the past conflict will have no bearing, while new effort will have to be made to resolve it. We see conflict as normal and try to teach our clients to use their conflicts as motivational ploys to benefit themselves.

In Chapter 3 we provide a very brief overview of some of the major and minor therapies with an attempt to show how SET pervades them. It is not impossible for existing therapies to build self-esteem but without a clear understanding of self-esteem, it is haphazard at best. Our treatment is not meant to be exhaustive but relies upon the valuable work of Corsini for its model.

3

The Parsimonious Explanation

Psychotherapies may be classified into two groups, those focusing on theory and those focusing on process. Freud's psychoanalytic system is basically a personality theory whereby we see abnormal behavior as resulting from flaws in the developmental and/or socialization process. In juxtaposition to the psychoanalytic model, we might look at the eclectic approach, whereby the clinician examines the various systems and attempts to identify the various valid elements of each and combine these into a consistent whole which he/she then uses in his/her paradigm for helping the client.

Professor Randall Florey, noted for his work on adjunctive behavior at Hollins College, Virginia, commented that it is his belief that systematic desensitization, a therapeutic paradigm, is nonproductive theoretically in that when it works, it only works to the extent that the individual's locus of control is increased as a by-product of the therapeutic process. Locus of control is a point of major consideration in the development of psychoanalytic techniques. Corsini, in his book *Current Psychotherapies* (1973), lists 12 major psychotherapies and in his *Handbook of Innovative Psychotherapies* (1981), he covers 66 lesser but still well-known therapies. This vast proliferation of therapies has done much to muddy the waters and what we need to do is attempt to pull together the various therapies and develop a parsimonious explanation of therapeutic effectiveness and ineffectiveness that can function as a theoretical model for any therapy using any given technique.

Research without a theoretical orientation is sterile; theory without research is barren. Theory should guide the researcher and the function and results of the research should be to strengthen or weaken a given theoretical system so that the researcher begins to develop a stronger, more productive theoretical outline which can then serve as a guide for more productive theoretical and therapeutic endeavors. It is our major contention that in therapy, as in the physical and social sciences, we need a productive, functional, and theoretical focus if our therapy is to be more effective. We hypothesize that with the given proliferation of various therapeutic models, each of these models, as utilized by a clinician, is effective for some individuals, if it has the serendipitous effect of increasing the locus of control. Thus it is the locus of control which then benefits the client, not the actual desensitization.

Generally in psychotherapy, the emphasis has been upon the intrapsychic factors providing the basis for maladaptive behavior. The psychotherapist is usually seen as focusing on the intrapsychic factors, whereas to some extent the clinical sociologist is more prone to look at and emphasize the societal factors as providing the basis for maladaptive behavior. We would like to provide an example showing the interrelationship of the interpsychic factors in the development of maladaptive behavior and in the treatment of the same behavior. The particular example to be cited is utilized earlier in Steffenhagen and Burns' *The Social Dynamics of Self-Esteem: Theory to Therapy* (1987), but the emphasis there was different. The individual whom we are discussing is a client who had progressed to the point in the development of his maladaptive behavior that he was both suicidal and manifested all the characteristics of agitated depression. The background information was such that one could see that in the development period he lacked love and nurturance, having a father who died in a mental hospital and a mother who was an alcoholic. He was raised by relatives and was never given the opportunity to go to college, although he had the intelligence and the desire to advance his education. Despite that he had a reasonably good blue-collar job, his salary was not sufficient to cover adequately all the household expenses and frequently, in order to meet the bills, the grocery list had to be greatly curtailed. His family had to go without many of the necessities of the average middle-class family, which were luxuries for him. He had internalized a belief that he was genetically predisposed to mental illness, that he would either succumb to it and be hospitalized or possibly develop into a problem drinker. He was able to control the latter fear by not drinking at all. His work was of a routine monotonous kind that was tremendously boring and intensified the inner psychic conflicts that raged within him. Over a period of several months the individual was able to bring about great changes in his belief system and the depression began to diminish. Then we reached a plateau where further gains were not forthcoming.

I would see him weekly and we would make strides during the therapeutic session only to see these totally undone the next day (within a few hours at work). His job was so monotonous and so boring that it had a very destructive effect on him. It became evident that if further success was to be forthcoming, he would have to quit that particular job and find one that he would find rewarding. He did quit his job, went through about a year of intense change, including a rehabilitation program, and eventually was retrained in the area of the helping professions. The change in this particular individual was absolutely dramatic over a two-year period. He went from being an incredibly angry, bitter individual to one who was loving and caring with much to give to society. It should be noted that, in this particular case, the individual had the potential for developing into a problem drinker or an alcoholic, as well as a suicidal/homicidal manic-depressive. During the year of change he worked at a job in which most of the men were given to stopping at the bar on the way home. Feeling in need of the camaraderie, he found himself engaging in similar behavior, stopping at the bar and then not leaving until he was drunk. He found that if he went into the bar for one drink he could not leave until he was drunk. This behavior did not manifest itself until he was approximately 30 years old, because up to that time he remained a teetotaler. Since going through the job-training program and having found a job he truly enjoys, he rarely drinks, although if he does have a drink, he still tends to drink to excess. We believe that this case clearly identifies the function and the importance of the inter- and intrapsychic factors that affect the individual.

In the area of alcohol rehabilitation, it is already evident that the various models function differentially in relationship to the socioeconomic status of the client. The AA model (Alcoholics Anonymous) was originally founded by two hopeless alcoholics, a surgeon and a stockbroker, in 1935. AA has no specific religious dogma, but is founded upon a strong spiritual approach, a belief in a higher power greater than the individual. For many years the AA model probably was the most (if not only) effective therapeutic model for the rehabilitation of alcoholics. It is only recently that the prognosis for successful treatment has increased. It is generally estimated that, of the skid row type of alcoholic, success is limited to 5–10 percent of the population, whereas for those in business and industry, the potential rehabilitation rate may be as high as 80–90 percent. Counselors of alcoholics like other psychotherapists generally operate within a specific treatment modality with which they are comfortable and for which they have background training. Some utilize a single modality, whereas others may use a variety of methods.

In the treatment of alcoholism, a general systems theory has been developed that provides the most comprehensive and potentially most successful therapy for rehabilitation. A general systems theory includes: (1) the biological component of the organ body and the biochemical function of the body; (2) the intrapsychic; (3) the interpersonal; (4) the societal—small group, large group, and societal influences. The difficulty with the general systems theory approach is that it is so all-inclusive that the cost factor and the ability of therapists and rehabilitation counselors to work together on these various levels make it extremely expensive and difficult.

Alcoholism and/or problem drinking is merely a type of compensatory mechanism, a form of deviance, a type of maladaptive behavior. As we have stated, the type of deviance or the compensatory mechanism that the individual chooses or falls prey to is a function of the milieu-exterior in which he/she is socialized, pressures of the peer group, and further pressures from the Zeitgeist. A college student with a neurotic predisposition who comes from a teetotaling family background and goes to a Southern Baptist College is most unlikely to develop problem drinking behavior. However, if the same individual were to attend a larger state university and be thrown into a highly secular social group and brought in contact with other students for whom drinking is the acceptable norm in the campus environment, he might turn to alcohol. His private attitudes regarding drinking might well undergo a change and drinks, not necessarily as a rebellion against his parental upbringing, but as a function of a need to be part of the peer group. Further, drinking provides a ubiquitous approach to problem solving. It is a tranquilizer and provides an immediate release from tension. When we examine maladaptive behavior, we need to look to the social milieu in order to understand why the individual has chosen this form of compensatory mechanism to deal with his/her inner psychic conflicts. The value of the general systems theory approach is that it begins with the basic physiological organism and wends its way to the broader societal level. We have already mentioned Dr. Florey's comment as to the value of desensitization, but Dr. Florey also made a statement to the effect that he believes all major therapies have something in common, something parsimonious, and that someday someone will put it together. This is a pregnant idea, and it suggests the need for simplification within the psychotherapeutic field and simultaneously a broadening of its concepts and ideas. In the sense of broadening, we find this manifest within the general systems theory approach but in the need for parsimonious development we are still at a total loss. H. Gilman McCann (1983) discusses the role of self-esteem theory as a theory of deviance in relationship to other theories and how self-esteem theory is able to explain forms of deviance that are not explainable within many of the theoretical frameworks, especially middle-class deviance. In this chapter we wish to show how self-esteem ther-

apy (SET) contains all the basic tenets that exist within the other theoretical perspectives. First, we will look at the 12 major psychotherapies
in an attempt to show how self-esteem theory is addressed by each.
For our purpose, we will utilize Corsini's two works, *Current Psychotherapies* (1973) and his *Handbook of Innovative Psychotherapies* (1981) to
contrast SET with the other 66 psychotherapeutic models using the ideas
of the chapter authors as our source. The following 12 therapies will
be discussed in relationship to the ideas presented by the authors of
the chapters found in Corsini's *Current Psychotherapies* (1973).

TWELVE MAJOR PSYCHOTHERAPIES

In the development of the psychoanalytic model Freud attempted to
utilize a scientific approach to the development of a personality theory.
Ruben Fine (1973) defines eight major concepts in the psychoanalytic
model: The first is topographic, referring to the unconscious. Freud
emphasied the role of the unconscious as a motivating force in behavior. This unconscious is also utilized in the Adlerian approach as the
apperceptive mass. We have commented previously that the apperceptive mass is a broader concept than the Freudian unconscious, in that
it is not merely a reservoir of suppressed/repressed materials but is the
reservoir of all knowledge and experiences the individual has acquired
up to this point in time. The next concept referred to is the genetic
developmental, which includes Freud's sexual stages of the oral, anal,
and phallic. We do not deal with the sexual stages of development but
rather begin with the Adlerian concepts of inferiority, in which the
individual is born into an inferior position physically, mentally, and
socially. The striving for superiority is the basis of all motivation, it is
the striving for superiority or an alleviation or diminution of inferiority.
Freud's third point is the dynamic—the interplay of emotional forces.
SET itself is a totally dynamic therapy, focusing on the interplay between the intra- and interpsychic components. Rubenstein defines
Freud's fourth concept as economic, and speaks in terms of cathexis
and energy. In SET we do not deal with energy per se but rather utilize
Adler's degree of activity; in SET this degree of activity is not fixed but
is a function of perception. If an individual feels inferior, he will manifest a low degree of activity, thus the degree of activity is in direct
relationship to an individual's self-esteem. If he feels inferior, he has a
decrease in the available energy that he has to expend; if he feels good
about himself he has a greater reserve of energy to be manifested in
activity. The important concept is the degree of activity and not energy, per se. The fifth concept refers to the structure of the interplay
of id, ego, and superego. In SET we have a similar condition, in which
we deal with three levels of the ego; the world-emersed, the transcen-

dental, and ego strength. It is level three, the awareness/integration level of ego, ego strength, which is identified as the mediator between the world-emersed and transcendental levels of ego. Ego strength is equated with awareness, that element which has been identified by the philosophers as the real goal in life, and "awareness" in the Gurdjieffian sense. The sixth concept is referred to as interpersonal or transference. This transference is a projection of feelings and thoughts onto the analyst who represents a figure of the client's past. This transference then can be positive or negative. The need for transference does not exist in SET, due partially to the fact that we do not emphasis the role of the past but concentrate on the present and the future. The emphasis is upon the client's goals and not upon his or her past failures. The seventh concept is cultural and in part becomes somewhat concomitant with Kardiner's (1939, 237) basic personality structure. Each culture creates a certain basic personality type that can be distinguished from those of other cultures. The eighth point is adaptive and refers to the need to adapt to the environment. Here in SET we deal with adaption and place emphasis on the social milieu because it is only within the social milieu that the individual can reach a degree of functionality to achieve his striving for superiority. We believe SET includes all of Freud's important basic concepts while eliminating many of the pitfalls.

The Analytic Psychotherapy of Jung is discussed by Whitmont and Kaufman (1973). Simply put, Jungian analysis relies upon symbolism and is a reformulation of much of Freud's work. The emphasis of Jung is upon the dialectical interrelationship between the conscious and the unconscious as seen through the role of symbols, especially in terms of dream archetypes. The conscious and the unconscious interact in an attempt to compensate each other. For Jung, the personal unconscious is similar to the Freudian repressed unconscious and the nonpersonal unconscious includes the archetypes, which he considers to be inborn psychic predisposition for perception, emotion, and behavior. Jung sees man as being both masculine and feminine with each sex having a greater degree of his/her own sexuality present. The goal of the Jungian analysis is to move toward a greater wholeness or individuation. Further, for Jung the ego is the center of consciousness, the experiential being. In SET, we would also agree that the core of the individual is a function of the three levels of ego. Jung's emphasis on the dialectic is also crucial to SET. However, where Jung emphasizes the dialectic between the conscious and the unconscious, we emphasize the dialectic in relationship to what we call tendencies toward behavioral expression, such as aggression/passivity, and so on.

Client-centered Therapy, discussed by Meador and Rogers (1973), emphasizes the importance of a motivational force described as self-actualization; thus the goal of client-centered therapy is self-actualization. In SET the self-actualization is concomitant with ego strength (the total awareness) and once the individual has achieved the unity between the levels of ego, through ego strength, (the total awareness), he or she then becomes a whole person and the need for compensatory behavior is eliminated. One of the most important basic concepts of the client-centered therapy is the notion that if the therapist is positive, then change will occur. In SET we likewise emphasize the importance of the positive and diminution of the negative. Some of the concepts expressed in client-centered therapy include; actualization tendencies, feelings and experiencing, awareness, emphasis upon self-concept and self-worth, locus of evaluation, intentionality, and others. In SET we feel these basic concepts are largely contained within our three levels of the ego as manifest through the components of the unified self and measured by the respective elements. We would hypothesize that the concepts contained in the three models are organized in a tight theoretical framework, as against the loose conceptual framework of client-centered therapy. Further, in reference to personality, the client-centered therapist focuses on self-concept and self-worth. In our model self-concept is one component of self-esteem. Self-worth, we might hypothesize, would be contained under model two and be a by-product of the transcendental level of self-acceptance. The core of client-centered therapy lies in the empathetic relationship of the therapist to the client and the positive feedback that the therapist gives to the client, which we consider essential for the development of self-esteem. The client-centered therapist focuses upon the rationality of human growth, which is contained in the development of good self-esteem vis-à-vis the successful striving for superiority.

The next therapeutic model is the Rational Emotive Therapy of Albert Ellis (1973). It should be noted that RET draws heavily from the Adlerian model focusing upon the quotation of Adler, *"Omnia ex opinione suspensa sunt"* or literally, "Everything depends upon opinion." This summarizes the major focus of SET and RET, in that it is one's perception of one's accomplishments which leads to the development of the healthy personality. We have commented continually throughout the book that it isn't important how someone else perceives you in relationship to your accomplishments, in other words, I may think you have succeeded and compliment you on your accomplishments on graduating with a 3.8 grade point average, however, if you perceive the 3.8 as not a real accomplishment, in that the courses were too easy, you didn't do all the required readings, you should have learned more, and you wasted too much time, then in your opinion you have not been successful—leading to low self-esteem. RET basically includes the mental, the emotional, and the experiential, focusing upon the cognitive, emotive, and behavior change. One of the basic concepts is the uniqueness of man, a concept fundamental to Adlerian psychology. Some of the other basic concepts include the importance of suggestibility, the fact that people act on immediate perceptions and attempt to prevent transference; the use of role playing; the fact that emotional problems result from irrational thinking, and the focus upon the fact that people are responsible for their own thinking, that we indoctrinate ourselves, and that only we can bring about change in ourselves. RET, in that it draws heavily upon the Adlerian framework, is consistent with SET. However, we feel that SET has expanded the concept of self-esteem far beyond the original Adlerian paradigm and that through this expansion and understanding of self-esteem, therapy will be greatly facilitated. Without question, RET builds upon the soft determinism of the Adlerian model and consequently allows for change that can only be brought about by the individual, resulting from a change in cognitive endeavors. The appellative "rational emotive" indicates that the focus is upon rationality, a rationality related to a feeling state. RET contends that the rational individual does not 'esteem' and therefore does not develop disturbed personality parameters. We contend that to 'esteem' is universal, that human beings will never be totally rational, and should never attempt to be. SET accepts the nature of one's irrationalities and effectively deals with (not eliminates) them. We see no conflict between RET and SET as cognitively based therapies, only in the fact that SET has attempted to create a parsimonious theoretical structure.

Behavior Therapy, as developed by Wolpe, is discussed by Alan Goldstein (1973). The basic concept in behavior therapy is that behavior must be understood in relationship to past learning, present motivational forces, and individual biological differences. These three components are basic to SET. Past learning is certainly a fundamental part of the Adlerian apperceptive mass. Present motivational forces can only be understood in terms of current perceptions in relationship to goal striving, the basic component of Adlerian psychology. Adler's work on organ inferiority is relevant in relationship to understanding individual biological differences, such as an individual who is 5'6", 130 lbs., who strives to be a linebacker on the college football team, and is creating what we will call godlike goals and is doomed to failure. In order to set realistic goals, the individual's ability must be taken into account. Generally speaking, behavior therapy is based upon laws of learning and to this extent it has a practical base. The behavior therapist, as in SET, deals with the present and feels that a change in present functioning can produce long-lasting therapeutic results. SET allows for the past, deals with the present, and focuses upon the future. We suggest that there is no change within behavior therapy that cannot be accounted for, as SET can be largely classified as a cognitive-behavior therapy.

Gestalt Therapy will be reviewed briefly; we will focus upon the material presented by Walter Kempler (1973). Gestalt Therapy is built upon a phenomenological approach and to that extent is consistent with SET. We will examine some of the basic concepts inherent in Gestalt Therapy. The first is process, which is seen as a dialectic—a simultaneous attraction and repulsion (yin/yang)—or our shared emphasis on the role and function of the cognate dialectic. Kempler stresses the fact that process and action end when the two points of the dialectic emerge, which is consistent with our emphasis on the Hegelian dialectic. Further, the gestaltist stresses the fact that, in order to conceptualize, we need to polarize, which is consistent with SET's emphasis upon the dialectic and the need for an innervative correspondence. The gestaltist sees the task of therapy as a rearrangement of forces into a functional process, or what we have also called the functional unity of opposites, to bring about the innervative correspondence of ideas and to develop the functional unity of the three levels of ego. In Gestalt Therapy, awareness follows experience and thus the focus of the therapist is upon experience or becoming is the process of being. The gestaltist sees man as an integrated unity of processes which we call behavior and further sees energy and matter as the two major poles representing man. In SET, we would not refer to energy and matter as the two major poles but speak in terms of yin and yang and see people's behavior as resulting from the dialectical process. We have no basic quarrels with Gestalt Therapy but feel that it lacks a tight theoretical structure and that there are missing components which are inherent in SET. Without question we feel that behavior can only be understood in relationship to self-esteem and that, therapeutically, success can only be achieved to the extent that self-esteem can be raised. If the increase in self-esteem is built upon a solid base, then therapy will be successful in terms of long-lasting change. If, however, the increase in self-esteem is transitory, then the individual will quickly slide back to a former state of reduced functioning.

The Reality Therapy of William Glaser will be reviewed as discussed by William Glaser and Leonard M. Zunin (1973). Reality Therapy is based upon the basic proposition that the individual must accept responsibility for his or her own actions, which of course is totally consistent with the basic assumption of SET. The six basic propositions discussed by the authors are: (1) behavior is geared to meeting individual ends; (2) it focuses on the present; (3) transference is eliminated; (4) unconscious motivation is not allowed to excuse present behavior; (5) one is responsible for one's own actions; and (6) patients are guided to adopt better ways of achieving their desired ends. By contrast, we contend: (1) that there is nothing in Reality Therapy that is not consistent with the goal orientation of SET; (2) we focus on the present but add an additional component, the future, since goals are always futuristic and if we are to bring about a change in behavior, this change can only be achieved vis-à-vis an understanding of what the individual wants and desires; (3) SET also eliminates transference; (4) the apperceptive mass is never used as an excuse for behavior in SET; (5) the individual is always seen as responsible for his/her own actions, which is contained within the soft determinism of the Adlerian model; (6) the goal of SET is to bring about change by guiding people to develop new behavior patterns to achieve their goals. The concepts basic to Reality Therapy are: identity, goal clarification, and alternatives, all of which are inherent in the SET model. Also inherent in Reality Therapy are the pathways of love and self-worth in terms of needs, and delinquency and withdrawal in terms of identity. While we don't use these same concepts in SET, we would hypothesize that self-worth is but one component of self-esteem and that love, delinquency, and withdrawal in terms of needs and identity are not inconsistent with our model.

Experiential Psychotherapy is discussed by Eugene Gendlin (1973). Experiential Psychotherapy emerges out of the tradition of the existentialists and the phenomenologists. It focuses on the present and holds that we change only in relationship to the present. The basic concepts inherent within Experiential Psychotherapy are existence, encounter, authenticity, and value—all basic to existentialism and phenomenology. In essence, existence is seen as preconceptual and experiential in relationship to body sensations. Encounter refers to an interacting within the world; authenticity is tied to the mind/body, the person/environment, all as relates to past, present, and future; and value suggests a focus that is experienced itself as purpose, even though the present condition may be one of discomfort. Gendlin suggests that other systems can be identified fundamentally within two modalities; first, those older theories that are highly theoretical but include little on technique (he would identify these within the Freudian and Jungian paradigm); and second, he would classify as single technique types those that are short on theory and focus just on technique—usually a single, narrow, procedural focus. He further suggests that the single-technique types work only some of the time, which is what we hypothesized at the beginning of this chapter. We suggest that when they work, they work only because they have brought about a resultant increase in self-esteem and that this increase in self-esteem is due to the fact that the particular focus zeroed in on one of the weaknesses within our three levels of ego and that this is a purely change happening. Glendin further suggests that in the psychoanalytic model transference is the basic tool but that the theory does not in any way provide guidelines for the therapist for either overcoming or dealing with the transference that is projected onto him. The Jungian model suggests that the patient should negotiate with his dream archetypes but again provides little or no technique to accomplish this. SET is based upon the phenomenological foundation used in Experiential Psychotherapy while developing it further.

Eric Berne's Transactional Analysis will be considered next. Glen A. Holland (1973) provides the material for this brief overview. The basic concepts underlying Transactional Analysis appear to be motivation (based on needs), strokes (referring to the therapist's providing the encouragement and support), structure, excitement, recognition, and leadership. The therapeutic model is basically built on the stroking of positive behavior and largely ignoring the negative. Transactional analysis suggests that the client must be the one to decide what he is to achieve from therapy. This is clearly stated in SET, where we suggest that therapy begin with a goal clarification and that nothing can be achieved until certain goals are identified. Then therapy proceeds by focusing on what is desired, what exists, and the skills or abilities that either allow for the attainments of the projected goals or do not; therefore, one of the functions of therapy should/could be a reorientation of goal structure. In transactional analysis, again, we see that the individual decides what his or her life will be. This is called one's life script and is certainly concomitant with Adler's *Lebensplan* (or life-style). Berne suggests that there are three egos or ego states, which he calls child, adult, and parent. At this level SET departs from the transactional approach in suggesting that the egos of Berne are not egos at all but roles that affect the development of self-esteem. Berne defines the ego as a structured set of affects together with their resultant behavior. Fundamentally SET does not disagree with any of the basic tenets of Transactional Analysis except for placing less emphasis upon the aspect of the "games people play" and differences in ego formulation.

The next psychotherapeutic model to be considered is the Encounter Group as described by William Schutz (1973). Encounter, itself, is based on the concept of group dynamics and the basic concepts include awareness, voluntarism responsibilities, contact, naturalness, and an encounter culture. It basically suggests that the individual has a certain inherited potential for growth, but that this potential may be curtailed by physical or emotional trauma that interferes with the natural growth process. Much emphasis in the encounter approach is based upon emotion, a releasing of emotion, and change through emotional response which is brought about by the encounter group itself. Schutz suggests that the encounter group should be grounded in openness on the part of the participants, honesty, and self-awareness, with emphasis upon emotion and a present orientation. We suggest that the basic concepts underlying encounter are not inconsistent with SET but rather that encounter lacks the necessary theoretical structure of SET and changes may not always be directed optimally. The lack of understanding of the role of self-esteem appears to be one of the major hindrances to an effective therapeutic approach within encounter.

The basic theory behind Eclectic Psychotherapy as discussed by F. C. Thorne (1973), if one can call this a theory, is a selection and identification of the concepts and elements contained within other (not all) systems in an attempt to develop a more meaningful therapeutic system. Some of the basic tenets are: (1) that neuroses or psychopathology may be highly resistant to change; (2) that no single method is universally applicable; (3) that, in reality, maybe only a few therapists actually bring about real change; (4) that not only do we have the individual differences of the client in the Adlerian framework, but cognitions themselves may be totally difficult to evaluate in terms of therapeutic results; (6) that the eclectic approach may be even more difficult to evaluate than a single therapeutic model; (7) that ideology is difficult to assess, as is the need for quantification in order to be able to make judgments of therapeutic success. We would suggest that none of these tenets is inconsistent with our model. We have indicated consistently that therapy is difficult to evaluate and assess, that diagnosis is difficult and sometimes erroneous, that therapists are actually capable of making the client worse, and that many clients get better in spite of therapeutic efforts of the therapist rather than as a result thereof. We would basically suggest that the eclectic approach has the advantage of helping to gear the therapeutic process to the needs of the client, while its weakness is that it is not a consistent theory and as such makes diagnosis and evaluation doubly difficult since one cannot evaluate within a single framework.

The final psychotherapeutic technique to be discussed is that of Adlerian Psychotherapy, as presented by H. H. Mosak and R. Dreikurs (1973). The basic assumptions presented here have all been discussed in the first chapter wherein the differences between humanism and mechanism were presented. The emphasis is on social milieu. The basic concepts utilized are the social milieu; individual psychology; holism; the function of the conscious and the unconscious; the cognitive function life-style; social embeddedness; the striving for superiority; self-determinism; freedom of choice; emphasis on process rather than on diagnosis; the basic life tasks presented by Adler which include society, sex, work, and spirituality; self-coping, courage, and meaning of life. The position is put forth that the basic position of Adler is, of course, that the individual is not sick but discouraged. We need not spend any more time discussing Adlerian Psychotherapy since SET is basically an expanded derivation of this model. We find nothing inconsistent in the technique, as presented by Mosak and Dreikurs except that we would suggest that, generally speaking, Adler does not present a consistent theory of personality although he tends to provide the majority of the basic concepts necessary for the development of a theory. We have said that, within SET, personality is a dynamic configuration of the three levels of ego.

Corsini's book, *Handbook of Innovative Therapies* (1981), covers 66 individual psychotherapies and is not exhaustive. In the first part of this chapter we summed up the 12 major psychotherapies discussed in Corsini's book *Current Psychotherapies* (1973) and discussed each one of them briefly in reference to SET. We will, again briefly, look at each one of the 66 therapies discussed in Corsini's *Handbook of Innovative Psychotherapies* (1981) in a brief paragraph and then combine them in categories to show the relationship of these therapies to SET and to show that SET provides all the basic components inherent in the individual therapies. Previously we commented that many of the therapies provide either a reasonably coherent theoretical base with little reference to technique, or concentrate on technique while being relatively devoid of a theoretical overstructure within which the technique operates. It is further our general contention that these various therapies are successful to the degree that they raise self-esteem and not generally for the reason hypothesized within the frameworks of the theoretical structures. This tends to explain why there are successes within each therapy and failures. The individual therapies themselves are not geared to explaining success or failure but merely accept success as a reinforcement or proof of the fact that their theoretical structure is adequate. The converse of this is that each failure weakens the validity of the theoretical structure. It would seem that the number of clients receiving real benefit from any given therapy is relatively low and that the majority gain benefit only from the value of supportive therapy. We would hypothesize that many apparent successes are not truly successes, but rather short-term successes, and would explain this in terms of our conflict theory. We suggest that conflict is normal, that it can be used constructively as well as functioning destructively, as is usually the case for the client when he comes into the therapeutic situation. It is our contention that there is a need to reevaluate the conflict, that the individual learns to adapt to the conflict situation and not attempt to resolve it. Let us assume that the client coming into the therapeutic situation is manifesting dysfunctional behavior as a result of conflict. Let us further assume that the orientation of the therapist is to focus on the conflict and to help the client work through the problem in an attempt to resolve the conflict. And let us further assume that at the end of two to four months the client is able to resolve the conflict, feels better, and terminates therapy. At this point we would suggest that if we were to evaluate the therapy, we would call this a successful therapeutic endeavor. However, it is our contention that at a later point in time a new conflict situation may arise, different from the first, and that the client may be back to square one, in that he does not know how to deal with the new conflict situation. All of his work resolving the first conflict may be totally irrelevant to the new situation. Further, since self-esteem was not the focus of attention, the individual does not have the ego strength to work through or to deal with the new conflict and must return to the therapeutic situation. We feel that when self-esteem is the focus of therapy, two things are essential—one, that we raise self-esteem so that the individual has the inner strength to deal with the conflict, and two, that the individual come to understand that conflict is normal, that there are times when a conflict situation cannot be changed but must be dealt with or accepted and he/she is able to do this when he or she has good self-esteem. It has been our experience that when the focus of therapy is to develop self-esteem, we find that the problem is not a point of major issue. We have dealt with clients who have been depressed for years and who, within four to eight sessions, have bettered their self-esteem, resulting in drastically reducing or eliminating the depression. We have commented previously on one client who had been in a therapeutic situation for a year, came to me, and indicated that she was more depressed now than when she had started therapy. We began by using therapy to increase self-esteem and within six sessions the client terminated therapy with me, the depression was gone, and she was feeling great. Granted, while we cannot help all our clients in six sessions, we suggest that a successful therapy must deal effectively with self-esteem issues.

Now, let us look at the 66 innovative psychotherapies in relationship to self-esteem therapy and consider briefly how the focus of these various therapies can be parsimoniously subsumed under SET.

SIXTY-SIX INNOVATIVE PSYCHOTHERAPIES

1. Self-Actualization, as presented by Abraham Maslow, in itself implies growth, and when an individual truly becomes self-actualized we might suggest that he or she has good self-esteem. Underlying Maslow's work there is a basic theory which consists in the development of trust, growth, emotion, self, and dependence leading to independence. The focus is on helping the individual to restore a sense of trust in him- or herself rather than to cure an illness. It is our contention that this self-actualization and restoration of trust ultimately lead to better self-esteem.

2. Aesthetic Realism emerged from philosophy and was developed by Eli Siegel in 1944. It focuses on work and sees the self, art, and work as one. Evil is merely a form of discontent and is itself caused by contempt for the world. The focus is generally upon opposites, in other words, opposites exist within every facet of reality and we need to accept and understand these opposites. The similarity to the dialectic of SET should be evident.

3. Aqua-Energetics is a multidisciplinarian approach and evolved out of nude marathon work. It generally is atheoretical and is built upon the process of rebirth. In death the ego dies, in rebirth self-identity emerges. It generally focuses upon increasing the flow of energy and to that extent is somewhat similar to the work of Wilhelm Reich. Aqua-Energetics may help the individual develop an increased sense of self-worth and, accordingly, would be successful because of the increase in self-esteem. However, without a broader focus, it is questionable whether self-esteem will truly increase, or which facet or component of self-esteem might be ignored within that particular process.

4. Art Therapy is based upon the theory that art, as a form of spontaneous expression, releases unconscious material. The focus, here, is psychoanalytic, and suggests that most neurotics express problems through their art. Their emphasis on polarity is similar to the dialectic feature of SET. One goal of Art Therapy is to strengthen the ego but there is no emphasis upon building self-esteem. It is psychoanalytic in focus and does not suggest how these goals will be accomplished.

5. Autogenic Training is generally associated with the work of Oscar Vogt in Germany in the late 1800s and early 1900s. It is generally based upon studies of sleep and hypnosis and is a forerunner of the current work in the area of autonomic nervous system control through relaxation. It uses positive affirmations and also focuses on the use of the white light as a healing component. We suggest that any success would be haphazard, since there is no theoretical focus to the therapy.

6. Biofeedback is itself a process and in essence goes back to Zen Buddhism. It focuses upon the body in relationship to the ecto-, meso-, and endoderm and suggests that the client must accept the body and its relationship to thought and emotion. Thus, when we learn to control emotion we can change bodily functions.

7. Body Therapy has a rather vague theoretical focus. It builds upon the work of Eastern cultures, assumes energy and matter to be interchangeable. Under body therapies we might include yoga, aikido, t'ai chi ch'uan, acupuncture, rolfing, and rebirthing. The general theory calls for a psycho-structural balancing in the organism and sees the personality as a composite of ego states. The goal or focus of Body Therapy is to return to the *Solham* which means "That I am." It basically postulates that the true or perfect state, "That I am," is concealed

within *Ko/ham*, "Who am I?"—and thus the purpose is to return to the original state of perfection, *So/ham*. It suggests an integration of mind, body, and emotion, basically consistent with SET.

8. Brief Therapy # 1 generally focuses upon symptoms and an alleviation thereof. It is built upon the premise that dysfunction is a result of social inaction and persists as long as the conflict situation persists. It is based upon Bertrand Russell's theory of logical types and suggests that you teach the client to solve easier problems and ultimately he or she will progress to solve harder problems. SET also focuses on the alleviation of symptoms but we feel that this is achieved through building self-esteem.

9. Brief Therapy #2 is similar to # 1 and generally suggests that life's problems result from: (1)denial, (2) trying to solve problems that cannot be solved, and (3) taking wrong action. It suggests that the way of working with these problems is to operationalize the problem, devise a plan of action, implement the plan, and terminate the problem. This is fine to the extent that the individual has sufficient good self-esteem and sufficient ego strength to follow through with the proposed solution.

10. Cognitive Behavior Therapy is built upon conditioning and learning theory and generally focuses on problem solution. We would suggest that this particular approach would have merit only to the extent that the individual has the self-esteem to operate on a cognitive level and work within the modality.

11. Comprehensive Relaxation Training is nothing but a process, a composite of many relaxation techniques. Further, it emphasizes the importance of abstinence from a variety of foods and beverages that may have an adverse effect upon the body. The focus or goal is on reducing stress.

12. Conditioned Reflex Therapy emerges from the work of Pavlov, Bechterev, Watson, and Hall. It generally utilizes autohypnosis and systematic desensitization. We suggest that this technique is successful only to the extent that the locus of control is increased, albeit accidentally, as a result of the therapeutic endeavor.

13. Conflict Resolution Therapy suggests basically that psychopathology results from or is a by-product of conflict, and so the focus is conflict resolution. The general emphasis is on increasing self-esteem, which, of course, is the core of SET. We would suggest that its weakness lies in its inaccurate focus on conflict resolution and a lack of clear understanding of the complexities of self-esteem.

14. Covert Conditioning Therapy likewise addresses conflict and resolution, and focuses on behavior modification using mime and imagery, the assumption being that when covert psychological and physiological changes are made, overt behavior can be changed.

15. Creative Aggression is based upon frustration-aggression hypotheses and suggests that aggression can be used to bring about change. It generally postulates that two opposing life-styles, the hawkish and the dovish, interfere with self-actualization and the focus is ultimately upon development of self. It lacks a major theoretical focus, however. The process utilizes the marathon group as a vehicle for change.

16. Crisis Management is a form of short-term therapy which focuses on the immediate crisis in an attempt to reduce trauma and thus bring the client back to a precrisis level of functioning. It lacks both theory and process.

17. Dance Therapy focuses on the mind and body and utilizes dance as a technique for bringing the mind and body back into a functional growth. It suggests that we get in touch with blocked areas in order to facilitate growth. We suggest that, to the extent that the individual progresses and becomes proficient in movement, there may be an increase in self-esteem, especially at the material-situational level.

18. Direct Psychoanalysis is built upon the premise that the ego and superego are in a relentless battle with the emphasis on treatment rather than investigation. It emphasizes the role of the unconscious and suggests that the therapist be a loving mother. In this respect, self-esteem is develped on the transcendental level in terms of the therapist functioning as a support figure and providing encouragement to the client. To this extent, Direct Psychoanalysis can be effective when the problem in ego development lies on the level of the transcendental ego.

19. Ego-State Therapy, as discussed by Watkins and Watkins, suggests that there are different ego states and that these ego states are like part persons, and the goal of therapy is to integrate the parts into a unified whole, not provide a fusion. They further suggest that hypnosis can permit the therapist to manipulate the ego but they lack theoretical structure or focus to indicate in what way hypnosis should be used. Further, they suggest that the heart of the problem of disassociation is discerning what is object and what is subject in relationship to the individual's perception of self. They see the ego as a confederation of states. We suggest that their focus on ego can permit the development of self-esteem and does so when by chance the therapist connects with the deficient ego state as they would hypothesize. The weakness in Ego State Therapy is not so much the focus on the ego and the importance of the ego as on the lack of theoretical structure within which the weakness or deficit is ascertained by the therapist and thus becomes the focus of therapeutic management; further, it fails to address the importance of the interrelationship of ego to self-esteem. We suggest that SET does provide the theoretical structure and a more consistent whole, and that Ego State Therapy is a part of SET.

20. Eidetic Psychotherapy, as developed by the Marburg Institute in

Germany, emphasizes the role of eidetic imagery as a stepping stone to higher consciousness. It is based upon the assumption of Ashem's that personality is the result of a genetic tendency toward wholeness and that this wholeness is influenced by coded holograms that contain a library of eidetic images in each individual. These eidetic images provide the self-organizing nucleus of the psyche. The role of therapy is to help the client to resolve conflict. We suggest that rather than disparage the role of eidetic imagery in personality formation, SET actually provides the same theoretical focus vis-à-vis the apperceptive mass. The apperceptive mass contains all the material that the individual has ever perceived vis-à-vis experience and is consequently the library providing the material for the interpretation of current sensory data. We suggest that Eidetic Psychotherapy lacks the broader structure necessary for effective therapy and that, when success occurs, it is as an accidental result of change rather than an accurate indicator of inherent weakness.

21. Encouragement Therapy generally develops from the work of Bertrand Russell, as formulated by Robert White. He found encouragement to be the essential ingredient in any effective therapy. It presupposes that the neurotic is basically a discouraged person (as in Adler) who is unmotivated to change vis-à-vis the discouragement (as opposed to being incapable of change). The fundamental goal of the therapist is to motivate the client to change and this change can be brought about by helping him or her visualize or become aware of perceptual alternatives to reorganize his or her thinking. It assumes that a person's interpretations provide a pattern for action and the problem then lies in the interpretation. SET would have no disagreement with Encouragement Therapy except to point out that it is but one small component of the total process. Its emphasis on interpretation is similar to our emphasis on the function and role of the apperceptive mass. Encouragement is one of the elements of the transcendental ego and of course reorganization is fundamental to any therapeutic success. We find that W. I. Thomas' basic proposition that "If an individual perceives something as real it is real in its consequences" provides the underlying basis of Encouragement Theory.

22–23. Feminist Therapy I and II are sociopolitical types of therapy which suggest that deviance in women may largely be due to their marginal role and that successful therapy with women needs to be seen in relationship to the *Volkgeist* (spirit of the people) and *Zeitgeist* (spirit of the times) and how this provides a basis for discouragement in the female. We have suggested through SET that culture provides for the development or the retardation of self-esteem and that advertising and the mass media have not given women their rightful place in society. Adler emphasized this many years ago. SET maintains that the orientation in therapy would be different for men and women clients, as for example the sex role interpretation is important in understanding the basis of anorexia nervosa. SET addresses those concerns within the purview of Feminist Therapy.

24. Fixed Role Therapy is a therapeutic model deriving from G. A. Kelly's Psychology of Personal Construct. As the name implies, Fix Role Therapy emphasizes the importance of the function of role in that each person plays a hypothetical role. The goal is to teach the client to become sensitive to others' responses based on their role interpretation. Our basic concern with Fix Role Therapy relates to the fact that the focus is on only one aspect of personality, role behavior. Role behavior is fundamental to SET and of course is fundamental to the world-emersed ego through the function of status.

25. Focusing Therapy is a special form of introspection. The focus is on how symbols and persons interact. We suggest that the function of focusing is contained within SET and that the focus on symbols is fundamental to the apperceptive mass.

26. Functional Psychotherapy is more closely related to SET in that its founders are William James, John Dewey, and George Herbert Mead. The goal of Functional Psychotherapy is personality change with the emphasis upon the role of social action. It suggests that personality needs to be exercised, that fitness needs contact, and thus, to stay fit, one needs to be stressed. SET, through its emphasis on conflict, addresses the role of stress in the development of a healthy or neurotic personality. We suggest that stress is not the culprit in the development of a discouraged personality but that it is the interpretation of stress which is the culprit. Again, we basically suggest that Functional Psychotherapy is too limited in its theory and that the emphasis on action is an essential within SET.

27. Holistic Education, as developed by William Schutz, is a collage of action-oriented therapies. It includes Feldenkais, meditation, and encounter, and change is brought about through teaching. Its emphasis is on the physical, intellectual, emotional, aesthetic, social, and spiritual components of the individual and attempts to bring these into a functional integration. Holistic Psychotherapy suggests that all therapeutic techniques are usable in holistic education. Our major point of contention with Holistic Education is not that various techniques may be valuable in the educative process but rather that Holistic Education lacks a theoretical focus and that when it is successful it is due to the fact that the technique has been successful in the development of bettered self-esteem and that this improved self-esteem is due to chance rather than by design.

28. Immediate Therapy is based on Heider's theory of interpersonal relations and Festinger's theory of cognitive dissonance as well as Zei-

garniks' incomplete gestalt. It basically maintains that every individual has the potential for improvement, that the body heals itself. Psychodrama is a technique that can help facilitate Immediate Therapy. Here again we suggest that the emphasis on interpersonal relations, cognitive dissonance, and incomplete gestalt are all contained within SET and that Immediate Therapy basically lacks the broader theoretical perspective necessary for a functional psychotherapy. We again feel that the value lies in the development of self-esteem and that success, encouragement, and support are inherent in Immediate Psychotherapy.

29. The Impasse Priority Therapy of Nira Kefir is based on Adlerian principles. It assumes that we go from the minus to the plus or, in Adlerian terms, from inferiority to superiority. The theory suggests that people are in constant motion, that change is inevitable and that it is the form that change takes that is essential to successful therapy. It suggests that we need a reprocessing of childhood patterns and that the personality may be divided into four dynamic patterns: the controller, the pleaser, the moral superior, and the avoider, all of which are a part of Adler's paradigm. Again, Impasse Priority Therapy's weakness is its weak theoretical structure in that it fails to provide the necessary guidance or focus in therapy.

30. The Integrative Therapy of Walter Urban is an integration of all major personality theories. It has no basic theoretical structure of its own, but focuses on freeing natural energy, and suggests that when natural vital energy is recaptured, self-concept is modified in a desirable fashion. The focus is on development of a clear identity. Integrative Therapy lacks its own theoretical focus and consequently is too all-inclusive: Not all the major personality theories are, or can be, successfully integrated, despite the promise of its theoretical structure, and in consequence it lacks diagnostic value and therapeutic focus.

31. Integrity Groups is basically a therapy based upon mutual aid and self-help groups. It suggests that modern technology has eroded our interpersonal support systems and that neuroses stem from blighted interpersonal behavior due to the fact that people are alienated. We suggest that its value comes from changes in self-esteem, that it lacks a broad theoretical focus, and that a bettering of self-esteem through the self-help group may well affect group self-esteem alone, and that improvement is transitory and exists only as long as the individual remains part of that self-help group—which is one of the weaknesses of Alcoholics Anonymous (AA).

32. Interpersonal Process Recall Therapy, as developed by Kagan and Associates, is based upon the constructs from the analytic therapies of Horney and Sullivan as well as the behaviorists. The two basic dynamics underlying the therapy are that people need each other and that

group interaction can be the greatest source of pleasure as well as a source of pain. Additionally, the therapy stresses that people learn to fear each other and that relationships can become a source of intense pain. Without question, this therapy is based upon the assumption that the focus of the orientation to action is the culprit in the development of neuroses and that it is important for the client to come to know where his or her fears lie and how these fears provide the basis for less adaptive behavior. Again we suggest that the success of Interpersonal Process Recall is in the chance development of self-esteem, brought about by helping people relate more successfully to each other and consequently develop better self-concepts.

33. Mainstreaming, a technique of Mendel and Goren, focuses on teaching the patient to use community services. It basically suggests that all people use formal and informal resources and that the neurotic lacks the skill to use his or her resources successfully. Further, it suggests that the mentally ill too often use other patients as role models rather than healthy normal persons. The focus is on the rehabilitation model and it utilizes the technique of supportive care. Within SET, support is a part of the transcendental ego and, further, SET emphasizes role modeling in the development of a healthy personality in that it is role behavior that develops status essential for the world-emersed ego.

34. Meditation is a type of discipline based upon the teachings of Buddha more than 2500 years ago. It implies that our usual state of consciousness is suboptimal and that our goal should be the development of an optimal state of being.

35. Morita Psychotherapy derives from the work of Shoma Morita in Japan. It suggests that all neuroses are the result of an obsession with the self, a preoccupation with oneself. As the Adlerian paradigm suggests, behavior is controllable, one is responsible for one's own actions, and through this responsibility one is capable of changing. The theory underlying Morita is that the flow of awareness in the neurotic is blocked or turned inward. The client learns to accept his or her symptoms as reality and learns to live a constructive life despite weaknesses. We suggest that in SET this is included under our conflict theory, that conflict can be used destructively or productively, that the role of therapy is to teach the client to use stress and conflict to benefit rather than to destroy oneself and, further, that the aspect of learning to live despite weaknesses is addressed more adequately by Adler's Goal Theory.

36. Multimodal Therapy, as developed by Lazarus, is based upon behavioral and verbal constructs. It suggests there are seven interactive modalities and that these modalities include behavior, affect, sensation, imagery, cognition, interpersonal relations, and biological factors.

These modalities are all consistent with SET. Multimodal Therapy further suggests that each therapist tailor his or her treatment to the needs of the client, which again is consistent with SET.

37. Multifamily Therapy emerges from individual and group family therapy and the work of Dr. Laqueur of the Vermont State Hospital. It is based on a support system and focuses on an educational model. Its weakness is probably due to its lack of an integrated theoretical system.

38. Multiple Impact Training is based on an educational model. It sees neurosis as a life skill deficit, which is consistent with SET.

39. Mutual Needs Therapy includes any of the so-called self-help groups, such as Alcoholics Anonymous, Gamblers Anonymous, and so on. It sees the person as a function of physical, mental, and spiritual needs, all essential within SET. We have commented previously that the weakness of this type of orientation is that its focus is on rehabilitation and not cure, that it lacks a theoretical substructure, and further that the increase in self-esteem is due to a group self-esteem and not the development of a stronger individual self-esteem; that when the individuals leave the group they tend to revert back to their previous inadequate behavior vis-à-vis low self-esteem.

40. Naikan Psychotherapy is a meditative type of psychotherapy focusing on the importance of the role of self-sacrifice and the service of others. We would suggest that this emphasis upon self-sacrifice is part and parcel of Adler's function of the role of social interest. Naikan Psychotherapy focuses on the role of existential guilt as a mechanism for creating social interest. Its goal is to create a shift from self-centeredness to other-centeredness or, as we would say in SET, from self-interest to social interest.

41. The Natural High Therapy of Walter O'Connell is a therapy based on Adlerian principles. The aim is to increase self-esteem and social interest. The goal of Natural High Therapy is the removal of natural restrictions to help the individual develop his or her natural potential and focuses on the role of humor in helping the client develop and increase self-esteem; it is consistent with SET.

42. Identity Process focuses upon the concept of bonding or close relationships with other people. It focuses on happiness and pleasure and suggests that excess emotions must be discharged for success in therapy. It provides the basis for adaptational psychodynamics and Synanon techniques, but it basically lacks a broad theoretical basis (although beneficial if self-esteem is strengthened). Certainly the concept of bonding is essential to Adler's concept of social interest.

43. Nondirective Psychoanalysis is a conglomerate of traditional analysis and client-centered therapy. It has no explicit personality theory and the patient decides what direction the therapy will take. Suc-

cess can only emanate from an increase in self-esteem which may result from a successful talking out of problem areas by the client. We would suggest that the lack of theoretical focus makes Nondirective Psychoanalysis a rather weak modality.

44. Orgone Therapy, as developed by Wilhelm Reich, is based upon psychoanalytic principles and suggests that success is achieved by removing the blocking or physical armoring the patient may use to protect him- or herself and that the removal of this blocking and armoring provides for the free flow of energy essential for the free flow of a healthy personality. Reich's emphasis on orgone energy is interesting and could easily become useful within SET.

45. The Personal Construct Psychotherapy of George Kelly is based on the theory that each person uses his or her own system of constructs to categorize, give meaning to stimuli, and thus provide determinants for his or her behavior. The basic proposition is that the personality results from construct arrangement—all essential to SET vis-à-vis the function of the role of apperceptive mass. The goal of Personal Construct Psychotherapy is to promote change by helping the client to create new meanings, and it is through these meanings that the individual is able to achieve better adjustment. Within Kelly's theory each construct has two poles made up of construct and contrast, which is all contained within SET, in relationship to the dialectic, and contained within the concept of contradictory tendencies and the function of an innervative correspondence. The basic weakness results from the focus on the role of the construct alone and a failure to understand the role of self-esteem. We suggest that the therapy's value derives from the serendipitous development of self-esteem.

46. Plissit Therapy is basically an intensive therapy focusing on one or two problems within a given time frame. It utilizes attitude reinforcer discrimination (ARD), but lacks any theoretical structure. We suggest that its value is rather limited due to the fact that self-esteem may be temporarily increased as a result of the client's learning to deal with a particular problem, however it gives no basis for the individual to deal adequately with future problems as they may arise.

47. Poetry Therapy is merely a merging of poetry and therapy to help the client develop better self-awareness regarding his or her own body feelings and to accept the here-and-now life experiences. It is more a process for using poetry to help complement some other basic therapy than a discrete therapy.

48. The Primal Therapy of Janov is based on a belief in the organismic rightness of the individual. Its position is that we need to reclaim repressed feelings and that these feelings need to be integrated into a total functioning. The basic assumptions underlying Primal Therapy are generally included in SET but with a difference in technique and

Primal Therapy's emphasis upon the repressed content. In SET we maintain that repressed material is relatively unimportant, that it is the present orientation toward future action which is the key to successful therapy in the development of good self-esteem. Primal Therapy may be beneficial in that, by releasing some of the pent-up feelings and energies, self-esteem may be temporarily increased, but we suggest that it lacks the theoretical focus necessary for the development of a solid self-esteem oriented to future action.

49. Primal Relationship Therapy is based upon Adler's work as revised by R. Postel. It is a reparenting form of individual psychotherapy and suggests a minimum of 60 sessions are necessary in which 30 are geared to the role of mother as therapist and 30 to the father as therapist. Its value lies in helping the client to allay his/her fears of emotional closeness and consequently to develop a healthier life-style through social interaction. Generally speaking, it is directed toward those clients who have experienced rejection and consequently would be limited in its use.

50. Provocative Therapy, as developed by Frank Farrelly, is based on the idea that the client has developed false ideas and assumptions that provide the basis for action which he/she then is provoked to continue, maintaining the neurotic condition. It is based on the idea that we change if we choose and, consequently, it is important for the therapist to help the client to develop a new orientation when he or she decides to change. The goal of Provocative Therapy is to provoke the client into change. It suggests that adult experiences are more important than those of childhood and consequently, as in SET, focuses on the present and the future rather than on the past. Generally speaking, Provocative Therapy lacks a broad theoretical outline and, again, would be productive to the extent that the individual increases self-esteem through change.

51. Psychoimagination Therapy is phenomenologically oriented. Its focus is on the need to help the client understand how he defines himself in relationship to others. It emerges from the work of Laing and Sullivan. The two premises underlying the theory are, first, the need to make a difference to someone and, second, the need for confirmation or acknowledgement of the self. Imagination is the kernel of consciousness. Images can be reshaped into healthier self-concept development. To this extent, Psychoimagination Therapy utilizes the importance of imagination or fantasy in the Adlerian model in helping to develop better self-esteem.

52. The Psycho-synthesis of Robert Assagioli stresses the integration of the personality. It tends to focus on making the unconscious conscious and, through this process, helping the client to develop a superconsciousness or, in essence, a healthier personality. It focuses on the

contradictions in each individual, emphasizing the contradictions in our desires. It further stresses the function of body, emotion, and mind and the need for an integrating center of the "I" and the "self" with an emphasis on the importance of developing purpose in life. We suggest that the tenets of Psycho-synthesis are all contained within SET, but that the emphasis is largely on the transcendental ego in SET.

53. Radical Psychiatry focuses mainly on the function of alienation as the basis for developing neuroses. It suggests that all functional psychiatric difficulties result from alienation coming from power abuse, and fundamentally call for a politically oriented psychotherapeutic technique. It further suggests that alienation appears as a result of aggressive influences.

54. Raix Neo-Reichian Education (RADIX) emerges from the Reichian model with the emphasis on both muscular armor and life force. The body armor is seen as objective, and mind/emotion subjective. Fundamentally blocked emotions provide the basis for neuroses and these emotions are seen in antithetical pairs, pain/pleasure, longing/fulfillment, anger/love, and so on. It suggests that all feelings are acceptable and that the function of therapy is to discover oneself, and through self-discovery the individual is able to bring about change. The emphasis on antithetical pairs is quite similar to SET's emphasis on contradictory tendencies, but we suggest that SET contains a more comprehensive theoretical structure, whereas RADIX therapy is too restrictive in content.

55. Rebirthing is based on breathing rhythms, and suggests that our belief systems are founded upon a set of imprints regarding self, which have resulted from the birth experience. It follows the psychoanalytic theory that assumes we are responsible for the birth process itself. Rebirthing references negative self-concepts and suggests that through Rebirthing there can be the development of a more positive self-concept. Breath is seen as the rainbow bridge between the subjective and the objective which is not too inconsistent with the concept of breath as *prana* in Hindu philosophy. It is one of process, a process that is safe, seen as effective, simple, and enjoyable by the client. We suggest that rebirthing is generally weak in theory and that its value is somewhat tenuous in the development of good self-esteem.

56. The Re-evaluation Counseling of Harvey Jackins emphasizes the function of flexibility as the key to successful therapy. It suggests that the difference between rational and irrational behavior is a function of flexibility. In SET we maintain that flexibility is but one facet in the development of good self-esteem and thus the value of Re-evaluation Counseling is in the development of flexibility; it would be successful if flexibility were the exclusive are of weakness, however, focusing on only one facet of self-esteem, it consequently ignores the other 17.

57. The Self-Image Therapy of Camillia Anderson focuses on the role of self-image in all behaviors. It suggests that self-image actually replaces personality and that each self-image is unique. This is totally consistent with the Adlerian model. It further suggests that the self-image creates a patterned response for each individual, that every action is associated with a dialectic, and emphasizes the importance of role behavior. Further, it suggests that there is no such thing as bad self-image but, rather, identifies weakness in our grandiosity or development of a bigger-than-life self-concept, which is consistent with Adler's godlike goals. Self-image Therapy, again, is weak in theory and focuses on only one facet of the Adlerian model, as well as that of SET. In the instance of a client not compensating for inferiority feelings but rather merely acting in terms of his or her perceived self-concept, we suggest that Self-Image Therapy is in error in not understanding the importance of the role of compensation.

58. Sex therapies are basically therapies focusing upon process and cognition where the goal is to help the individual to increase satisfaction and where dysfunction is seen as the result of attitude and emotion. We suggest that the importance of attitude and emotion can be identified through SET and that, by developing self-esteem and helping the client to sharpen self-awareness, the same goals may be achieved.

59. Social Influence Therapy provides no theory of personality and focuses instead on a client's changing his or her attitude about the self and understanding of the social situation. It generally focuses on the role of social influence in relationship to behavior, which is consistent with the basis of SET.

60. Stress Management Therapy basically focuses on the reduction of tension, on cognitive restructuring, and on the role of education in helping the client to learn coping skills. Included within Stress Management are biofeedback, hypnosis, behavior therapies, inside orientation, and other techniques for handling and reducing stress. In SET, we suggest not so much the reduction of stress but rather reinterpreting stress so as to make it functional rather than dysfunctional.

61. Structured Learning combines modeling, role playing, performance feedback, and transfer of training. It basically sees behavior as skills acquired through learning. It emphasizes role modeling and role playing as important in the therapy process. The concept of role is but one aspect in the development of SET.

62. Triad Counseling emphasizes the function of crosscultural differences. In theory, it focuses on stress, response to stress, and ameliorated intervention. It comprises the client, counselor, and anticounselor, emphasizing the functions of articulation, resistance, defensiveness, and recovery through the utilization of psychodrama and socio-drama.

Again, the function and importance of stress are fundamental to the development of SET.

63. Transcendence Therapy, or a going-beyond, is a group process. The emphasis is on formation—to shape ongoing processes and, through a holistic development, to move beyond the pathways of life and give greater meaning to a new spiritual formation. SET, likewise, emphasizes the role of the spiritual and of transcendence in the development of good self-esteem. We further suggest that although Transcendence Therapy is theoretically very weak, the emphasis on the spiritual is valuable.

64. Twenty-four Hour Therapy is not in essence a true psychotherapy but an intensive team approach to help the individual meet an immediate crisis. We see Twenty-four Hour Therapy as being especially basic to the development of self-esteem through its emphasis on success, encouragement, and support. It utilizes a team approach and has value in the development of transcendental self-esteem.

65. Verbal Behavior Therapy rests on classical and instrumental conditioning theories. The basic assumption is that a change in one category in life brings about a change in another. It is basically eclectic, lacking its own theoretical structure. It emphasizes the overt categories of action, speech, and physical activity and the covert categories of perceptions imagery, thinking, and emotion, all of which are contained within SET. It suggests that you influence your milieu and your milieu influences you, a reciprocal arrangement consistent with SET theory.

66. Z-Process Attachment Therapy focuses on bonding, or what we believe would be consistent in SET in relationship to social interest and the importance of social interest to the development of good self-esteem. It totally lacks, however, an understanding of the importance of self-esteem, per se, although it focuses on perceptions, cognition, emotion, and sensory behavior, all of which are included in SET.

CONCLUSION

We have defined the personality as a dynamic configuration of the three levels of ego (the world-emersed ego, transcendental ego, and ego strength) as developed parsimoniously from the integration of contradictory behaviors. Our three levels of ego include nine components and nine elements. These elements and components form three Stars of David, combining to move in the direction of a circle forming the core of the personality. The personality is an integration of the three egos, as developed from an integration of the contradictory tendencies which include the various opposing forces. We can describe the personality as a circle of the three egos, around which the contradictory tendencies revolve. Aggressivity and passivity function as two traits inherent in each individual but which vary in importance individually. The functions of these traits are affected directly by the egos and, in turn, the strength and development of the egos reflect the function of these opposing forces or contradictory behaviors. Self-esteem is a composite of the functioning of the three egos.

Self-Esteem Therapy is a therapy built upon a personality theory developed out of the Adlerian model emphasizing the dialectical nature of the universe. In this chapter, we have briefly attempted to show that the various therapies that have developed can all be parsimoniously combined through the theoretical structure of SET. The three major forces in psychology have been listed as the humanistic, the psychoanalytic and the behavioristic. We believe that SET, while emerging from the humanistic tradition, can include all the basic assumptions underlying the others and we have attempted briefly to indicate how they interrelate with SET.

The 66 psychotherapies listed by Corsini as innovative psychotherapies we believe can be subsumed under six major headings: (1) creative, (2) body, (3) cognitive, (4) emotion, (5) relaxation, and (6) social learning. The creative includes art, aesthetic, dance, and imaginative therapies. The body therapies include aqua-energetics, Reichian, rebirthing, among other therapies. The cognitive therapies probably include the vast majority, for example, brief, cognitive behavior, conditioning, direct psychoanalysis, educational, integrated, impasse, nondirective, construct and psychosynthesis therapies. The emotional therapies would include actualizing therapies; identity-seeking therapies deal directly with affect. Relaxation therapies include all the meditative, relaxation and bio-feedback therapies. The social learning therapies are all those which emphasize the function of society, including conflict resolution, fixed role, immediate, family, mutual need, and those therapies dealing directly with integrating the individual with society.

We believe that SET theory reflects the theoretical framework that exists for all psychotherapies as developed so far. This chapter is not meant to be perceived as a definitive statement of the all-inclusive nature of SET theory, but to show briefly how the various therapies can be subsumed under SET theory, and how these therapies may in fact derive their effectiveness, or lack thereof, from the manipulation and management of self-esteem.

4

Self-Esteem Therapy (SET)

To maintain a consistency of thought, we begin this chapter by comparing the Freudian mechanistic approach to therapy with our Adlerian-based humanistic approach. Consistent with our dialectic theme, we have placed these two modes of therapeutic process in juxtaposition to each other while postulating that the one is largely sterile and nonproductive, the other vital and creative. Utilizing a Freudian approach to discover the beginning of the client's problem can prove to be a long, drawn out therapeutic process, and relatively useless. Knowing when and how the client's self-esteem was destroyed or what factors were present during the socialization process that prevented the development of good self-esteem does nothing to help rebuild a dangerously weak self-esteem. There is little wonder why psychoanalysis and many forms of therapy require such long-term involvement when the orientation largely focuses on the understanding of the basis for the condition or the cause of the malady. A more positive approach to therapy is needed: If A represents the past, B represents the present, and C the future or goal, then in the Freudian model, instead of moving from B to C, the emphasis is largely on A, the past or causal element presumed responsible for B, the present. It is assumed that successful therapy is contingent upon the understanding of the preceding causal motif, and it is only when this is understood that the disturbance will disappear. Little or no time is spent with C, the goal or the future. In Freudian therapy the movement then is from B back to A before moving to C. In the Adlerian model, we begin at B but place the emphasis on C, the goal or that which is desired. Our orientation to therapy, then, is the movement from B to C with little or no concern for A.

We once worked with a client over a six-month period and only once (for an hour and a half) did the client discuss his past as the historical antecedent of his neurosis. The emphasis upon the past was totally nonessential in achieving the goal of successful therapy, but since the client wanted to talk about the past we allowed him to discuss it and get it off his chest. Our purpose in therapy is to increase self-esteem; the focus is upon the future. It is our belief that in most cases, and especially in this particular case, if we had focused upon the past in an attempt to draw out all the various contributing factors involved in the development of the neurosis, he could easily have developed a psychosis. A very close relative of our client had died in a mental institution and he had actually internalized the idea that his particular disturbance was genetically inherited and that he too was ultimately destined to become psychotic. To reiterate, therapy began with the client being very depressed, barely maintaining a degree of functionality. The fact that he had internalized such a defective individual construct was not precipitated by his knowledge of the relative's illness, but rather, his lack of self-esteem resulting in faulty reasoning. This individual had created a convenient rationalization for failure, thereby safeguarding a weak, fragile self-esteem. The psychoanalytic approach in this case would consist in exploring the individual's past to determine why such a fear was internalized. Months of psychoanalysis might not convince the individual of his psychological normality, but rather reinforce his feelings of abnormality.

From a Self-Esteem Therapy perspective, we go from B to C, a much more parsimonious approach than going into the past, which may very well weaken an already fragile self-esteem. If low self-esteem is the problem, then, for example, dealing with unresolved Oedipal complexes, and so on, will do nothing to rebuild self-esteem. Consequently, it is not a solution, when the desire in therapy is to help the individual either to establish or rebuild a good self-esteem. We need not concern ourselves with the past but must, of necessity, concern ourselves with the future. Knowledge of when or why self-esteem development was interrupted is of only historical interest to the therapist, and has no power to determine therapeutic outcomes. A future orientation is essential to successful therapy; it is the basis for the development of good self-esteem which is achieved through the successful playing out of one's striving for superiority. We need to look at the individual now and help him/her build his/her self-esteem, forgetting the past, concentrating on the present, with an eye to the future goals of the client.

Neo-Freudians have identified many defense mechanisms or ego-protecting mechanisms used by the neurotic. These are essentially the same defense mechanisms utilized by the so-called normal person in his or her daily behavior. The difference between the normal person and the neurotic is not necessarily a matter of quality but of quantity, in other words, we all use many of the same defense mechanisms but the neurotic uses them to excess. The neurotic then, is only distinguished from the normal person in that the former spends a disproportionate amount of time and energy defending the ego at the expense of constructive character development. Pathology exists as an imbalance in the system. In the Freudian model, therapy consists of helping the individual to understand what defense mechanism he or she is using and for what purpose. Rationalization is only useful or effective as an ego defense mechanism to the degree that the individual is unaware of its use. Once he or she is confronted with the fact that he/she is rationalizing, the rationalization becomes useless and the ego is again vulnerable. A strong ego is essential for healthy personality development in the Freudian model. If either the id or superego achieves too much power, the personality disintegrates. If there is too much id, the individual tends to act like a spoiled child, wanting his own way at whatever cost. If there is too much superego, he becomes a puppet to social restraints. In our model the defense mechanisms, which we all use, are not ego defense mechanisms but are self-esteem–protecting mechanisms. When self-esteem is low, the individual resorts to compensatory mechanisms to safeguard or protect a vulnerable self-esteem. Thus, defense mechanisms are, or become, self-esteem–safeguarding mechanisms. We have distinguished between the mechanistic and the humanistic models as they apply to therapy. We will present Self-Esteem Therapy as a Marxian-Adlerian approach to self-esteem enhancement through heuristic management.

THEORY AND CAUSE

What differentiates a successful therapeutic modality that develops our so-called 'innervative correspondence of functional opposites' and unsuccessful therapy, where these same conflicting forces may become debilitating? To answer this question one needs to look at the concept of cause and effect. We have stated that the basic psychodynamic mechanism underlying deviance is low self-esteem and that the effect is the compensatory mechanism, or the deviance, for example, obesity, anorexia, alcoholism, crime, rape, neurosis, and so on. We have developed our model to illustrate how compensatory mechanisms fall largely into major subdivisions, which we have referred to as individual and social deviances. Such a subdivision is more apparent than real but has the heuristic value of helping us to delineate types. All deviances are ultimately individual, some are more socially visible, while others tend to be hidden.

We will develop what we call the concept of the *hierarchy of causes* in relationship to therapeutic models. The behavioral character deviance we will use as an example will be homosexuality, where the client's goal of therapy is to change his or her mode of sexual orientation (only one possible goal) to social action. We will briefly, and simplistically, list several therapeutic modalities in an attempt to show their development in relationship to cause. The hypnotist (use of suggestion only), as opposed to the hypnotherapist, might well place the client in a hypnotic trance and suggest to the individual that he or she will no longer enjoy sex with a member of the same sex but rather desire heterosexual relationships. The focus is on changing the orientation to social action without considering the basis for the action. The emphasis is on behavior change and not on cause.

In the behavior modification model one might find the therapist using positive and negative reinforcement in an attempt to bring about change in the sexual orientation of the individual. He or she might show the individual nude pictures of men and women. When showing the picture of the nude male to a male (whether there is an arousal or not doesn't matter) he/she may well give mild electric shock or aversive stimulus while when showing the picture of a beautiful nude female to the same male, he/she will not administer an electric shock and may give some form of positive reinforcement. Such a modality does nothing to deal with the cause of the behavior. Behavior modification does not theorize as to why the individual is homosexual, but rather merely attempts to bring about a change in sexual orientation based on positive and negative reinforcement principles. Similar to hypnotic techniques deprived of therapeutic context, behavior modification used in this way is generally not very successful in dealing with problems of a sexual orientation.

Under the psychoanalytic model, as we suggested, the analyst is concerned with going back into the early childhood period and determining the causation—when the problem had its inception, even though it did not become evident until much later in life. In the case of homosexuality, one of the theories within the psychoanalytic model is that the individual never resolved his Oedipal complex during early childhood development. The focus of therapy is then to take the individual back in time to help him understand why his love attraction for his mother was never resolved and why he has always seen himself in conflict with the male figure, his father, for the love object, the mother. In reference to the love object, since one cannot love one's mother, he cannot have sex with another adult woman because he will perceive her as a mother figure. Consequently, sex with the male becomes the only safe avenue to follow. If this theoretical orientation is correct, then working through an unresolved Oedipus complex should result in a change in sexual orientation. The literature would suggest that success through psychoanalysis in changing sexual orientation is relatively rare if not totally unsuccessful. Furthermore, therapists today are not primarily concerned with helping the individual change his or her sexual orientation but rather helping them reach a point in their development where they can accept it without fear, anxiety, or guilt.

In SET we will not concern ourselves with sexual orientation, per se, but primarily work to enhance self-esteem. Low self-esteem is the problem of the disturbance. In our model we assume low self-esteem to be the basic causal factor in the development of compensatory mechanisms. In our paradigm, homosexuality may be a compensatory mechanism used to safeguard self-esteem. I have had occasion to work with several young gay men in the past. I will discuss several case histories to show the role of self-esteem and its effect on the sexual orientation of these young men. One of them felt threatened by society; he evidenced severe anxiety and desperately needed help as he was suicidal at the time. He had been a sexually active heterosexual when he started college and developed several close intimate relationships. On an occasion when a very close intimate relationship had just dissolved he felt very alone and was approached in one of the university lavatories by a gay male. Because of his feeling of loneliness and sexual frustration resulting from terminating an active sexual relationship, he allowed himself be used sexually. He did not take an active part in the sexual liaison and, although he reached orgasm, he did not experience any enjoyment from the act. A couple of days later this experience was repeated, with the same lack of enjoyment from the act. Some time later he was approached by a gay male in town and was literally raped and the experience was not only unpleasant but extremely painful. It would seem that, since his early sexual behavior was all heterosexual and enjoyable and his recent behavior with homosexuals was unpleasant, that he would have rejected any further advances by gays. However, this was not the case and shortly after being raped he became an active male homosexual.

The literature says that very often when a young male is raped by an older male he resorts to homosexual behavior and becomes homosexual himself. Because our client was suicidal, we decided to work on his self-esteem. We decided that the first goal of therapy would be to help him develop an attitude of acceptance—acceptance of his new identity—and through this new identity, become more comfortable with his new life-style. Therapy lasted about four months and during this period of time his depression and anxiety abated. He became happy and content with himself, he began to renew his heterosexual behavior as well as maintaining his homosexual behavior. We considered the possibility of attempting to bring about a behavior change utilizing hypnosis, but he decided that he was content and happy being bisexual, enjoying both men and women, and that he would remain bisexual until a later point in time when he felt he would meet the right women, want to get married, and begin a family. As stated, the goal of therapy was not to change his sexual orientation, per se, but rather to focus upon building self-esteem. When his self-esteem increased, the individual was able to deal with his own sexual orientation, and accept or reject it through his own volition.

In another case, I worked with a gay male in an academic relationship. At one of our academic sessions he mentioned that he was gay and hoped that it would not affect our relationship. Hypnosis was employed to help the young man increase his self-esteem, but in no way was the sexual preference discussed. In this case the individual's early sexual experience was homosexual and he had never had a heterosexual experience. As a child he was a rather sensitive individual and his father decided that sending him to an all-male camp would be good for the development of his masculinity. However, one of the counselors at the boy's camp was gay, and he was used sexually; he began to enjoy the experience, although he did not reciprocate. Before therapy he was living a rather active gay life-style. As a result of a few sessions his self-esteem increased significantly. Then, one afternoon he told me about his most recent sexual experience. He had picked up a male the night before, gone home and been unable to complete the sex act with him; his comment was: "I looked over at him and asked myself what the hell was I doing in bed with a strange male?" Shortly after that, he called to say good-bye at the end of the semester, not only to say thanks for helping him but to tell me that he had been downtown the night before and picked up an older woman, had sex with her, enjoyed it tremendously, and was looking forward to an active heterosexual life-style. In the case of homosexuality we postulate that extremely low self-esteem may be crucial in the development of an attitude of risk aversion, which predisposes the individual to the development of an appropriate compensatory mechanism, in this case, homosexuality.

We are suggesting that not only is low self-esteem a factor in the development of homosexuality, but that it plays a role from two different perspectives. In the second case history, we postulated that the individual became an active homosexual not as a direct result of being used by an older male while at a boys' camp but as a result of low self-esteem. He found that being brought to orgasm was an enjoyable experience that he continued throughout the summer. In this particular case we say that the individual had low self-esteem and that this low self-esteem was originally manifested in a shy, somewhat effeminate behavior. It should be noted that most males begin their sexual activity with a certain degree of anxiety and trepidation. Will they perform adequately? It is certainly normal for the male to be concerned. Consequently, when a young male has extremely low self-esteem, he may have unusual fear of being rejected by the female or being inadequate and ridiculed. As has generally been the case in our culture, the female submits to the male. In the case of homosexuality, the male is able to play the female role, he submits to the advances of another male and is not threatened. Usually, when the male is initiated into homosexuality, the first experiences are precipitated by the active partner and the novice merely submits without participating or, if he does, the other initiates the action. Homosexuality is a compensatory mechanism, a safeguarding mechanism for one's own sexuality—a type of self-esteem risk aversion.

In the first case we have an individual who was heterosexually active but who switched to a homosexual role. The behavior change took place when his life-style was threatened, when his girlfriend broke up with him and because his self-esteem had been affected he was vulnerable. We are not suggesting that this individual had extremely low self-esteem but that due to the particular environmental circumstances, his self-esteem was threatened, so that he allowed himself to be used and then began to develop a gay behavior pattern. In this case, self-esteem was extremely threatened by the participation in homosexual acts. Because of cultural pressures to conform, he felt threatened, his self-esteem diminished, and he became suicidal. We are hypothesizing that gay behavior may actually be affected by self-esteem in two particular ways. One, low self-esteem may be the basis for the development of homosexual behavior, and two, homosexual behavior, even when not directly precipitated by low self-esteem, may bring about a lowering of self-esteem as a result of societal pressures.

TRANSFERENCE

We have found through the utilization of SET that rarely, if ever, do any of our clients develop a transference. We are not referring to all five types of transference listed in the psychiatric literature but generally to the attachment of the client to the therapist in the traditional therapeutic relationship. We have found that when we are able to help the client raise his or her self-esteem, the problem of termination in the therapeutic relationship is automatically taken care of through the betterment of self-esteem, in other words, we have never had to discuss termination but find that when the client's self-esteem is strengthened, he or she automatically determines the point of termination. This is handled simply by the client saying, "Well I feel so good that I think I'll skip our next session" or "I'm feeling so good now let's say we skip a week or two and I'll call you when and if necessary."

THERAPY AS A COMPENSATORY MECHANISM

Let's consider the value of therapy. Is therapy beneficial or would the patient's improvement have been just as good through the passing of time? We suggest that when self-esteem is the focus of the therapeutic relationship, and when the therapist's role is that of helping the client build self-esteem, therapy is valuable. Too often, the client develops a dependency on the therapist and the therapeutic relationship itself functions as a compensatory mechanism for dealing with low self-esteem. When the therapeutic relationship functions only on the basis of dependency, we suggest that it is a compensatory or safeguarding mechanism for dealing with threatened self-esteem. When therapy focuses on building self-esteem, the therapeutic relationship is not a compensatory mechanism but a learning experience in which the client plays an active role in the therapeutic process. Further, it is only through the development of a dialectic that the individual will develop a sense of adequacy and fulfillment.

Therapies that do not deal with causality or low self-esteem as the basis of the problem tend to function as dependency relationships, albeit, at times they are necessary. We suggest that, even in the Freudian model, the Oedipus complex is not the real culprit but causality itself exists in a hierarchical relationship in terms of the patient's past. The real cause of homosexuality, the compensatory mechanism, is low self-esteem. In our model, the compensatory mechanism is the effect and low self-esteem is the antecedent cause.

PURPOSE AND GOAL OF THERAPY

We have discussed the function of causality in the development of deviant behavior. Causes can be arranged in a hierarchical order: Each cause has an effect and the effect becomes a cause for another effect, which is a continuing, nonending process. Compensatory mechanisms are self-esteem–safeguarding mechanisms and generally have been labeled by society as deviant. It should be noted that what is deviant in one society may well be the norm or the standard in another society. Thomas Szasz, in *The Myth of Mental Illness* (1961), suggests that mental illness does not exist but rather that what we as a society label mental illness is little more than eccentric behavior. He would have us believe that if we were more tolerant of eccentric behavior, not only would many people be happier, but much of the deviant behavior would be eliminated.

To a large extent Szasz is correct. What we label as deviant is deviant by definition. All laws are social in that they are enacted to control or guide behavior. Society has even gone so far as to want to control behavior that may have no social consequences—what are referred to as victimless crimes, one of the most obvious and widespread today being smoking marijuana. Marijuana smoking is a form of deviant behavior and the actor is a social deviant. As far back as 1969, it was estimated by a Washington bureaucrat that 20 million Americans smoked or had smoked pot. Today that figure must be many times that amount; therefore, a significant proportion of the total population is deviant. It has also been stated by Harry E. Barnes in his book *Social Institutions* (1946) that an average individual breaks the law one or many times a day with behavior known or unknown to be illegal. Maybe Szasz is correct—this is little more than eccentric behavior. When does one behavior, smoking pot, become more or less eccentric than another? Certainly this is a matter of degree rather than of kind. Many of our leading citizens smoke pot—doctors, lawyers, professors—does this make them unacceptable deviants? Of course the answer is no, they are acceptable deviants, but nonetheless deviant. We can make them nondeviant simply by passing a law, the legalization of marijuana; then by law they become normal. Proof of this has historic precedent. In Victorian England, and back through history, masturbation was considered unnatural, abnormal, and sinful; it was the major sin of middle- and upper-class adolescents (masturbation being less common among lower-class youth who more readily and at a younger age engaged in fornication).

Parents, physicians, and the clergy took strong action to prevent their sons and other youth from masturbating, although most males probably did it in secret. However, the admonition was so great that many males were adversely affected by guilt even to the point where some of them were known to commit suicide because they could not quit masturbating. Physicians warned of the dangers of masturbation, attributing sundry illnesses to it, physical and mental deterioration, and especially insanity. Is it any wonder that some youth were adversely affected by such admonitions? Menninger (1973, 34) says, "The doctors really believed this theory, and of the official adjudications in cases of mental illness, many were officially based on 'masturbation.' I have examined many old state hospital records in which the etiology of case after case is so ascribed." Then, by the mid-to-late 1900s, the medical profession (including psychiatry) decided that masturbation was normal, that probably more than 90 percent of males masturbate, so now they are no longer deviant or eccentric; they are normal, with the non-masturbators becoming the deviants. Without changing behavior the deviants become normal. Every individual is unique, is his or her own prototype, and he or she is normal to that prototype. This proposition provides the underpinnings of SET. Sometimes therapy consists of little more than convincing an individual that he/she is normal to him- or-herself, that it is the worry that is of concern, not the behavior.

More and more people concern themselves with the past like the worry bird; they are not interested in where they are going but rather where they have been. Christianity has wreaked havoc upon society with its emphasis on sin and guilt. The concept of guilt has created untold suffering; man is born in original sin. On the issue of masturbating, Menninger (1973, 36) says masturbation was a solitary vice, "the sin of youth", which has become less a vice, no longer sinful, no longer dangerous but a form of normal, healthy, pleasurable experience. Even today, college youth find it difficult to talk about masturbation. We take the position that normal is a relative concept, relative to the Volkgeist and the Zeitgeist and, as we have shown, what was abnormal and sinful, masturbation, is now normal and pleasurable. In Chapter 5 of *The Social Dynamics of Self-Esteem: Theory to Therapy* (Steffenhagen and Burns 1987), we discuss in great detail the role of culture and its effect on the development of self-esteem. Like the worry bird, when we are busy worrying about the past we will never progress. We will define normal as any behavior that is acceptable and/or pleasurable to an individual, that is not detrimental to him/her or society. Some individuals do engage in behavior that is detrimental to their own health but is pleasurable and not detrimental to society. Normal sexual behavior is nonexistent; what is normal to one may be unacceptable to another; as therapists we need to emphasize the concept of uniqueness. The unhappiness created from sexual mismating is more the result of perception than behavior. If each partner would realize that what is normal to the one might not be normal to the other, they could then resolve and accept these differences. Our modern emphasis on sex (the sexual revolution), with its openness, is less than healthy. It is our contention that pornography and even the R-rated movies are responsible for the increase in rape and date rape. The incidence of rape is increasing rapidly. Young people are constantly bombarded with the idea that women are to be used sexually. A large majority of the movies show a couple in bed having sex on the first date. Pornography further exploits the female and also creates envy in many young men because their sex organs do not measure up to those of the reigning porn stars who are heavily endowed. Millions of dollars are being made from pornography. Where has censorship gone? This new openness, although statistically normal, is not necessarily beneficial to the individual or society as the incidence of VD and AIDS are becoming increasingly prevalent. The openness and emphasis upon sex is also creating self-esteem problems. The fear in the young male of not being virile enough or not being adequately endowed can lead to feelings of inferiority or lowered self-esteem. The female is equally plagued. In our model the goal of therapy is to raise self-esteem, not focus on the problem or attempt to eliminate the problem via reduction of conflict. We teach the client how to use conflict successfully to enrich his or her life. Too often, the goal of traditional therapy is problem oriented with the therapist concentrating on the problem.

The Freudian model suggests that abnormal behavior may well result from repressed materials that come from the unconscious into the conscious in disguised form, manifesting as aberrant behavior. The goal of Freudian therapy is to bring the traumatic event back into consciousness so that it can be dealt with consciously and thus extinguished. Although psychotherapies may differ, the cause of the behavior usually becomes the focus of attention, whereas in behavior modification the cause may actually be ignored while the behavior is dealt with directly in terms of change. We agree with this orientation but suggest that one of the weaknesses of behavior modification is the focus on eliminating or terminating a habit. We suggest that if a habit is terminated, a new habit will develop to fulfill the same need as the original or a new compensatory mechanism. Recently I became aware of an M. D. who suggested to a patient undergoing hypnotherapy for drug abuse that an elimination of the drug habit would not be effective and that he would merely develop a new habit, probably becoming an alcoholic. Many years ago I came across a reference in the literature of a patient who went to a hypnotist for smoking. Through the hypnotic process the patient was able to eliminate the smoking habit but began to eat excessively and put on weight. She again returned to the hypnotist with the problem of gaining weight and was hypnotized again for weight loss and the weight gain was brought under control. However, it wasn't long before the individual began drinking and again returned to the hypnotist with a budding alcohol problem. The hypnotist, not to admit defeat, used the hypnosis process to deal with the drinking. The final chapter of the story occurred when the patient was admitted to a mental hospital as a classic schizophrenic. This particular case history drives home the fact that the client's ability to eliminate the drug habit would not be successful as he would merely restructure his addiction or develop another compensatory mechanism to deal with the original problem (what the doctor failed to identify was low self-esteem). This particular criticism of hypnosis is not unwarranted when hypnosis is used merely as a technique for the elimination of a habit without consideration of the underlying dynamic cause.

Therapeutic endeavors should not be used to eliminate a habit but, rather, to develop good self-esteem. In conjunction with the development of good self-esteem, we suggest that a new and positive habit be developed to replace the old habit. Habits are basic structures of behavior and once developed become autonomous unto themselves, forming the basis for much of our behavior. They are developed by a trial-and-error method whereby a given behavior, if satisfying on any level, will be perpetuated and thus a habit will emerge. Habits are the foundation of behavior—rather, let's refer to them as bricks in an arch—and if we remove a brick without replacing it with a new one, we weaken the entire structure, ultimately leading to its collapse.

Gurdjieff (1872–1949) was a metaphysician and an occult evolutionist who was concerned with psychic pathology and health. Gurdjieff's most important contribution to our methodology was his emphasis on the fact that therapy would largely be geared to the normal for the individual's highest intellectual and spiritual development. He was a guru and a therapist who maintained that most men never achieved consciousness but remained in a state of sleep. The goal of therapy should be the higher development of the spirituality of man, freeing oneself from an emotional determinism. The purpose of therapy should not be to dig out the basis of the neuroses but to help the individual to open the latent and higher centers of the mind, to develop a higher consciousness. This development is part of the evolutionary process, physical and spiritual, and the goal of therapy is the creation of a healthier personality. Most people never achieve consciousness or, as we have said, they never reach awareness but always remain on a lower level. Therapy should constitute an evolutionary process in the Darwinian and Marxian sense as well as in De Chardin's sense, whereby the individual is brought into a state of cosmic reality. Through this he will become aware of the infinite realities of the material plane as well as the infinite realities of the cosmic level. Therapy, then, should have its focus on the development of the higher centers of man; not on the elimination of problems, the termination of conflict, but the development of a higher awareness. Conflict can be beneficial, when it is understood. It can then be utilized positively rather than negatively to help man achieve a higher potential. It is only by emphasizing the higher potential that effective therapy can be achieved. In conclusion, the goal of therapy should be positive, and the therapist should not allow his weakness to interfere with the client's development.

THE ORIGINS OF SELF-ESTEEM THERAPY (SET)

SET is based on an integrated philosophical approach, utilizing the ideas of Adler, Marx, Husserl, Simmel, Gurdjieff, and others. It is seeing the universe as composed of opposites, the yin/yang, positive and negative. In sociology, Herbert Spencer developed a theory of social Darwinism in which he saw society as a product of evolution. If we were to apply a structural approach to this analysis we would see all the individuals in society as composing the cells of the organism and together beginning to form structures, organs, and systems, ultimately comprising society. It is a product of inductive reasoning, whereby we reason from the particulars to other particulars or to generalizations. Individuals form groups and ultimately form the social system of society. In our analysis we will utilize a deductive approach and reason momentarily from the general to the particular or to other generalizations. The universe is comprised of the dialectic; each individual unit is comprised of the dialectic. SET is based on the premise that each individual unit, each person, is a function of dialectical forces and that psychically each is composed of opposing traits. In SET, we see the universe as a function of opposing forces and then generalize to the individual, seeing each unit as a dialectic. In therapy we reverse the process (in the inductive framework); we reason from particular to other particulars or to the general. Behavior is a function of the dialectical movement: Cells form tissues, tissues organs, organs structures, structures systems, and ultimately the individual, so behavior is likewise composed. Individual units of behavior group together to form certain complexes and these complexes ultimately form the life-style of the individual, or in essence the personality. In our discussion of organ inferiority, we postulated that if an organ of the body is weak or "inferior," then it is most likely to become the organ to be diseased or to malfunction in the broader system. It is impossible for an organ to malfunction without putting strain or stress on other organs, beginning to create a complex. In the behavioral realm, no behavior is discrete or separate unto itself, but a behavior that is neurotic or malfunctions in one area phases over and begins to affect other areas. Consequently compensatory mechanisms are not isolates but are conglomerates of individual units.

One aspect of the dialectic is unity, or the law of strife. In the Simmelian framework, unity is preceded by conflict and contradiction. Within unity there is always the element of contradiction in relationship to social process. For Hegel, every phenomena has an opposite tendency, a contradiction that makes the development of the theory of unity of opposites a vital aspect of the dialectical process. Can individual behavior be devoid of contradictions when the social process and the universe itself is an expression of contradiction? The fundamental difference between dialectics and metaphysics is that the former is dynamic while the latter is static; metaphysics is timebound, dialectic is universal. Any therapy that focuses on the resolution of conflict is doomed to failure, because conflict is normal and inherent within unity. If we are to achieve unity (an integrated personality), then therapy should focus on contradictions and the dialectic force. Therapies are dynamic only in respect to the fact that they accept contradiction and conflict as normal and see that the successful outcome of conflict is to develop an innervative correspondence of functionary opposites. It is not conflict that is disruptive to the individual and social behavior but rather the lack of understanding of the positive element of the negative force. Engels considered the dialectic to be a living guide for action, *both individual and social*.

Another Hegelian concept important to the cognitive emphasis of SET is the law that quantity may be transformed into quality. As quantitative changes accumulate in respect to given qualities, new qualities arise out of these quantitative changes that are new and different from the original qualities. Two units of behavior are never the same as the sum total of two individual units. As units of behavior increase, new and totally different qualities begin to emerge. As an example, the behavior of individual Germans under the Third Reich began to take on a totally different qualitative characteristic as the doctrine of Nazism emerged. Utilizing the Siegfried legend, Hitler hypothesized that many of the problems of the German economy were due to the economic practices of the Jews. While this particular lie was not accepted in toto by the German populace, it began to form the seed for the manifestation of racial prejudice. While Germans individually accepted Jews as Germans, as good God-fearing law-abiding German citizens, in consort and under the influence of Nazi propaganda, they began to stone their most beloved friend and neighbor, the Jew next door. These individual Germans would have totally abhorred their own behavior if they could not have justified it on the basis that their other friends engaged in that same behavior. Thus, we see that, as units begin to increase, the qualitative outcome of such quantitative changes begins to develop new complexes of behavior that were previously nonexistent, unpredictable, or abhorrent on the basis of a unitary measure. New and different qualities begin to emerge out of the quantities that differed from the original qualities. Following the law of the transformation of quantity into quality is the law of negation of the negation. The change of quantities into qualities is unending; each stage of development is the negation of the previous one, a synthesis that resolves the contradiction contained in the thesis (the previous synthesis). Each produces its own contradiction, each unit of measure has the seed of the contrary borne within it. This movement of change is normal and any attempt to arrest the process is negative. Change is normal, whereas fear of the new, although common, is abnormal, stultifying, and the basis for the continuation of neuroses. The neurotic, although displeased with his own behavior, is even more fearful of change, and yet his neuroses were borne out of the contradiction which he so fervently fears. Personality is a result of the dialectic process, just as phylogenic growth is a result of the dialectical process of Darwinian evolution. Personality and ultimately spirituality (ontogenetically) are borne of the dialectical process contained in cosmic evolution (see Birx 1972). The negation of the negation is sometimes seen as the Hegelian premise of thesis, antithesis, synthesis. The thesis is actually the status quo, the situation as extant. In society it would be seen as the prevailing Weltanschauung. Inherent within each social condition lies the seed of the opposite or its antithesis. This antithesis then creates or becomes the basis of the conflict, the yes becoming no and the no becoming yes. The no becoming a no and a yes and the yes becoming a yes and a no. Each containing two contradictory thoughts within itself. These conditions, individual and social, contain the seeds of their opposites and ultimately contain the basis for their own destruction. The antithesis is the basis of change and a culmination of the struggle of the antithesis creates a new set of conditions, a new quality, the new synthesis. As we have stated previously, culture is dynamic, ever changing and yet static. Personality is static and yet changing. In essence this is the basis for thesis, antithesis, and synthesis. If everything were in flux, then the force would become so dynamic that it would create ultimate destruction socially and/or individually. If on the other hand the condition is so static that it does not change, it ultimately also destroys itself. It is the dynamic aspect of change which is the very essence of life; when the sperm and ovum meet the zygote is formed, the fertilized egg. The egg then divides, forming two; the two ultimately divide, forming eight, and so on. Life itself begins as function of change like the dynamic element of the yes becoming the no and no becoming the yes, and each simultaneously becoming both no and yes, yes and no. It is the function and the understanding of the dialectic that is necessary to build a dynamic theory of individual change on the therepeutic level. The three basic laws of the dialectic process are important to SET: (1) the law of strife (interpretation and unity of opposites), (2) the law of transformation of quantity to quality, and (3) the law of negation of the negation—these are then thesis, antithesis, and synthesis; or position, opposition, and composition; or affirmation, negation, and negation of the negation.

The concept of homeostatis becomes applicable to our concept of contradictory tendencies or opposing forces, in other words, the process of achieving psychological homeostasis will be referred to as the function of the innervative correspondence of opposing tendencies. This innervative correspondence does not just create a functional unity of opposites but rather creates a new awareness, a function of the negation of the negation. This new awareness then becomes not only the goal of therapy but, in the Gurdjieffian sense, should be the goal of life itself, a culmination of the socialization process, a type of spiritual reality, superceding the materialistic secularism of our culture. Innervative correspondence refers to the strength of the various forces of the opposing tendencies and their particular applicability for each individual. We use Weber's concept of ideal types to label our constructs. If each construct is laid out on a continuum, the innervative correspondence is an attempt to achieve homeostatis as a unique configuration for each individual, which leads us to the understanding and utilization of conflict. It is the unity created out of conflict, the synthesis created out of opposition. This is the dialectical process, having opposing forces operating within each individual so that the individual becomes a living dialectic synthesis.

Let us digress momentarily and look again at the Freudian paradigm in the mechanistic model. Important to an understanding of the dialectic process is an understanding of the Freudian concept of the ego as the administrator of the personality. Freud's psychology was frequently referred to as ego psychology. A process of the id, the basic psychic energy, the basic pleasure principle, is free of conflict until the development of the restrictions of social behavior, as manifest through the superego. The id processes are free of conflict before the superego creates an intrapsychic conflict, where the ego's purpose is to maintain a balance? The defense functions of the ego arise from the need to resolve conflict and protect the ego from threat. A partial list of defense mechanism is denial, rationalization, repression, identification, compensation, protection, displacement, and so on. These functions are seen as relatively normal and only become abnormal when pushed too far. We all rationalize when we fail to realize the truth; we are in jeopardy of losing contact with reality. Many elderly people regress because they were happy and felt needed in the past. Active, creative, elderly people do not need to regress and seldom do. How do we deal with the untoward effects of these defense mechanism? We help the client to build his or her self-evaluation so that this won't be needed to resolve conflict. However, does this really create a homeostatic balance?

Freud concerned himself with the ego, while we focus on self-esteem. Ego strength and self-esteem are not the same. We have indicated the difference and have shown that compensation is a broader category than the ego defense mechanism, and in our Adlerian framework we will refer to it as a safeguarding mechanism for dealing with low self-esteem. These mechanisms are used to protect a fragile self-esteem but do not protect a weak ego, which we have indicated in Chapter 3 of *The Social Dynamics of Self-Esteem: Theory to Therapy* (Steffenhagen and Burns, 1987) may actually be strong. In the dialectic we do not suppose that we can resolve conflict. Conflict is seen as a normal state of the organism, the basis for which unity can ultimately be achieved. Conflict is change, change is dynamic and can lead to a healthy personality. The healthy movement from inferiority toward superiority involves conflict and change, whereas remaining in a state of inferiority is static and abnormal. Therapy should not focus on the resolution of conflict, which ultimately would result in another state of abnormality, a state of static balance, but it is the dynamic balance of the dialectic that is the truly normal. The focus of therapy should not be to eliminate the divaricated tendencies or the opposition but to bring it into a creative opposition, an innervative correspondence.

In the dialectic we need to see conflict behavior not in terms of the class of opposition but in terms of dynamic movement. It is a mode of therapy derived from social, psychological, and philosophical theories applied to the individual in the therapeutic model.

DEFINITION AND CHARACTERISTICS OF SET

Rational Emotive Therapy (RET) takes the position that it is unique in the field of psychotherapies to the extent that it does not require the individual to concern him- or herself with achievement, goals, complexes, or social approval, and further, that the individual need to evaluate him-or herself in any way whatsoever. It states that to construct a self-image is detrimental to the individual. Although we perceive SET to have many of the characteristics of RET, we suggest that the difference between them is crucial. RET maintains that people do not have to rate themselves and, actually, that to rate is undesirable. However, people are social animals whose thought processes are the result of socialization and internalization: All social organization is based on status distinctions and behavior is the result, the ability not to rate is impossible. Within a phenomenological perspective, no empirical statement (a statement of fact) can become credible or have meaning without a reference to experience. It is this experience which then becomes subjective vis-à-vis the apperceptive mass. What is real is that we perceive, believe to be real. The brain as "computer mechanism" perceives the stimulus. It sees a bottle marked "Pepsi" but what is this "Pepsi"? Pepsi is nothing. It is a name constructed out of someone's subjective consciousness that has become identified with a substance, a liquid, identified by taste and color. Further, the name Pepsi is perceived differently by different people. One sees it positively, another negatively. The basis for the negative and positive interpretation lies within the apperceptive mass. Our response to the bottle, the Pepsi, is not based on perception but, rather, judgment. There are two types of judgments; terminating judgments and nonterminating judgments. A terminating judgment is an experience that is capable of verification or falsification by the scientific method. Moreover, the non-terminating judgment can never be completely scientifically verified. Perceptions without judgments are sterile and it is the judgment that creates the difficulty in terms of maladaptive behavior. It is how we judge an act, an event, or a condition that allows for healthy, normal personality development or maladaptive, destructive personality development. If we did not judge, we would not react. Judgments are the basis for expectations which are the determinants of behavior. The perception, a stimulus, a neural pattern is the brain, is of no consequence until we give it meaning. The meaning we give the stimulus ultimately becomes a judgment leading to expectations and resulting in behavior. A person says "fuck off," a statement which is subject to a judgment. The judgment is based on the apperceptive mass, the Volkgeist, the Zeitgeist, and is an evaluation of the person making the statement. However, given the change that has taken place in our culture in relation to the Volkgeist and the Zeitgeist, this becomes a statement which may be used openly today, whereas it would have been used very infrequently in the past or most likely only in all-male company. The judgment is largely a function of an evaluation of the immediate set of circumstances surrounding the person making the statement. If one is to make this statement in friendly jest, it is taken without critical evaluation. If, on the other hand, the statement is made in a situation of hostility, anger and annoyance may immediately transpire. The statement can be seen as demeaning, in which case one is viewing it in relationship to some form of estimation of self. Is the individual being demeaning in this retort? We maintain within RET that it is impossible to react totally rationally given the affective consciousness of man. The very name Rational Emotive Therapy, implies that one must perceive behavior as both rational and emotional, implying the pain/pleasure principle in terms of people's hedonistic behavior. RET maintains that it deals with beliefs, attitudes and values and to this extent SET deals with these same three components. However, we additionally deal with judgments, and it is on the level of a judgment that the difference between RET and SET becomes most pronounced. SET is a cognitive behavior therapy (in essence all therapy, if successful, is a type of behavior modification, but it is the focus which is different). It sprang from the seminal work of Alfred Adler, from the phenomenological approach developed by Husserl, and from the dialectical foundation of Marx and Hegel, and from the work of Georg Simmel. It is through these philosophical focuses that SET develops into a unique therapy within its own right. As a cognitive behavior therapy, we focus upon behavior and the need to change behavior, but we achieve this end through the cognitive mode. We focus on interpretation, the interpretation that emerges from the apperceptive mass, eventuating in judgments and expectations, and, as a result of these, the given behavior. It is not always the behavior that is important. We have seen in many of our clients, not an inappropriate behavior but an inappropriate affectual state of consciousness. We once worked with a client for anxiety whose given social and vocational behavior were appropriate but whose response to stress was destroying his stomach. In this case we did not need to change behavior, but change thinking, create an interpretive response that reduced the function of the autonomic nervous system through a change in stress reduction. It was not the stimulus that needed to be changed—the behavior was appropriate—rather, it was the interpretation that needed revamping. A behavior modification approach in dealing with this client for stress would be totally useless. It was not the behavior that needed modification, but his interpretation of the milieu exterior vis-à-vis the apperceptive mass. Isn't it true that two people evaluate a given stimulus completely differently? The difference in evaluation ultimately becomes a function of self-evaluation or self-esteem. If we perceive our behavior as adequate and appropriate, then we have no need to build up internal tension. If, on the other hand, our self-esteem is low, then we tend to perceive our behavior as less than adequate and respond with a negative judgment. We are judging our behavior as less than adequate, and consequently we feel the need to accomplish more in a given amount of time than is: (1) necessary, (2) appropriate, or (3) possible. When we have good self-esteem, we feel good about ourselves and our judgments of our behavior become positive, leading to good self-acceptance. SET is a cognitive therapeutic approach dealing with change on the cognitive level, helping the individual to reevaluate his or her behavior and bring about a change in judgment and expectations.

In essence, SET might be thought of as containing the basic premises of RET plus the component of judgment, given that the human being will never, nor should ever, hope to attain a completely rational, scientific orientation to problem solving. This latter component, judgment, is what makes SET unique in the field of psychotherapies. SET contains the following characteristics: (1) it focuses on beliefs, attitudes and values, but we concentrate upon judgment, since without judgments these are meaningless; (2) we focus on freedom of choice but do not posit humanity as the center of the universe, which would be a position too anthropomorphic for our modality; (3) flexibility becomes a key focus of SET; (4) we have already discussed the philosophical nature of SET and our entire focus is reeducative; (5) one of the elements of our ego number 3 is social interest, the opposite of the self-indulgence therapies; (6) SET is humanistic and phenomenological; (7) we do not focus on hedonism but rather on goals—short-, mid-, and long-range goals—as a focus; (8) we utilize existing psychological learning theories in an attempt to bring about a change in the apperceptive mass to create a change in judgment, expectations, and ensuing behavior; (9) we focus on reduction of pain through the building of self-esteem and feel that our therapeutic modality is probably one of the shortest; (10) we accept the uniqueness of people and focus on getting the client to accept his or her own special uniqueness.

Both behavior therapy and behavior modification tend to reject the medical model of pathology without considering deviant behavior a symptom of underlying pathology. Abnormal behavior is seen as a behavior that is learned and as such is nonjudgmental. For example, deviance, social or individual, is learned in much the same manner as Sutherland (1947) posits, which is social deviance in relationship to his differential association theory of crime. If an individual spends more time with the deviant culture, then his behavior will take on the characteristics of that subculture and will be deviant. Accordingly, if he were to spend more time with a "normal" subculture, then this behavior would tend to be normal. Both these behaviors are seen as following the same laws of learning. In the case of a phobia, the view is that at some time the object of the phobia, the fear, was accidentally paired with an undesirable unconditioned stimulus, normally producing fear or anxiety. Avoidance of the undesirable stimulus is itself self-reinforcing for the individual. Therefore, both behavior therapy and behavior modification reject the notion that behavior is unconsciously controlled, but rather take the position that it is environmentally conditioned. Behavior modification is an attempt to utilize the principles of positive and negative reinforcement, de-sensitization, and so on, to remove the undesirable response (fear). Behavior modification focuses on the response, specifically targeted and counter-conditioned with a more desirable response. The difficulty however, is that while the effect may be desirable, as is the elimination of fear in the case of a phobia, the technique does nothing to get at the function of the interpretive process in the apperceptive mass. Therefore, if as in SET we see self-esteem being the focus of the compensatory mechanism (a safeguarding mechanism), then the elimination of the behavior, while desirable, is not sufficient. If we do not reeducate and bring about a change in the individual's evaluation of him- or herself and environment, he/she will merely succumb to another environmental stimulus with another undesirable behavior response.

SET utilizes similar principles but in a more nondirective fashion. Instead of a specific behavior being targeted and modified, the client reestablishes goals and determines what is to be accomplished. Behavior therapy is a process of reeducation where the client is an active-passive participant, with emphasis on making the client more capable of dealing with the problem, low self-esteem. SET, while utilizing a conditioning model, relies implicitly on reinterpretation of the content of the apperceptive mass in a future orientation; mediates desirable judgments, cognition, and expectations leading to behavioral responses. Direct behavioral education may be mediated through the use of biofeedback, relaxation, desensitization, flooding, and other behavior therapy techniques. Because behavior therapy produces a certain insight, it is assumed that the chance for symptom substitution is reduced, and once self-esteem is bettered, the need for the compensatory mechanism (the undesirable response) is eliminated.

In essence, SET is a cognitive behavior therapy with additional emphasis on the process of interpretation and the formation of judgment. We have postulated that all successful therapies are in reality therapies that overtly or covertly, explicitly or implicitly, cognitively or unwittingly bring about a bettering of self-esteem. After developing the self-esteem theory of deviance, I began to apply this knowledge in a therapeutic setting and found that while originally I worked on self-esteem in drug abusers, I began to see that by developing self-esteem (in my clients who manifested a broad spectrum of behavior problems), I achieved remarkable success. I found that when dealing with phobias, by developing self-esteem, they tended to diminish and fade out. I found that when working with patients who manifested deep depression, the depression abated when self-esteem was developed. Working with schizophrenics, I found that when I was able to develop and expand the base of self-esteem, the dissociative behavior began to decrease. Thus far, I have found no behavior disorder, be it neurosis, psychosis, character disorder, and others, that has not been amenable to self-esteem therapy. This does not mean that I have had successes exclusively—although my success rate is eminently high. There are, of course, some individuals who do not relate to the technique or me as a person. I further suggest that all therapies are effective only to the degree that they do raise self-esteem and since the focus of SET is a conscious cognitive approach to the building of self-esteem, SET has an advantage over the other modalities. Further, given any modality, we find that therapist A may be successful while therapist B may not, utilizing the same modality for the same condition. It is essential that we always keep in mind that the therapeutic process is an active process and that as such there are certain characteristic personality dimensions of both the client and the therapist that either enhance the therapeutic process or detract and negate the process, regardless of the modality. It is our contention that SET is a therapeutic modality that is effective in eliminating any major disorder, given an effective therapeutic process vis-à-vis the didactic relationship.

In our discussion of personality, we have considered the function of contradictory tendencies as trait complexes that form a configuration around which the personality develops. We have considered the various polar concepts and stated that there is no mid-point but that each individual personality becomes a unique configuration of the individual positioning on each continuum. When taken as a whole, these form the unique configuration of each individual. Whether an individual has in excess or a deficit for each trait tendency is unimportant but, rather, what is important is how these integrate into a total configuration identifying the degree of normalcy for the individual. We have commented that, on the trait complex of aggression and passivity, the two major social classes (lower and middle) internalize norms which create a variation in terms of the degree of passivity or aggressiveness that the individual will manifest. It is not that the individual is to the right or left, but rather if he or she moves too far in either direction, it may cause problems in individual or social adjustment. If the individual is too far in the aggressive component, he/she may likely come in conflict with society (especially the law) and may find himself/herself identified as incorrigible or violent. If the individual is too passive, he/she may find his/her courage threatened because of an inability to stand up for his/her rights, self-esteem will become threatened, and this will have a negative impact upon his/her social adjustment. The ideal is not the mid-point, but rather how the individual internalizes a particular trait in relationship to his/her social behavior. An individual in the lower class needs to be street-wise if he/she is to survive. On the other hand, an individual from the middle class will function quite adequately in a more passive capacity. The point is that the goal of therapy is not to make an individual who is aggressive passive, but rather to identify the two tendencies, point out the relationship of these two tendencies, and create a functional balance or innervative correspondence between the two opposing forces.

ASSESSMENT

The basis of SET are Adlerian, Husserlian, Marxian, and Simmelian. The emphasis upon the dialectic and the need to create an innervative correspondence of the opposing forces is a major focus in SET. We need to create an innervative correspondence between opposing tendencies. Personality is the dynamic configuration of the three levels of ego developed parsimoniously from the integration of the contradictory tendencies. Table 4.1 lists 16 contradictory tendencies. These are neither exhaustive nor traits in the usual sense of the word, but are seen in the dialectic as opposite tendencies. We have stated that the correct balance for each individual is unique.

If we are to function effectively in a therapeutic setting, we need to have some measure of assessment. Table 4.1, an assessment questionnaire, is provided in order to make a behavioral trait assessment. It covers three areas: contradictory tendencies (question 1), cognition (questions 2, 3, and 4) and goals (questions 5, 6, and 7). Under contradictory tendencies we have taken 16 opposing tendencies and asked the subject to rate him- or herself in terms of the extreme or neutral

Table 4.1
Assessment Questionnaire

Name_____   Age_____ Sex_____ Date_____

Check the following:

					Neutral
1.	☐	I am too aggressive	☐	I am too passive	☐
	☐	I can't make decisions	☐	I make decisions easily	☐
	☐	I am sexually aggressive	☐	I am sexually too passive	☐
	☐	I am too defiant	☐	I am too compliant	☐
	☐	I am very rational	☐	I make decisions	☐
	☐	I criticize myself too much	☐	I feel good about myself	☐
	☐	I tend to be depressed	☐	I tend to be hyperactive	☐
	☐	I tend to like to fantasize	☐	I tend to be realistic	☐
	☐	I like to be with other people	☐	I am a loner	☐
	☐	I am introverted	☐	I am extroverted	☐
	☐	I am highly structured	☐	I feel unstructured	☐
	☐	I often feel life is painful	☐	I feel life is enjoyable	☐
	☐	I tend to organize	☐	I am unorganized	☐
	☐	I am very productive	☐	I lean on others	☐
	☐	I protect myself	☐	I feel vulnerable	☐
	☐	I feel harmonious	☐	I feel discordant	☐

2.   What thoughts do you have that make you uncomfortable?

3.   What are things that you or others think you should do more, for example, compliment
      others, be more productive, make more time for recreation, and so on?

4.   What thoughts make you happy?

5.   What are your goals?

6.   What do you expect to accomplish from therapy?

7.   What do you want to change most (look at the lists in items 1 and 2)?

position; for example, I am too aggressive / I am too passive, or neutral.

Under cognition, number two then asks what areas of the thought process tend to create further problems for the subject. Number three asks what the subject perceives as being an area of deficit; and number four asks what thoughts make you happy. These three questions help to clarify what the individual perceives as major sources of pleasure or areas of deficit in his or her life-style.

Under goals, question number five asks what are your goals? We follow with two questions: (six) What does the client expect from therapy and (seven) What does he/she want to change most? These last two questions bring to light the conscious motives of the individual. The questionnaire focuses on the conflict and the dialectic.

We still have a need for an assessment of self-esteem. In Chapter 1, "What Is Self-Esteem?", we attempted to define self-esteem nominally, really and operationally. Further, we offered a simple definition of personality, stating that it is an integration of the three levels of ego. Of what use is the idea of an integration of three levels of ego unless these levels can be meaningfully and operationally utilized? In *Hypnotic Techniques for Increasing Self-Esteem* (Steffenhagen 1983), we have the first self-esteem sub-test based upon the first model (see Appendix B, this volume). We have created two more self-esteem sub-tests (Appendix B), testing self-esteem at each respective level of the ego (material, transcendental, and ego strength). Self-esteem Sub-Test 1 is based on the material level of ego. Sub-Test 2 is similar to Sub-Test 1 but operates on a higher level of abstraction and subjective analysis. Self-Esteem Sub-Test 3 (ego strength) serves an integrative function.

Thus, for assessment purposes we have a questionnaire and three self-esteem sub-tests which measure self-esteem on three levels comprising an aggregate measure of self-esteem. These assessment instruments can be used to help understand the areas of weakness and what the focus of the therapeutic process should be.

As ego strength increases, the correlation between Sub-Test 1 (material/situational) and Sub-Test 2 (transcendental) will increase positively. Further, and conversely, as ego strength decreases, the correlation between Sub-Test 1 and Sub-Test 2 will increase negatively. In other words, as the strength of the ego increases, the situational ego will operate more harmoniously with the transcendental ego. A functional reality orientation/integration will define and prevent the individual from attempting goals likely to diminish his/her self-esteem.

In Figure 4.1, 18 facets of self-esteem are represented, each model represented by a Star of David. Superimposition of the situational, transcendental, and ego strength models produces an 18-faceted model of aggregate self-esteem.

These sub-tests, consisting of 27 questions each, comprise the 81-item Steffenhagen/Burns Self-Esteem Measure (SSM). Response is measured by a five-point Likert-type scale on a continuum from 'strongly agree' to 'strongly disagree', or 'very often' to 'almost never', depending on the nature of the question. Self-esteem has been defined in terms of three levels of ego: the world-immersed (material/situational), the transcendental, and ego strength (awareness/integration) level of ego. The three sub-tests are trifurcated to correspond to the operationalized concept of self-esteem introduced by Steffenhagen in 1983 and elabo-

Figure 4.1
Integrated Model of Self-Esteem

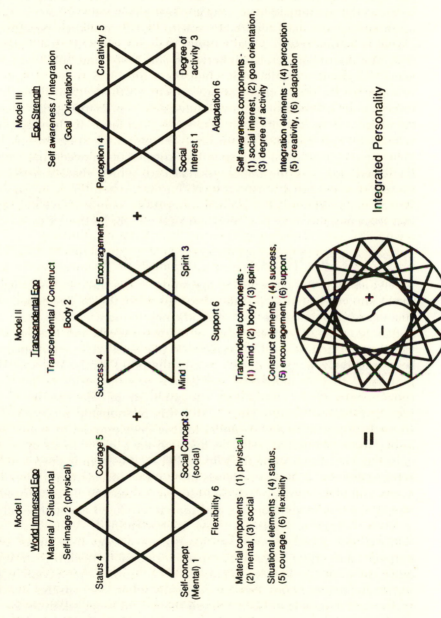

Model I
World Immersed Ego
Material / Situational

Courage 5

Self-image 2 (physical)

Status 4   Social Concept 3
                            (social)

Self-concept
(Mental) 1

Flexibility 6

Material components - (1) physical,
(2) mental, (3) social

Situational elements - (4) status,
(5) courage, (6) flexibility

+

Model II
Transcendental Ego
Transcendental / Construct

Encouragement 5

Body 2   Spirit 3

Success 4   Mind 1

Support 6

Trancendental components -
(1) mind, (2) body, (3) spirit

Construct elements - (4) success,
(5) encouragement, (6) support

+

Model III
Ego Strength
Self awareness / Integration

Goal Orientation 2   Creativity 5

Perception 4   Degree of
                              activity 3

Social
Interest 1

Adaptation 6

Self awareness components -
(1) social interest, (2) goal orientation,
(3) degree of activity

Integration elements - (4) perception
(5) creativity, (6) adaptation

=

Integrated Personality

rated on in 1987 by Steffenhagen and Burns. Each test measures three elements and three components of self-esteem at their respective levels: Test 1 measures the elements of status/courage/flexibility and the components of mental/physical/social. Test 2 measures success/encouragement/support and mind/body spirit. Test 3 measures perception/creativity/adaption and social interest/degree of activity/goal orientation. The degree of correlation between Sub-Test 1 and Sub-Test 2 will show the greatest significance when the score on Sub-Test 3 is high. Our operationalized concept of self-esteem postulates that those individuals with low ego strength will have either an inappropriate reality orientation or an inability to integrate this orientation to develop more self-satisfying personality parameters. Therefore, when ego strength is high, there should be a corresponding correlation between the world-immersed ego, and the transcendental ego, which characterizes self-esteem at the internal construct level. Further, when the score on Sub-Test 3 (ego strength) is low normal, population samples have indicated that the variability between Test 1 and Test 2 will be the greatest.

FUNCTION OF THE THERAPEUTIC PARADIGM

Personality is the dynamic configuration of the three levels of ego—world-immersed, transcendental, and ego strength—as developed parsimoniously to integrate the contradictory tendencies. We have hypothesized that self-esteem exists on all three levels and that an individual may manifest good self-esteem on one level while simultaneously being relatively weak in one or two of the other levels. We originally postulated that an individual could have good self-esteem and weak ego strength while considering ego strength in relationship to the Freudian model, but we have found this relationship incorrect. Ego strength is crucial to and essential for the development of self-esteem in our model; therefore, SET begins with an a priori focus upon the development of ego strength. Within SET, self-esteem is postulated as being composed of the three levels of ego, each divided into three elements and three components. Self-esteem is theoretically comprised of nine independent components and nine interrelated elements—subsequently 27 facets of self-esteem have been identified.

Life is not a bed of roses, things do not always flow in an even tranquil manner, and we need to be prepared to deal with trauma, catastrophe, and adversity. Trauma, catastrophe, and adversity are seemingly strong nouns, but are not really when we consider that the apperceptive mass is the key. Stimuli that might seem relatively inconsequential to us may be viewed as catastrophic by the client. What is traumatic for one may be mild or unimportant to another. We need to individually prepared, as Adler would say, to deal with our life processes in a constructive manner. Ego strength is comprised of Adler's components of social interest, goal orientation and degree of activity. Within our model, we see individuals manifest a high degree of individuality in their development of self-esteem. An individual can be high or low on any of the nine components or nine elements. It is possible that a person may be very low in one while being very high in another, and, as we have indicated, character types may vary in terms of their self-esteem; consider, for example, male athletes manifesting a higher degree of self-esteem in the physical area and female athletes a higher degree of self-esteem in the social area, while they may both have areas in which they are low. In the development of our three levels of ego we move from the highest to the lowest; ego strength can only be achieved on a higher, and more abstract plane than that of the transcendental ego, which is of course consistent with the importance of the function of the material/physical universe. Therapy should never be devoid of the importance of the function of ego strength; once self-esteem is developed on this level, the individual will be able to deal with adversity on either of the other two levels. Our three-level self-esteem test can be used as an adjunct to assessment. We shall discuss the various components and their measurement elements briefly in relationship to their function in terms of diagnosis. In Model I (see Figure 4.1), the situational elements are status/courage/flexibility. These three characteristics are essential to good self-esteem on the world-immersed or material level. Status and courage are important in all cultures, whereas flexibility is especially important in modern technological societies manifesting rapid cultural change, demanding change in both recreational and vocational areas.

Self-esteem exists on the material level of the physical, mental, and social components of the unified self. The physical is frequently referred to as the self-image. In the traditional literature, mental refers to an individual's assessment of his/her cognitive processes, or self-concept, and social refers to the assessment of the individual's social behavior: All assessments are made as the individual judges how others perceive him. The physical level refers to self-image, what we think others think of our body. This is especially important in the United States, where television has created such an idealized version of the male and female forms. Few of us can come close to such an idealized version and yet we feel we are expected to compete on this level. It implies competition as a social process. Anorexia nervosa becomes a classic example of an underassessment at this component level.

The mental, or self-concept, level refers to the evaluation one makes of intellectual capacity. Again, this evaluation is mediated to the subject through intentionality, what one thinks others think of one's intellectual capacities, which of course is dependent on one's degree of social activity and basic character traits as set forth in the conflict theory of personality. The cultural level, or social concept, is the assessment of social participation. Man is a gregarious animal and social interaction is essential to our mental well-being. Social interaction requires communication, both verbal and physical. Kurt Lewin's (1948) work on the material and social differences between Americans and Germans presents the notion that social distance operates on the peripheral and central areas. Americans appear to have less social distance than Germans, but the level of integration is much more peripheral than that seen in Germans. We further suggest that this rather superficial level of social interaction, accompanied by relatively little social change or distance, has been further increased due to television which fosters one-way communication; the individual becomes a receiver rather than a communicator. Sexual promiscuity is an indicator of this trend. Many youth turn to sex as a means of communication. Since they cannot communicate verbally, they do so on a physical level. They find, however, that such physical communication still leaves a void in their need for meaningful communication. This is supported by clinical evidence of the author.

So far we have discussed self-esteem in terms of the first six points of the paridigm at the material level of the ego. In relationship to the transcendental level of ego, we present internal construct elements of success, encouragement, and support. It doesn't matter what others think of us so much as what we think of ourselves. The he-man may be seen as macho by his friends, and yet he may feel like a 'wimp.' The brain surgeon may feel unsuccessful if he looses a single patient under a complicated surgery. These elements of success, encouragement, and support are espoused by educators as the three factors most important in the development of self-esteem vis-à-vis the educational process. As stressed earlier, man is a social animal, and in terms of his psychological needs, these elements are necessary. We need the encouragement and support of our friends and relatives, but when an individual needs excess chronic encouragement and support and feels unsuccessful, this is an indication of low transcendental self-esteem. Success has too often been hypothesized as the most important factor in the development of self-esteem. If a student succeeds, he will feel good about himself, but, as we find in clinical practice, this often is not the case. We are aware of many students who certainly succeed academically and socially, yet have low self-esteem.

The body, mind, and spirit are the tripartite unification of man. We have discussed this in relationship to the body as the physical structure, the mind as the computer component, or cognitive element, and the spirit as the psyche (the life force, the essence), and then the socialness of man. The body, mind, and spirit differ from the physical, mental, and social on a somewhat higher transcendental level. The body is seen not only in terms of its physical form vis-à-vis the mirror, but as a structure that is essential to life and to having a higher purpose than that of the actual physical image. The mind is certainly the key to an understanding of our habits and their effects. In the Johnsonian framework the mind is the servant of the spirit. It functions much as a computer functions. It is a robot, an automaton and it is guided by the inner force of a deeper essence, which we call the psyche or spirit. The West has geared itself to mind/body dichotomy, the East to a mind/spirit dichotomy. Both these dichotomies lack an extremely important component. To illustrate this weakness on the component level we would like to discuss a case history of a student who manifested suicidal ruminations. We found that he was particularly immersed in the Madison Avenue success interpretation of money as the key to happiness. In part, while he had internalized this value from his parents, he further became immersed in the values of the drug culture of the late 1960s and rebelled overtly to the American emphasis on money as the key to success and happiness. The dissonance between two divergent values, one based on material success and the other on the need for higher spirituality, created an inner conflict that served as the basis for depression and anxiety. He could not disassociate himself from the value of material possessions yet spiritually he rebelled against this ideology. Through therapy we found he had no understanding of the third component of the transcendental spirit. We discussed in great detail the tripartite unification, the importance of the body as a temple which houses the spirit, and gave meaning to this reality. Several times he became extremely agitated and had serious suicidal thoughts, but was able to refrain from acting on thee impulses. He said the only thing that prevented him was the fact that he was beginning to accept a higher reality, that he could begin to see and accept the idea that the material level was only one level, and although he had not been socialized within a traditional religious setting and rebelled against religiosity, he could accept the concept of spirituality, or purpose and meaning of life that transcends material acquisition. We stated many time that the function of this life was the development of this transcendental quality. De Chardin's (1962, 23) cosmic evolution states that one needs to experience the material reality so that one can grow and evolve on the basis of a higher reality. Again we see the importance of values and their impact on behavior. The result: The patient's acceptance of the fact that there is a possibility of another reality kept him from committing suicide. The body is the superstructure for the transcendental level of the ego. The mind is its computer component and interpreter of the physical universe, and the spirit the inner life force, be it called soul, spirit, essence, or transcendental socialness.

In model III (see Figure 4.1) ego strength is the result of what we call the epoché performing level of ego. The development of the epoché reduction culminates in true awareness, the goal cited by the philosophers throughout the ages. Awareness of self leads to awareness of others, and vice versa. Without the phenomenological orientation of reality, the final goal of life as espoused by Gurdjieff cannot be achieved. Without the development of true ego strength, man is constrained within a sleeping state of consciousness.

The integration elements of model III (Figure 4.1) are perception, creativity, and adaptation. Perception refers not only to the stimulus but to the interpretation on the basis of judgment. A negative life-style presupposes one to interpret behavior negatively, even when it is positive in its origin; in other words, when someone is being positive to us in a helping fashion, we would interpret this as condescension and a put-down. This is not the perception on the level of the world-immersed ego, but perception as judgment on the level of awareness.

We have discussed creativity in relationship to right brain activity and if instincts exist on the human level, or if we are to postulate an effective basis for human behavior, then the instinct has been basically socialized out of modern man as a result of the scientific revolution. Colin Wilson (1973), says that the Age of Magic was destroyed by the advent of the scientific revolution. The basis of creativity, a reality on a higher level, whether it be called parapsychology or something else, is not lost but has been deprogrammed from individuals (by the family and other institutions) so that they do not believe this reality exists. In the arts we are finding decreased attention and increased stultification in today's *Volkgeist* and *Zeitgeist*.

Adaptation refers to the characteristic of being able to adapt to a changing *Umwelt*. Our Umwelt (or social world) is constantly changing as a result of modern technology and science. These changes need to be incorporated within the life-style of the individual. Adaptation to this higher level depends on one's ability to integrate the various changes that occur within the ego and between the three levels of ego.

The components of ego strength include goal orientation, social interest, and degree of activity. The basic psychic energy of the individual we call degree of activity. The striving for superiority is the basic motivation for all behavior and this striving is aimed at reducing inferiority. The dialectic between inferiority and superiority provides the energy source for the behavior of the individual, and this energy is then directed toward goal orientation. When this striving is reduced, possibly in response to a lack of goal orientation, the individual manifests a low degree of activity; he has little psychic energy. Within our therapeutic model, the beginning point of therapy is a discussion and clarification of the individual's goals. We cannot strive unless we strive for something, and what we strive for is seen within the overt and covert goals we set. We can only achieve superiority in relationship to achieving goals. Adler often stated that a client's neuroses served a purpose, and suggested asking the client, "What would be different in your life if you didn't have this problem?"

Social interest exists in the apperceptive mass and would have a relationship to the *Gemeinschaftsgefühl*, or a sense of community, which can only be achieved through a positive orientation to social action. In therapy a sense of *Gemeinschaftsgefühl*, or lack thereof, is of major importance in helping the client to develop self-esteem. Social interest, as with self-esteem, is not developed in a vacuum but is created out of a socialization process from the primary institutions. If there is an apparent lack of social interest in the client, then a deconditioning/reconditioning process must be instituted in which the client is helped to develop a sense of social interest. Social interest in and of itself is not value laden, in other words, we are not imposing our values on the individual but are rather helping him or her to understand that selfishness and selflessness make a dialectic which, when understood, can be used by the individual to further his/her own integration and awareness. Selfishness in and of itself is not always negative but may provide the positive kernal for the development of selflessness, or, as we shall refer to it in this paradigm, social interest. The energy of the individual is concomitant with the striving for superiority, the basic motivation. The degree of activity and goal orientation are intricately interrelated. Degree of activity is not the energy, per se, in our model, but rather is observable in the life-style of the individual. The degree of activity is then manifest in the behavior of the individual on the on the overt level; he is seen as being active, constantly moving forward. We feel that the degree of activity is a function of goal-directed behavior. The apperceptive mass provides the interpretive data that allow for an integration of goal orientation and social interest. This integration is then identified as the degree of activity manifest by the individual.

Ego strength identifies the integration of the three levels of ego. The final integration allows for self-awareness—"this above all: to thine own self be true" (Hamlet). The true awareness can only emerge out of the final integration achieved through the epoché reduction on the phenomenological level. The elements and components of ego strength can be quantified by the use of our self-esteem Sub-test 3 (Appendix B), and may also be observed through the diagnostic process.

Self-esteem, then, can be high or low on any level of ego. The therapeutic process may raise self-esteem on any of these levels, or all three simultaneously. When ego strength is high, the prognostication for success in therapy is high; therefore, in SET we make ego strength an a priori focus on attention while attempting to delineate inadequacies at other levels during the process.

GOAL ORIENTATION

Within the Adlerian paradigm, one of the important components is a discussion of goal clarification. We have indicated throughout the book that self-esteem emerges from the striving toward superiority and that this striving is ultimately goal oriented. Without goals we are amotivated. In fact, if there were a classic amotivational syndrome, it would be the result of a lack of goals. The basic energy force in the Adlerian model is the movement of superiority, the striving. We have further commented on the importance of realistic as opposed to godlike goals. These two are, in actuality, polar opposites, although the opposite of the godlike goals is a realistic goal, and in this particular instance would be the ideal for the focus of therapy. Godlike goals are those which are often borne of a pampered life-style and so exultant, they defy achievement. We call them godlike because the individual sets goals so high they they are beyond the pale of human achievement. Obviously, godlike goals vary in terms of ability, in that a godlike goal academically for someone with a 100-110 I. Q. would certainly not be godlike for someone with an I. Q. of 150.

It is our contention that the most common client problem, depression, generally stems from faulty social relations. Man is a gregarious animal who needs social contact. We have stressed the importance of social contact by indicating that one of the most severe forms of punishment devised by man is social isolation, solitary confinement. Without question, most people cannot endure solitary confinement and break down mentally. This punishment has also been used for brainwashing in order to totally destroy a person's values and attitudes in order to establish new ones.

Individuals create fictional goals. Ultimately, all goals are fictional in respect to the fact that they are projections into the future. Whether these projections are realistic or not doesn't alter the fact that they are projections of a desired accomplishment. We have stressed the importance of realistic goals vs. godlike goals in the development of good self-esteem. On the level of social relations, we are constantly creating these fictional goals, and when the actual behavior of the other person does not conform to our fictional goal there is the tendency to search our apperceptive mass for the answers. If one finds that he or she has had previous failures in the area of personal relationships, the person tends to live out a self-fulfilling prophesy and ultimately undergoes additional failures. In relationship to the psychoanalytic study of the family, we find that certain individuals create an image of what their marriage partner should be, based on their own socialization vis-à-vis the mother or father. Very often, men develop unconscious fictions of what the wife should be, based on their original contact with and love for the mother. Consequently, what they may do is to seek out a partner who has all the characteristics of that parent. However, in the marriage relationship they frequently find that, while these characteristics may be totally desirable, they become intolerable on the conscious level in that they want a wife not a mother. Such relationships usually end in divorce and then the individual proceeds to develop a close relationship with another person who has the same characteristics, eventuating in the same conclusion.

Obviously the link between the past and current goal orientation is a function of ego strength. To what degree do we perceive reality realistically, and to what degree do we create illusions of what reality should be? Adler, borrowing from Vaighner, deals with the 'as if' concept. Fictions are a necessary part of our intellectual development and are very often one and the same. However, fantasy misguided may become the basis for depression in that we cannot achieve our goals, then begin to develop deep-seated feelings of inferiority, and consequently may begin to withdraw from social relations. Sometimes one develops a fictional goal and, in the process of working toward this goal, the dialectic of fiction and reality may create a new synthesis and the creation of a new goal; consequently, reality may become blurred. The human tendency will be to find what is most real (a function of ego strength) in order to adjust behavior appropriately. If what is not real has been synthesized from ambiguous goals, the individual will then have difficulty delineating fiction from reality. Every synthesis of the dialectic is a self-fulfilling prophecy; it becomes a new goal based on interpretation, and these interpretations are a function of the apperceptive mass vis-à-vis ego strength. Because it is natural to desire a resolution of conflict (pain/pleasure), the individual's level of self-esteem will function accordingly. Low self-esteem and ambiguous goal orientations will create a striving in which the individual seeks out realities or attempts to achieve goals that will fit his or her self-fulfilling prophecy. Although undesirable, the individual, when placed in a painful situation, tends to want to remain as long as possible to see if pleasure will ultimately develop. The neurotic, while wanting to change, is also afraid of change; he does not want to give up his previous malfunctioning thoughts, his fictional goals, which have become embedded in the apperceptive mass. Faulty thinking is the basis for depression. Frequently a depressed person is afraid of success. A neurotic invariably fears success or fears failure. In either case, he or she is inhibited and prevented from engaging in rewarding social contact. If we don't try to relate to other people, we prevent change and become mired in our own feelings of inadequacy.

The characteristics of friendship and love are very similar. They both are the only logical conclusion of close interpersonal, social relations. A list of some of the characteristics are: acceptance, respect, trust, confiding, understanding, spontaneity, mutual assistance, enjoyment, fascination, and others (Davis 1985). The passion cluster includes exclusiveness, sexual intimacy, giving the utmost, success ambivalence, among others, and includes a caring cluster of giving the utmost and being a champion advocate, although giving the utmost and being a champion advocate were also very typical of best friends. This *Psychology Today* article helps us delineate some of the interesting characteristics of friendships, best friends, and/or lovers. It is in the area of interpersonal relations that most people have their greatest problems. Too often we expect too much from friendships and/or love relationships. We create fictional goals and then, when the realities do not correspond with our fictions, we tend to become depressed. Often, one expects more than the other person is inclined to give, or give to a relationship more than someone else is able to return in kind. Too often, one enters a new relationship doomed to failure on the basis of a self-fulfilling prophecy developed as a result of low self-esteem and past experience included in the apperceptive mass. One has had failure in love and consequently when entering a new relationship assumes that the new relationship will result in the same failure on the same basis as the previous relationship; when we have low self-esteem we cannot enter a relationship on a positive foundation. We set the stage automatically for failure and then feel bad when it eventuates exactly as we had predicted.

When we have strong self-esteem, and good ego strength, we develop adequate orientations toward social action, orientations that are realistic and create new, positive self-fulfilling prophecies. In the framework of conflict theory and dialectic, we need to allow for various combinations relative to our goal orientation. We need to create a balance between social interest and self-interest, where self-interest itself becomes fulfilled through the medium of social interest. Ego strength determines our reality orientation and integration. Our self-fulfilling prophecies are our realities. The individual then expects that these realities will be met without corrective influence from the outside. Depression itself has a snowballing effect. It predetermines how we will interpret social relationships and, due to the negative nature of depression, it creates a barrier in communicating with others.

In Reality Therapy we can deal with disturbed thinking on the cognitive level and show a person how his inaccurate or disturbed thought processes are preventing him from active, fulfilling social participation. However, the knowing-how does not always precipitate the appropriate action. We need to break through the conscious level at times and begin to deprogram negative self-fulfilling prophecies on the unconscious level to start the process in motion. A number of years ago I worked with a client who had been extremely depressed and was failing in school as a result of the depression which was inhibiting her from working productively and, indeed, from studying at all. She had been in therapy for two years without success. Her comment was that she felt more depressed at the end of the two years than she did at the beginning of therapy; she was at a loss for what to do next. We utilized hypnotherapy as a way of implanting some positive thoughts at the level of the unconscious to create the initial change in thinking which was necessary to precipitate a change in action. During the hypnotic process we commented on the fact that she was a beautiful woman and that this was a positive asset she could use in her interpersonal relationships. After the session she commented on the fact that her previous counselor had often told her that she was attractive, and that all she needed to do was to allow this asset to spark social relationships. Her comment was that no matter how often the therapist told her that she was attractive, she refused to believe it because she felt ugly. After the hypnosis session she expressed confusion as to why the same statement now had an effect. The planting of the suggestion on the unconscious level was sufficient to change her mode of thought. She began to think of herself as an attractive, positive person who could have positive relationships with other people. We found that this particular case of deep depression was amenable to change through five hypnotherapeutic sessions. In fact, after the second session she was vivacious, enjoying life, and was absolutely ecstatic about the change in her thought process. The use of hypnotherapy expedites the process of normal therapeutic change available to SET practitioners.

It is not always possible merely to reinterpret our social relationships, but sometimes it is necessary to bring about a change in the social milieu. If we find an individual from the lower social class who has developed middle class values and aspirations, we will find the need to bring about a change in the social milieu, otherwise all efforts will be to no avail, since he/she will be caught between the ideal and the real. A middle-class individual cannot function adequately within the value systems of the lower class; hes/she needs the feedback from others who feel and express the same values that he/she does. Employment itself can often become the source of deep-seated depression. An individual who has an active, creative mind, who is intelligent, may not be able to function adequately in a blue-collar job that requires no intellectual thought. Years ago I had the occasion to work in a factory

for a period of time, before I went to college and after being discharged
from the army. Within a relatively short period of time I become so
bored from the monotony at work that I dreaded going to work each
day and if I had had to stay in this job for a longer period of time I
would most certainly have become depressed. A change in work may
be essential to bring about a break with the depression. Reevaluation
and reeducation are often essential in the therapeutic process, if success is to be obtained. We need to be aware of the community resources that can be utilized to help the individual develop his or her
potential.

Goal orientation and social milieu are intricately related, and consequently need to be seen in a single context. Our goals can only be set
in relationship to a given Umwelt, and their attainment can only be
derived from the social context. If we set a goal to become a professional worker in our society, we need to utilize the training of our
colleges and universities to prepare us to attain that goal. Therapists
need to look at the goal orientation of the individual in relationship to
his or her social milieu.

In another instance, I had the occasion to work with a client whose
abuse of drugs was reaching serious proportions. At the point when
he entered therapy, he had already completed a masters degree and
was slowly killing himself on "downers," particularly Quaaludes. During the course of therapy, it became evident that his background was
upper-middle class and both parents were professionals. He had a very
high I. Q., within the genius range, and his performance as an undergraduate was exemplary, graduating with honors. He was able to enter
the graduate school of his choice, and his work on the graduate level
was equally admirable. After a period of time in therapy he was able
to verbalize his true feelings about himself. To use his words: "I feel
like a piece of shit." This individual had all the successes that should
have provided him with the basis for good self-esteem. He was successful academically, as well as being a jock; he had a good build, was
very handsome, was successful in his relationship with members of the
opposite sex, had the encouragement and support of his family and
friends, had a successful career in a fraternity—all which should have
provided the basis for good self-esteem. However, it became evident
during therapy that none of the successes were seen as successes by
him. He developed goals of such proportions that they were totally
unachievable even by someone of his ability and intelligence. In examining the family background, we find the mother was constantly
pushing him to greater success. She would invidiously compare his
father with other successful men she knew or had known from her
past. She would comment that so-and-so was more successful than the
father. As a result of this emphasis upon success, he had developed

goals of such grandiosity that they were godlike and unachievable. The basis for his drug abuse was low self-esteem, and the primary cause of his low self-esteem was his inability to succeed, in accordance with the godlike goals.

In any therapeutic situation it is necessary to identify the client's overt and covert goals. In some individuals godlike goals may become the basis for low self-esteem. Some individuals may be unable to structure or identify goals for themselves because of an inadequate socialization process. Very often clients of social workers (the socially deprived) have problems that are not insurmountable but only seem insurmountable due to the social milieu—albeit we operate in a capitalistic society in which the social structure discriminates against the poor. However, there are social agencies that can be used to solve problems. It should be noted that most communities of medium to large size have health care facilities that can be utilize by the poor. One of the important components of problem solving is a knowledge of what facilities are available.

One of the functions, then, of SET is to provide the setting for an in-depth discussion and verification of an individual's goals. It is important to help the client not only establish goals but to become aware of his or her abilities and capabilities, and then help him or her set goals that can ultimately be achieved, so that through the successful achievement of those goals, the client may begin to raise self-esteem. Further, it is important to delineate a client's covert goals, those that become self-fulfilling prophecies, both negative and positive, the perpetuators of the neuroses (low self-esteem) and the *Leitlinie* (guiding line) for adjustment. It is important for therapists to realize goals exist from the negative valance of having no goals to the negative position of having godlike goals. A therapist should help the client to understand his or her abilities and capabilities and structure goals that can be achieved with this medium. Certainly teachers, in the academic environment, can help students achieve success through realistic goal development. Success exists only in the eye of the beholder, and it is not in our position as therapist to evaluate success, but rather see how the client views or interprets his or her behavior in terms of success or failure.

It is important to begin therapy with the question, "What are your goals?" The answer should include goals that are social, vocational, and therapeutic. As noted, clients often identify their goal in therapy as "I only want to be happy." This type of goal is godlike and therapy will be unsuccessful unless the goal is changed. Happiness is a by-product of social interest, goal achievement, and the degree of activity. Psychologists are now commenting that the people who are the happiest are those who are concerned about and serve others. All the books centering around the theme of 'I am number one' are detrimental and only promulgate self-consciousness, self-centeredness, and low-esteem. When an individual develops a totally selfish orientation toward social action, he or she is doomed to failure in that there is no gratification from success that has no social meaning. We might refer to this as a hollow or meaningless victory. Within the framework of SET, we recommend that the therapist begin with the consideration of goal orientation that can be overt and covert. One can ask the client directly what his or her goals are or, through the therapeutic process, begin to realize and understand the client's goals.

SOCIAL MILIEU

It is important to understand the *Umwelt* (the individual's social milieu) in its relationship to the therapeutic process. We will begin with a case history to illustrate the importance of the social milieu in relationship to successful treatment.

I have occasion to work with a client who was depressed. One day he commented on the fact that his particular job was incredibly boring and his way of coping with the boredom was to create mind games while at work. This sufficed for a period of time, however, when he entered therapy, he stated that he was no longer able to identify what was real and what was fictional. The mind game was a compensatory mechanism that he had been using to deal with boredom. However, the fiction became a dangerous technique that needed to be assessed realistically so that a more effective and productive technique could be developed to deal with the boredom. The individual had a very high I. Q. His self-esteem was very low. A goal he had established while a teenager of going to college was not reached. We discussed his interest and he began to take courses through Continuing Education. Although he did not set a goal of becoming a college graduate, the enjoyment he achieved from taking courses was beneficial. It became evident that his work was so demeaning for him that all that was accomplished in the therapeutic setting would be lost at work. We do not mean to imply that the job was at fault but it was detrimental to this particular individual's emotional well-being. One day he called saying, "I hope you won't be angry at me, but I just did something that I have to tell you. I just told my boss to stick it." After a rather protracted period of time he was able to enroll in a job orientaton program and developed a skill in the health care area that proved extremely gratifying for him and helped him to develop good self-esteem. Today, he is happy and no longer plagued with anxiety. In this particular case, certain goals had to be assessed and changed. At one point it was necessary for his wife to work in order to help supplement the income. When this was discussed, his first comment was "In no way will I let my wife work." We discussed this and were able to get him to realize two important considerations: first, that his wife was also intelligent and outside employment would be beneficial for her self-esteem, as well, and second, that within the middle class, husband and wife employment has become more the rule than the exception, and society sees this as the standard within the present era. He was able to reassess his values, his wife went to work, and it was beneficial for both. In this particular case it would have been impossible to have concluded therapy successfully without an understanding and revamping of the social situation. One of the advantages of SET is that the therapist focuses upon the social milieu as a crucial factor in the development of individual or social deviance. It is wrong to help a client reassess and redevelop his or her value system to one that is inconsistent with his or her immediate milieu or intellectual capabilities. Therapists should not superimpose their own value systems on someone whose social milieu is inconsistent with theirs. While each culture establishes basic norms, standards, and values that provide the Leitlinie for behavior, each complex society also creates subcultures that develop somewhat divergent value systems within themselves. These divergent value systems, especially notable in terms of class differences, are consistent with the broader system but are sufficiently divergent that they provide for variable behavior within the system. It is important in therapy to assess the individual's social milieu, to understand the basis of his or her value system, and then help the client set goals within that value system.

SOCIAL INTEREST

I had a student client who was seeing me regarding academic performance. He was taking an introductory psychology course and was doing very poorly; he was also doing poorly in his other studies. We began by examining his test performance in an attempt to delineate the areas which were causing the greatest difficulties. It became evident that he had the intellectual ability to perform adequately, but there was something acting as a stumbling block to his performance. He spent a great deal of time studying, was highly motivated, but manifested a great deal of anxiety and couldn't seem to concentrate. The young man came from a lower-middle-class environment and was an only child. His father died when he was relatively young. His mother, the sole breadwinner, wanted very much for him to become a college graduate, so he enrolled in a business degree program. His mother was the owner/manager of a small drinking establishment. He was highly motivated and wanted very much to please her. But at the same time, he felt guilty that she had to work so hard to support him and put him through college. It was a small bar, and she performed most of the necessary functions to run the bar in order to make enough money for their support and his education. In this particular case, social interest is the dominant theme. He was motivated to do well in college but his focus was on doing well to please his mother, not to please himself. The element of social interest, his concern for others, was predominating, self-interest having been pushed to the background. Viewing this within our conflict theory, we see that the conflict existed between two goal orientations: the goal of obtaining a college degree to please himself and the goal of obtaining a college degree to please his mother. In this particular case he was submerging his own interest in order to achieve the goal. It would seem that whatever served as a source of motivation for the achievement of the goal should be adequate, but within the dialectic, the wrong emphasis served as a deterrent to successful action. In this instance, we had to emphasize the selfish aspect of the continuum in order to provide the basic motivation for the achievement of social interest. The dynamic involved was the conflict of interest in relationship to the *Gemeinschaftsgefühl* and his self-interest. Although this self-interest was consistent with his social interest, we found that the conflict created a barrier to successful social action. He felt that he needed to do well in order to make his mother proud of him. Consequently, he had created a social pressure that functioned as a tension, thus reducing his performance. In this instance, we spent several sessions helping him reevaluate his goals and understand that in order to complete college successfully and make his mother proud, he had to develop what was seemingly a selfish interest of setting the goal for himself. The dynamic here suggests that we ultimately must direct our behavior in relationship to our own goals if we are to be successful. We cannot make the focus of our orientation the values of someone else. What we need to do is to internalize social values, thereby making them our own. After two or three further sessions and clarification of values, the student's performance increased dramatically and he no longer needed support. Self-interest is fine as long as it does not become a compensatory mechanism. Social interest usually mediates self-interest, whereas the reverse is not usually true.

Walter O'Connell, an Adlerian, stresses the importance of social interest in the judgment of good self-esteem. This is way we cannot emphasize too much the importance of the concept of *Gemeinschaftsgefühl* in its relationship to therapy. Our example of the client who says, "I merely want to be happy," cannot be overstressed. Selfish interest ultimately forms the basis for a continuing neurosis, and the faddish movement toward self-development, self-interest—'I am number one'— are all going to prove unsuccessful in building self-esteem. They will only perpetuate the neurosis and low self-esteem. In another particular case history involving a former alcoholic we received a statement from him to the effect that he was "happily married this time [this was his third wife] but AA is No. 1 in my life, not my wife." If AA did not remain No. 1 in his orientation toward social action, he would have fallen off the wagon and returned to being an alcoholic, which would ultimately have led him to a termination of the marriage. Thus, in order for his wife and his marriage to remain No. 1, he had to create another goal and make AA No. 1. It is necessary to utilize some of these inherent contradictions if one is to achieve success in therapy. Self-interest does not always prove to be detrimental in successful therapy, but in reality may form the basis for social interest.

DEGREE OF ACTIVITY

There are four types of social activity listed by Adler. The first three are not only lacking in social interest, but probably are identified with low self-esteem. The dominant type with the ruling attitude is probably high in social activity and would be symptomatic of suicides, alcoholics, drug abusers, sexual perverts, and prostitutes. These people are identified as having a high degree of activity but they do not have sufficient social interest to develop good self-esteem. They tend to attack themselves in order to hurt others, for example, the suicidal person who desires to commit suicide in order to hurt a loved one. The second two types—the getting type and the avoiding type—tend to manifest a low degree of activity. The getting type will lean on and expect everything from others, manifesting a high degree of dependence, while the getting type, according to Adler, would be an individual who would certainly develop transference with his or her therapist. They will expect emotional support from their therapist and will lean on their therapist and expect to be provided all the answers to their problems, "You do it for me, I don't want to spend the time or energy to do it for myself." Unless this dynamic is clearly understood, therapy cannot be successful. They must be made to understand the contradiction in their orientation toward social action; no one can solve their problem but themselves and only they have the energy and the power to change their life-style in order to eliminate the neurosis.

I recently had a client who had been in therapy for three years and had developed an obvious transference and dependency on the therapist. The client manifested an agitated depression and was given Elavil (Amitriptyline) in order to sleep. The dependency was obvious not only in the fact that she was additionally seeing a psychiatrist once or twice a week but further, she commented on the fact that previously she could not have survived without her therapist. Her method for dealing with the problem was in fact a compensatory mechanism: she leaned on the therapist and expected the therapist to provide the answers while she expended very little energy. With an increase in self-esteem, we found that she was able to terminate her psychiatric relationship within five weeks, and was further able to terminate therapy with me in eight weeks, while having eliminated Elavil over the same period. Part of the therapy merely consisted of emphasizing the fact that the ability to change lay within herself and that she was a good and positive person: Therapy need not be elaborate or complex to be effective. Her degree of activity began to increase dramatically. On the Elavil, she slept very poorly, was never able to get up in the morning refreshed, and constantly felt tired. Without the Elavil, she was able to get a good night's sleep, woke up in the morning refreshed and anxious to participate in the day.

The avoiding type is the person who attemps to deal with problems by sidestepping them in order to avoid defeat. Such a person manifests a low degree of social activity. It is necessary to stress the importance and function of goals with this type of client. The actual achievement of goals is less important than the action engaged in, in striving to achieve the goal. The means become more important than the ends for the avoiding type. It is important to get him or her to realize that the action is more important than the goal as a starting point for successful therapy. For example, take the individual who desires a college education but, because he/she is afraid of failure, finds a substandard service job and then uses this as an excuse for not being successful. He or she avoids success by failing to attempt to achieve success, and the result is a self-fulfilling prophecy. One of my clients who manifested low self-esteem had developed the notion that she was incapable of achieving a college education. Consequently she avoided college and would lie about the importance of its worth, making her work seem much more important in order to cover up for the felt inadequacy. In this particular instance it was important to emphasize the fact that she did not have the ability to do college work and as a starting point we convinced her to enroll in a college course through continuing education. Although she had inadequate secondary school education, her interest and motivation were sufficient for her to perform adequately. With the successful completion of several courses, her self-esteem became stronger and she began to think in terms of going to college. As her self-esteem bettered, the avoiding technique was diminished and the degree of social activity began to increase.

Within the first three types there is a general lack of social interest. The fourth type includes those individuals who solve their problems in a way that is useful to others and who also manifest high activity. Within the SET paradigm, it is necessary for an individual to have a high degree of social activity and social interest in order to manifest normal personality development. The ruling, getting, and avoiding types (in terms of social interest), can be changed in the therapeutic setting by identifying the dialectical nature of their behavior in order to provide the basis for social change. We need to point out to the dominant or ruling individuals that it is through the dialectic that the goal can be achieved. Adler suggests that the degree of activity, the amount of energy available, is acquired in early childhood and becomes a constant supply throughout life. We feel that the amount of energy available is acquired in early childhood and that by increasing self-esteem, the degree of activity can and will increase proportionately. However, Adler's suggestion may be true in reference to most therapeutic modalities which attempt to bring about a change or eliminate neurotic behavior or a social symptom without concentrating on the development of self-esteem. Good self-esteem results from a functional integration of the three types of ego and will provide the energy for a high degree of social activity. We believe low activity levels generally result from neuroses. The more neurotic or depressed one becomes, the less energy there is to deal with change.

In therapy, it is sometimes necessary to create shock in order to precipitate change. A number of years ago I was working with a student who was a mother of two, self-supporting, and putting herself through college on a part-time basis. Her therapy lasted for a number of weeks and was largely a supportive counseling which she needed desperately. One day she came in and was about ready to quit school even though the semester was almost over. At this point I indicated to her that she was working hard, wasn't getting enough sleep, was spending energy on other work, on her family, and on school but that I thought she was a totally selfish, indifferent, and inadequate mother. This particular statement would have been enough to have destroyed her a month earlier, however, at this point it was necessary to shock her to show her the contradiction. Here again, in order for her to continue to be a good and caring mother, she needed to spend more energy on her academic pursuits, reduce the amount of energy she could spend with her children, making it appear as if she were being selfish. It should be noted that this particular statement was all she needed to get back on track. Successful therapy makes use of the contradiction apparent within conflict. Conflict and contradiction can provide the positive impetus for successful therapy. Some of the recent books on success suggest a dictum that we live each day as if it were our last. Utilizing this approach brings a positive goal to a successful life orientation, subsumed under the degree of activity.

THE USE OF FICTIONS IN THERAPY

What is reality? In the phenomenological sense, reality is the true subjective experience of the individual and it is especially this reality we wish to emphasize. We need to demarcate the objective reality of the scientific method from the subjective reality of the phenomenological approach and we suggest that it is the phenomenological approach which is important to successful therapy. True objective reality, the existence of a tree one hundred feet away, is of no or little consequence in the therapeutic model. We have discussed Becker's concept of cultural heroes and his premise that the cultural hero provides the basis for the very fabric of society. Cultural heroes are derived from the myths of the culture. Hidden within the myths of society are the key values of man's happiness and survival. According to Jung, the psyche creates its own reality, and it is this reality on which man's behavior is based. Similarly, according to W. I. Thomas, if a situation is defined as real by the actor, it is real in its consequences. The real reality is the subjective reality. Physical phenomena exists only intentionally, whereas psychic phenomena exist both intentionally and actually.

The issue of reality is not merely philosophical but pragmatic. Hallucinations are mental constructs and must be dealt with on the level of reality. They are not merely figments of the imagination: They have a reality of their own. The shaman who deals with evil spirits may have a better chance of curing the obsessed and possessed than the American psychiatrist, because he looks at the malady as brought about by forces exogenous to the individual. These can then be subjected to endogenous control. Emanuel Swedenborg, an occultist in the 1600s, was a true scientist in the modern sense until some dreams totally restructed his approach to reality. Swedenborg provided a basis for the understanding of obsession and possession which come up frequently in the psychiatric literature. The difference between the Swedenborgian approach and the scientific approach is the reality of the situation, in other words, with the scientific approach obsession and possession are functions of a maladaptive thought process. In the Swedenborgian approach, obsession and possession are due to outside forces that actually affect the individual, forces present on another plane of consciousness/existence. Possession is a situation wherein an evil or earthbound 'spirit' takes over a body of a living individual. This, in part, becomes the occult explanation of the split personality as manifest in the schizophrenic syndrone. Obsession, then, is caused by a spirit from the astral plane or another plane of existence that does not enter the body of the individual on this side but rather attaches itself to the individal's aura and by so doing creates a desire in the individual. The individual says I have an obsession to drink alcohol. In the Swedenborgian sense, the obsession is due to the desire of the entity. We are not suggesting that the Swedenborgian explanation be accepted but rather that we look at the true reality of the situation and deal with the subjective reality in a way that may be helpful to the client. The Amer-

ican psychiatrist deals with obsession and possession as malfunctioning thought processes, hallucinations, or figments of the imagination.
The shaman deals with the situation as if it were due to an 'evil spirit.'
We will discuss both paradigms, each in relationship to the therapeutic
process.

Paradigm 1: The American Psychiatric Paradigm

Patient (P): Doctor, you mean these voices I'm hearing are just in my head?

Doctor (D): Yes, you are creating them.

P: But why would I create them? I don't want to hear them.

D: You are probably punishing yourself for some behavior you have engaged
   in and are unconsciously feeling guilty about it.

P: If this is so, then help me.

D: I can guide you, but the change must come from you. You have to help
   yourself.

P: I know why I feel guilty. It's because a teacher told me that I was responsible for killing my grandmother. I know I didn't do it because all my family
   and friends said so, yet I feel guilty. Please help me.

D: Let's go back into your childhood.

(Six years later, the patient still has the compulsions).

In this particular case the patient was suffering from a form of ago-
raphobia, not in its most intense form, but rather a general fear of
leaving the house and engaging in social activity. The client for years
had evidenced a fear of going out and was suffering from continued
feelings of guilt—guilt feelings that she had actually participated in her
grandmother's death. As a result of the work of another therapist, it
became clear that a fifth-grade teacher had actually accused her of being
responsible for her grandmother's death. She had been living in a small
town, and the death and the circumstances surrounding the death were
known by everyone. The erroneous conclusion was drawn that her ob-
streperous behavior had actually created anger in the grandmother and
brought about a fatal heart attack. From that point on she actually believed that she was responsible for her grandmother's death, no matter
how much her mother, father, and friends told her that she had nothing to do with the death. In this instance we utilized hypnotherapy
with some initial effect. A local priest who was operating in the same
therapeutic framework took over and ultimately cured her of her phobia, whereas years of psychiatric care had no effect.

Paradigm 2: The Reality of the Situation

P: Doctor, do you think these voices are only in my head?

D: Do you?

P: No, why would I want to create them? I don't need them. They are making me go crazy.

D: Then let's suppose they are the result of some outside force which you are sensitive to.

P: Then what can we do about it?

D: We will work together to help you 'exorcise' them. What we mean is that we will help you to get rid of them. Now I want you to say ten times each morning and each night, "Every day in every way I am getting better and better. Every day in every way I am becoming more and more positive. Every day in every way I am becoming stronger and stronger" (the treatment espoused by Émile Coué).

P: Do you think it will help?

D: Do you want it to?

P: Yes.

D: Then it will because you are doing something to actively dispel the voices. Further, when the voices present themselves I want you to ignore them, or if you are alone you might comment openly and loudly: "I will not pay attention to you. You have no control over me. I will not respond to your suggestions. I am stronger than you are." Further, let's assume they are a negative force. You do not have to respond to this negative force. Let us take this negative force and turn it into something positive.

P: How can we do that?

D: By utilizing the energy of the negative force in a positive way. These voices, if they are an outside force, obviously have an energy content. You can use that energy content for your own purposes.

Discussion

This particular case involved a schizophrenic who had been hearing voices for four months. The voices, as usually indicated in the psychiatric literature, were constantly saying evil and disparaging things. "You are a no good asshole," and so on. The patient had been in treatment and each time she went to the therapist, he asked what the voices were saying. We suggest that this actually reinforced, intensified and strengthened her belief in the voices. Within the three-month period of the second therapeutic modality, SET, the voices were totally dispelled. We do not suggest that the voices are even voices, but rather that, if we allow for the fact pragmatically and phenomenologically that these voices may have a reality, then we can do something actively to dispel this reality. If, as in Paradigm 1, we assume that the voices are a figment of the patient's imagination, the patient certainly cannot work actively to dispel the voices when she created them. On the other hand, if the voices are seen as having a reality of their own, then the patient can actively engage in a behavior that becomes effective in helping to dispel them—self-actualized behavior conducive to the enhancement rather than diminution of self-esteem. We are suggesting that the work of Émile Coué should not be disparaged but rather that the power of positive thinking can (and most physicians would agree) be effective in the treatment of psychosomatic illnesses.

In Paradigm 1, the therapist inadvertently made the patient feel crazy, inferior, weak, and helpless. "It's your creation, therefore you must get rid of it." The patient's self-esteem was further threatened by virtue of the fact that she now had to assume that she was creating a maladaptive behavior that was totally of her own making. In Paradigm 2, the therapist gives the patient hope and something to work with. He offers help and provides some tools for self-help, giving her hope.

Some traditional therapists would argue that in Paradigm 1, working through the problem and getting at the 'tangible' symptom or the cause will help in eliminating the problem. They might further suggest that Paradigm 2 will only eliminate the symptom while leaving the cause untouched. If this is correct, they then suggest Paradigm 2 is wrong, since it produces only symptom abatement and does not get at the cause which will then only crop up in another form. At this point, let us examine a case history. This case involved a middle-aged married woman who came to the author with a complaint of constant headaches for the previous three years. She had had an automobile accident three years earlier and was seriously injured, in a coma, and on the critical list for months. There had been severe head injury with some apparent brain damage. After she finally recovered and was able to return home, she was left with these constant headaches. Some of the top neurologists in the country examined her and no one could find the cause or provide an effective therapy. One of the experts even suggested transcendental meditation. Nothing worked and she nearly OD'd on several occasions as a result of inadvertently ingesting too many pain killers. She was constantly in pain and doped up from the various drugs when she came to therapy and asked if hypnosis could help. I suggested we try since hypnosis frequently would work when other techniques had failed. We began and after several sessions the pain was less intense. I continued to work with her and taught her several relaxation techniques that she could do herself. I suggested that this pain had basis in reality, even though the neurologist could not find the focal point, and that by actively using relaxation and Émile Coué's positive affirmations we would be able to eliminate the pain. Eventually, the pain subsided and she now no longer has the pain (it is now ten years). Therefore, Paradigm 2 has validity in this instance in that it was useful in eliminating the pain, where all other techniques had failed. Although the case involved pain as the result of physical insult, it has the advantage of showing the usefulness of this technique for physiological trauma as well.

The development of self-esteem is a process, a function by which the individual can develop a sense of self-acceptance (transcendental) and self-worth (situational). Deviance theories cannot predict the form deviance will take. In the Freudian model, oral personalities manifest normal to gross deviant behavior, and we can say the same for anal or phallic personalities. Further, there are eminently successful people who can legitimately be referred to as oral personalities, who have found a compensatory mechanism that is socially acceptable. These individuals are able to function in society and put on a facade that only the most discerning analyst would be able to see through and be aware of their low self-esteem. Happiness can only come through the development of self-esteem, and an individual cannot be happy when he/she looks into a mirror and says "I cannot accept what I see." This statement begins to clarify what self-esteem really means. The majority of people are not truly beautiful or handsome, because these two qualifying adjectives only reflect the values of the culture. Further, they are qualifiers based on a relatively small minority. Self-acceptance must transcend these superficial cultural values. For example, Marilyn Monroe, who was truly beautiful in the framework of our cultural models, had low self-esteem. Rather than attempt to impute all sort of judgments as to the reason for her suicide, let's instead consider a client who now says "I can accept myself, whereas before when I looked in a mirror I thought I was ugly." Here is a case of an individual who was handsome, had built a delusion that he was ugly, but learns to accept himself.

Science has created a monster when it separates myth (fantasy) from reality. Science, dealing with the objective, tends to set aside the importance of the subjective. Psychiatry and education have fallen into the trap when they posit a value-free superstructure. Psychiatrists, psychologists, and counselors are told not to impose their values upon their clients, and further make no value judgments in regard to the client's behavior. Yet values are the basis of behavior and value clarification would be a crucial part of the therapeutic process; further, values exist dialectically, or as opposites. For example, sexual behavior is largely governed by the values of primary institutions that create the standard for acceptable behavior. In Western culture, premarital sex is still rather frowned upon, suggesting that the individual wait until marriage. However, in terms of ideal and real behavior, we find there is a conflict of values. While valuing chastity before marriage, actively seeking premarital sex for its physical pleasure is the rule of thumb for most men. Here, especially, we see a conflict between eros and agape—spiritual love as opposed to physical love. The importance in the therapeutic situation is not to tell the client that premarital sex is good or bad but rather to discuss its ramifications so that he or she can make a decision concerning behavior within the personal and social parameters of what is culturally acceptable. Certainly many behaviors are unacceptable both individually and socially, for example, rape. To try to exclude values from counseling and education is impossible.

America has created a myth that material possessions are more important than spiritual values, it equates happiness with things and deeds rather than what you are and what you believe. The King Midas myth shows the failure of wealth to buy happiness. Myths and fairy tales, written for children, contain the deep-seated values, the cultural heroes, the fabric of society. In our culture Jesus taught by parables, why not the therapist? Are myth and reality really different? We suggest that by adopting a phenomenological approach, we can say that they are not different but one in the same. This is a case of polor opposites being a false dichotomy, a dichotomy created by Western culture.

COGNITIVE REINTERPRETATION AND THE DIALECTIC IN SET

We want to turn our attention to the law of strife, interpretation, and unity of opposites. A number of years ago a swami from India stressed the point that during every hypnotic session the therapist should make this statement: Your body is a holy temple in which your spirit lives; your body is a holy city in which your spirit resides. It has become ritual with me never to hypnotize a client unless I insert this statement. I would like to comment that although this statement may seem relatively unimportant, it is capable of having important consequences in the therapeutic process. It is not religious, but rather transcends religion. Even an atheist would not take exception to this statement, in that the spirit can be explained as being a transcendental force in the cosmos capable of being put to productive use. It has been my experience that this statement alone can have a powerful effect on building transcendental self-esteem though cognitive reorientation. A number of years ago I worked with a client who came to me for depression. She had been in therapy for a year without benefit. I saw her three times, each time utilizing the 'body is a holy temple' concept. The change after the first session was dramatic and the depression totally abated after the second session. It should be note that she was a very attractive young woman who did believe she was good-looking. In fact, she commented that her previous therapist tried to get her to believe that she was a very beautiful young woman, but her comment was, "This never had any effect upon me. When you speak of my body as a temple, I now feel totally different about myself, and I can accept myself." We will discuss another case to show the powerful effect of these two statements.

Recently I had occasion to work with a young woman who had been raped. She came to me for forensic hypnosis, not therapeutic. The trauma of the rape was so intense that her ability to visualize the rapist's face and features was severely limited and, similarly, vocal recognition/ identification of the rapist was impaired. Our session was geared to helping her remove the barrier so that she would be able to identify the rapist. We discussed the use of forensic hypnosis and I clearly indicated to her that opening these channels would be extremely traumatic and might precipitate a need for immediate and long-term therapy. During the hypnosis process we were able to help her remove the barrier to the memory. More important, as she was describing the sexual experience, she was expression a strong psychic pain through her facial and bodily reactions. At this point I stressed in detail the fact that her body was a temple in which her spirit lived, that her spirit chose her body as its temple, that it was divine and was capable of withstanding the severest trauma. Further, I commented on the fact that her body, as a temple, could not be ravished, that a temple maintains a purity that cannot be destroyed. As I stressed this, I could see a wave of peace beginning to flow over her face and take the place of the pain that she had been expressing. I cannot overemphasize the therapeutic value of the law of strife—interpretation and unity of opposites, for example, that the body is a temple, as opposed to the body as a purely physical structure. I stress the importance of the body, mind, and spirit, a tripartite unification, not the dichotomy of mind and body, which is consistent with modern Western psychological thought. It is only through unity of mind, body, and spirit that the integrated personality can emerge.

Still, one might have a difficult time conceptualizing the difference between the mind and the spirit. Julian Johnson (1939) makes an important distinction between the mind and the spirit. He comments that the mind is a wonderful servant but a bad master. The spirit alone provides power for the mind. The function of the mind is to serve as an intermediary between the spirit and the body. The body represents the physical work and the spirit, the metaphysical. This description can be used in therapy in that is can provide the individual with the power and strength to bring about a change in behavior. The mind has no power of its own, and acts as an automaton through the development of habit formation. We use this analogy when we work in the area of habit change. It is important to understand that habits, once developed, continue under their own volition. The mind is like a phonograph record in which each groove is a habit. Once a groove is cut it is obviously much easier for the needle to follow the groove than to create a new groove. This concept of habit change is important therapeutically, since all behavior is habit oriented. The focus of SET should be to help the client develop the self-esteem necessary to create new habits to take the place of old habits.

In terms of the law of strife, we would like to consider the function of time. Time exists in terms of the past, present, and the future. It is important to keep in mind the old saw that time heals all wounds. One needs to learn how to utilize time to advantage, rather than see it as a barrier to change or productivity. Along with the concept of time is the emphasis on action, a new habit, the elimination of procrastination. Procrastination itself is a form of strife. It provides the basis for social inaction and the continuation of the untoward behavior. The law of strife is concomitant with our emphasis on conflict. It is not conflict which is detrimental, but the interpretation of conflict is crucial. Conflict provides the basis for social change. Inherent within each thesis, is the antithesis leading to a new synthesis or unity.

THE LAW OF TRANSFORMATION

Within the law of transformation of quantity into quality, we suggest than an individual start each day with the idea 'I begin a new day,' meaning that the new day can be set apart from the old day, that the neurosis of the past can be changed into an adjustment for the future. Also, positive thinking suggests that we deal with positive words, that we drop self-defeating words from our vocabulary. This is important in antismoking therapy when we suggest that the client begin his or her new behavior as a nonsmoker. When asked "Would you like a cigarette?", or "Do you want to sit in the smoking section?", the individual should state categorically "I am a nonsmoker," not an exsmoker. It seems as though these two prefixes are similar, non- and ex- both implying an absence of smoking. However, the difference is in terms of focus. A nonsmoker has never smoked, and does not deal with smoking. An exsmoker, in utilizing the prefix 'ex' is constantly being reminded that he or she was once a smoker, and with this constant realization one can easily revitalize the old habit. At this point we give an unusual illustration of dealing with a transformation.

A number of years ago I worked with a client who had developed a grudge against an old friend. The grudge, however, was perfectly understandable and 'rational.' After a number of years of friendship, this individual seduced his wife. At various times during the therapy he would comment on his need and desire for revenge. In a case like this it is extremely difficult to try to find something positive in the friend's behavior. However, in dealing with the concept of the law of transformation, what one can do is to change or minimize the importance of the situation. One session, when he was commenting on the need for revenge and how he had been hurt, I made the comment that obviously this 'best friend' (or exfriend) was still one of the most important people in his life. He became most incensed and demanded to know how I could possibly consider this person important to him when all *he* wanted to do was get revenge and then forget him. We examined this in detail and he was forced to admit that a large amount of energy each day was being consumed with the thoughts of hate that he was harboring. I commented that if this exfriend was not so important, then we could forget him, but, by the very nature of this harboring a need for revenge, he was blowing the situation out of proportion and making someone whom he despised one of the most important people in his life. After this discussion, the need for revenge dissipated, because even the revenge itself was built on the premise of the importance of that person to him. In therapy, one needs to deal with the law of transformation in order to achieve the goal of the functional unity of opposites. The function of goal setting should be considered in the framework of the law of transformation. Goals should always be amenable to change. We have commented that goals themselves exist in a hierarchical arrangement in that we have long-term goals, short-term goals, and intermediary goals. As short-term goals are achieved, we begin to see more and more of the concept of quantity changing quality. Two and two does not equal four, but rather in our development of self-esteem, small units of goal achievement begin to accumulate synergistically. Self-esteem is capable of compounding at greater multiples than the constituent individual units of goal achievement.

THE LAW OF NEGATION OF NEGATION

Turning hate into love, we negate the negative by making it positive. Love and hate are themselves opposing tendencies and operate throughout life. In essence, we could liken love to the positive and hate to the negative. It is of no value to tell a client he could love someone whom he thinks he hates, but rather, by utilizing the law of negation, we can begin to negate the force of the hate by minimizing it. Through the minimization of hate, we can dispel its power and allow love to develop. While we are in the throes of hate, we cannot hate X and love Y simultaneously. Each one of us has a cube of energy, which can neither be created nor destroyed, but neither can it be multiplied within itself. Thus, by negating the negative force, we can utilize the given energy constructively.

"When I experience sadness I will counteract it with laughter." This statement is part of my basic positive-thinking program. It consists of the law of the negation of the negation. We postulate that one can change behavior by turning one emotion into another. We all know that it is not difficult to be feeling good, have someone insult us, and then immediately feel bad. If we can go from the positive to the negative within a matter of seconds (as a result of our interpretation of a given stimulus), then it is equally possible to go from the negative to the positive through our interpretation. The body emits an aura which is made up of magnetic energy. This magnetic energy has various titles: It is the animal magnetism of Anton Mesmer, ode energy of Baron von Reichenbach, and organ energy of Wilhelm Reich—to mention some of the main theorists. From the 1700s to the first third of the twentieth century, we have had philosophers and scientists discussing the negative aspects of human energy and the utilization of this energy in successful therapy. Today, in modern parapsychology, there is an acceptance of this energy which is emitted and can affect us. We speak of this sometimes in terms of 'vibes'—'I felt negative vibes when I walked into the room." Whether we wish to accept this in its totality is not important, but we can utilize the concept as an adjunct in therapy. Again, we look at this in relationship to myths and reality and point out that energies do exist, although we may not understand their origins. Certainly we cannot even begin to comprehend all the cosmic complexities of human energy, but one can utilize the concept with the client, to give the patient a basis of control, especially in relationship to affectual states of consciousness. Energy exists both positively and negatively, and the fact that energy cannot be either created or destroyed but only transformed (an accepted concept of classical physics) is generally accepted and we utilize this fact in counseling. In SET we are constantly aware of the polar opposites; through reinforcement, negative energy can be transformed into positive energy for the benefit of the client. In counseling, we concentrate on the function of helping the client understand and reinterpret his disturbance turning negative energy into positive. This is self-evident, because people who think positively act positively. Negative energy is a functional requisite for the development of neuroses. I saw a client for depression who once commented that she never joined the other workers during the coffee break because she was repulsed by their negativity and what she considered to be cutting remarks directed at her. These remarks might merely consist of, for example, "Well, we certainly haven't seen you in here for a long time," or possibly, "How are you doing, stranger?" These remarks, although not actually negative, were interpreted negatively by the client. Part of her therapy consisted in suggesting that she would be doing a service to humanity by bringing her positive orientation into the lunch room. We suggested that she could make positive remarks about others and that eventually her positiveness would be contagious, and that the others would begin to respond in a like fashion. She did this and, just as we predicted, she not only felt better but the others began to comment on the change in her. We are again dealing with the law of negation of the negation in which two things are operating: One, her negativism caused her to interpret the various remarks as negative, when in reality they were merely part of the coffee break patter one hears. These remarks are not actually negative in themselves but are phrased in such a way that the individual can interpret them positively or negatively; and two, when we are feeling good and a friend says, "Hey Dumbo, what have you been up to?," we interpret this positively, but when we are not feeling good we get angry.

We have discussed the importance of habit in relationship to behavior and in therapy, but we need to look at it again under the concept of the law of the negation. Habits cannot be eliminated, or changed, or broken; once developed, they are permanent, they have an existence of their own but new habits can be developed that will negate the function of the old habit. As an example, with regard to smoking, the individual desiring to change the smoking habit will enjoy breathing clean, fresh air. He will take three deep breaths of clean, fresh air and this will help negate any of the old desire to smoke. Obesity, as a result of excessive food intake, is of particular interest to us under the law of the negation. We find that individuals who join Weight Watchers must usually continue their association with the group if they are to be successful, as is the case with AA or Synanon. AA clearly maintains that an individual is always an alcoholic, must think of him- or herself as an alcoholic, and can remain alcohol-free only as long as he or she has the support of the group. Weight Watchers operates on a similar level, as does Synanon. We would like to point out that, as with Weight Watchers, this often produces the yo-yo syndrome, meaning that people join, lose weight, quit, gain that much back and more, then join again, and the process continues until they end up heavier than when they started. Under the concept of negation, one must realize that as long as an individual is on a diet, he/she is setting him- or herself up for weight gain. In essence, this is saying that a diet itself functions negatively in relationship to weight loss, because the individual constantly is thinking about food. In order to maintain a diet, one must either count calories or be particularly cognizant of the types and amount of food ingested. This particular approach is often self-defeating. Instead of dealing with the habit of overeating, the individual is constantly reinforcing the eating habit through his/her preoccupation with food. In SET, we show the client how to develop a new habit. One cannot break a habit. First, we postulate that weight control, smoking, and other addictions all result from low self-esteem. To deal successfully with these three compensatory mechanisms we must help the individual build self-esteem so that he/she can then take control over his/her life. Certainly, merely to remove one of these habits without building a new habit will not lead to a successful conclusion. Preoccupation with the thesis (being overweight) retards the development of the antithesis, thus preoccupation is self-fulfilling. Focusing on the compensatory mechanism and not the cause only intensifies the problem. Thus, the very behavior which is engaged in to eliminate the compensatory mechanism tends to negate itself and actually creates the antithesis for its own continuation.

It is important under the law of negation to realize that we do not attempt to eliminate a compensatory mechanism by merely eliminating a habit, because the elimination of a habit without the development of a new habit may ultimately lead to the development of a new habit, one that may also be antithetical to the client's desired goal. Our classic illustration was using hypnosis (not hypnotherapy) to quit smoking, which then led to overeating and so on. This particular sequence gives a perfect example of the function of the law of negation. We should never attempt to eliminate a habit in and of itself, but rather, if we wish to change, we want to concentrate on the development of a new habit that will fulfill the need of the old, and be constructive rather than destructive in its outcome.

In the case of neuroses, the individual is usually reluctant to engage in behavior that will eventuate in the elimination of a neurosis. This seems antithetical to the very goal the client has in mind when he enters therapy. Why should he pay for counseling when he, in reality, does not want to give up his old behavior pattern? In reality, it is not that he does not want to give up the old behavior pattern, but that he is afraid of change. Fear of change lies at the very heart of neurosis and a part of the therapeutic process should be discussion of the importance, the nature, and the function of change, to show how change is not threatening by discussing the nature of a neurotic pattern in relationship to its negation, in other words, what new behavior can be established that will not function as a threat but fulfill the need of the old behavior and increase the client's feeling of control. Fundamental to therapy, within our model, is the development of self-esteem. One needs to look at the function of the behavior in terms of its negation, so as to help the client develop his or her self-esteem. We suggest that when an individual's self-esteem is bettered, energy will be expended productively in making choices. We have the choice if we want to take this freedom. We are not bound by the rigid determinism of the Freudian model rather the soft determinism of the Adlerian model, where change is at the very heart of behavior and freedom of choice is one of our options. The function of therapy is to help clients understand and clarify their future options so that their choices can be effective in bringing about a change in behavior that they so ardently desire.

CONCLUSION

In Chapter 5 of *The Social Dynamics of Self-Esteem: Theory to Therapy* (Steffenhagen and Burns 1987), we discussed culture, the social processes, and their impact on self-esteem. We discussed competition as one of the major social processes in the Western Umwelt which hinders the development of good material self-esteem. We indicated that although competition, industrialization, and advertising, among other things, all have a negative impact on the individual and modern society makes it increasingly difficult to develop good self-esteem, these forces can be contradicted in the dialectical framework and be made to function for the individual. Our first law of the dialectic, the law of strife, involves interpretation and the creation of a unity of opposites. It is within the law of strife that these social processes can be interpreted positively by the actor. If we become aware of the function and the mode of advertising, then we can counteract some of the effects of subliminal suggestion. In fact, when the function of subliminal suggestion is understood, the individual can negate its effect through this understanding. Further, advertising itself can be seen like a parlor game, where the individual observes the advertising on television or in the print media and looks for the subliminal content. By becoming cognizant of the various conditions existing in modern culture, we can either utilize these in the development of our self-esteem or become able to negate their negative content. Therapists need to guide their clients, not direct them, in understanding what facets and factors of the Umwelt can be negated or positively utilized.

The law of strife itself implies the positive value of conflict vis-à-vis the conflict of opposing forces which are brought into unity and made productive within the social situation and on the individual level. We have noted how competition makes it difficult to develop good self-esteem by creating constant tension in the social milieu. Competition can be both positive and negative in relation to how it is used and its function. In bodybuilding, success is largely dependent upon having a weight lifting partner. The function of having a partner is both cooperative and competitive. All the authorities in the field comment on this dual social process in the development of a healthy mind and body. The interplay makes cooperation and competition interchangeable. In the therapeutic process, it is important to understand these social processes in the Umwelt so that the individual can utilize them effectively in his or her own behavior. In quitting smoking, two people can reinforce each other, and the positive aspects of the competitive process can be utilized in that each tries to outdo the other in terms of giving in. Sometimes even betting on who would give in first provides the stimulus for the successful elimination of the habit. Social processes, although social by definition, are obviously individual in terms of inception. We find all these processes existing on the individual level, group level, and larger social level. The social processes can be used effectively in the therapeutic process through the laws of strife, vis-à-vis interpretation and creating an innervative correspondence among the opposing forces, creating unity out of conflict.

Within the dialectic we further want to emphasize that, through SET, we have a further dialectic for dealing with conflict on two levels: First, change what we can, and second, accept that which we cannot change. This implies that conflict itself provides the motivation to bring about change or, as we have commented previously in reference to the soft determinism of the humanistic model, we do have freedom of choice and it is within our purview to make choices. We can choose to remain neurotic and unhappy, or we can choose to develop a happy, productive life-style. This choice itself is often precipitated by the conflict. I have worked with a client recently who came to me for the elimination of a cocaine habit. He had developed a very severe cocaine habit over a number of years and was reaching the point of no return, both economically and physically. He had used all his economic reserve and even his job was in jeopardy. After eight sessions of SET, he only had a craving, or urge, once and was able to deal with it successfully. He felt better, and there was a reduction in his alcohol and marijuana consumption, as well. Further, he was sleeping better and his work productivity had increased. The conflict of wanting to do the coke and becoming increasingly aware of the untoward effects provided the impetus which brought him into therapy.

We suggest that conflict is normal, that the goal of therapy should not focus upon a resolution of conflict, but rather on bringing about a functional unity of opposites, an innervative correspondence between opposing forces. This allows for two focuses within the therapeutic process. First, conflict always exists and can never be eliminated in relationship to opposing forces or the contradictory tendencies that are inherent within our personalities. We should not move from one polar opposite to another which could, in essence, work toward the elimination of one of the opposing forces. That force, of necessity, must always remain, but in balance. Certain conflict situations may be able to be eliminated and in doing so, the conflict may provide the motive force to bring about the desired change. If neuroses are habits in conflict with other social values, then it is more than appropriate to help the client to eliminate them totally. If, on the other hand, we find there are certain conflicts in the familial situation or immediate social milieu, then we may not want to eliminate the conflict but to accept the polarity, reducing the social stress. SET, then, focuses on the utilization of the positive function of conflict, created by opposing forces. The goal of therapy is not to focus on the elimination of the neurosis, per se, but to build positive self-esteem. SET should be as productive for the normal as the neurotic.

Second, within SET we can help the client to overcome problems without knowing the nature of them or their exogenous source. Rather, compensatory mechanisms result from endogenous low self-esteem and can be eliminated by the development of their antithesis, good self-esteem. When we build good self-esteem the compensatory mechanism is no longer necessary and is eliminated.

5

Innovative Hypnotic Techniques for Building Self-Esteem

In this chapter we discuss the role of hypnosis as a technique for building self-esteem. We need to clarify the hypnotherapy concept before we can truly understand the role of hypnosis in building self-esteem. *Hypnosis*, a term derived from the work of James Braid, 1848, comes from the Greek, meaning the state of sleep. This itself is a misnomer because even though hypnosis, a trance state, is referred to as somnambulism, or sleep-walking, and resembles deep sleep, hypnosis is actually a state of heightened awareness. Hypnosis is not anything new; it dates back to the Egyptians and Greeks, and probably the process itself was understood and used by many primitive tribes. The war dance of the American Indian was, in reality, a type of hypnosis that brought the braves into a state of frenzy. The beat of the tom-tom also had a hypnotic effect.

Hypnosis is not a therapy but rather a process. It is a process that can be used within the framework of any therapeutic modality, even hypnoanalysis within the Freudian paradigm. The state of hypnosis or the condition is a common-place occurrence and, in reality, when we use hypnosis therapeutically, we are often performing de-hypnosis rather than hypnosis, in other words, we try to undo much that has been inadvertently and detrimentally programmed into the client through mass media communication. We deprogram in very much the same way as deprogrammers work to undo the programming of cult members.

While there are various theories of hypnosis, we subscribe basically to the theory that likens hypnosis to a special state of relaxation wherein the unconscious is capable of being programmed. Since we do not utilize the concept of the unconscious, we will refer to the process as one that can bring about a change in the symbolic construction of the apperceptive mass. For instance, a number of years ago I worked with a client for depression and during the hypnosis pointed out that he was a very handsome young man, intelligent, and that he had much to offer humanity. He commented later that he really began to feel good about himself; he began to see himself as attractive and to believe it, whereas previously many people had made the same statement to him but he would not believe it. We see that within the special state of relaxation he was able to accept an idea unconsciously that he could accept neither consciously nor unconsciously previously in his normal state of consciousness.

All hypnosis is ultimately self-hypnosis in that in order to be hypnotized we must of necessity allow it to happen. We cannot be hypnotized if we do not allow ourselves to be hypnotized, that is, do not allow ourselves to follow the directions of the operator. The hypnotic process is extremely simple in that the technique can be taught to anyone within a five-minute period. However, while the technique is simple and can be learned by anyone from a two-dollar book sold in bookshops, its use as a therapeutic process is not that simple. Many top authorities say they can teach you how to hypnotize in a relatively short period of time but that it would take a lifetime to teach what they know about it. It is just as easy to do great harm by means of hypnosis as it is to do good. Throughout this book we have commented that hypnosis may be a negative influence when the hypnotic techniques are employed by advertisers, especially under the rubric of subliminal suggestion. Suggestion itself is frequently identified with hypnosis but we would qualify this by stating that conscious suggestions are not hypnotic suggestions in that, in order to produce the hypnotic suggestion, a special set of conditions must prevail which we, simplistically, shall refer to as a special form of relaxation, utilized for this purpose.

The literature is replete with many induction techniques ranging from those which are quick, almost instantaneous, to other very elaborate drawn-out relaxation methods. It is our particular position that one of these that is most effective for the development of self-esteem is a relaxation technique in which we can develop ideas through the use of metaphors and the use of visualization techniques to help the individual become relaxed and receptive to the positive suggestions that we make toward the end of the process.

Hypnosis, as we tell the client, is merely "a special form of relaxation which you will experience and will enjoy." It is not to be equated with stage hypnosis or that form demonstrated on TV, stage, and in the movies in which the performer tells his subject: "look into my eyes" or "follow the movement of my gold watch" and immediately the subject falls into a deep trance, unaware of what is going on around him and willing to respond to any suggestion the performer makes no matter how ridiculous or, we might add, detrimental to his physical or mental well-being. There have been many examples of the detrimental effects of stage hypnosis and it is our position that hypnosis wrongly used is capable of doing harm to the client. We premise two basic and contrasting theories regarding hypnosis; first, that you will never do under hypnosis what you would not do morally in a conscious state, and second, that within the hypnotic process you can be made to do things that you would not do under normal circumstances or that could actually be criminal in nature. We believe the second premise to be correct. Given sufficient knowledge about the subject and time, we believe one can construct the social situation in such manner that the subject can be made to do things that are against his or her moral character. For example, there was the case of a psychiatrist who hypnotized his daughter and asked her to disrobe. She refused, indicating that even under the hypnotic trance she would refuse to engage in a behavior that was against her moral predilections on a conscious level. He then hypnotized her again and told her that he was going to give her her physical for college the following month. At this point, she took off her clothes so he could give her the physical examination. It is not important which particular theory is correct but rather to understand that if we use suggestions wrongly, we can do harm. There are many examples in the literature indicating that if a client is asked to perform an act or to do something under hypnosis that he or she is morally predisposed to do, the client will become extremely agitated and possibly snap out of the hypnosis. While all this is true, it becomes evident that it is not hypnosis that is capable of producing immoral behavior, but rather that the nature of the suggestions can elicit deviant behavior. Under hypnosis, on stage, an individual will talk to an empty chair when told that his/her friend is sitting there. He/she will pat a "duck" which is perceived to be sitting on his/her lap. He/she will bark like a dog and run around the stage. These are all examples of behaviors which, although not in the normal repertoire of the individual, are not deemed as immoral or reprehensible by the subject. However, and I frequently ask my students this, if you come home and found a man raping your five-year-old daughter and I gave you a gun, what would you do? The answer from 99 percent of my male students: "I would shoot the bastard." Now let us reconstruct this. Let us assume that we have a subject who is capable of being hypnotized. Let us assume that over a period of time we are able to construct a situation where the individual believes this—that is, we tell him he has just walked into the house, his daughter is on the bed screaming and being raped. We put a gun in his hand and then we stand his friend in front of him and we tell him this person is the rapist. Need we say more?

In my lectures to naive audiences I point out explicitly that hypnosis is a process that is neutral in and of itself, but can be extremely beneficial psychologically and medically. However, depending on its focus and the expertise of the operator, hypnosis can be detrimental. I further make the suggestion to my audiences that they never let themselves by hypnotized by anyone they do not trust, and point out that if they would not go to a surgeon they did not trust, or a dentist, or psychiatrist, why would they go to a hypnotist about whom they have questions?

Frequently I have been asked by my students to recommend hypnotists in other cities and states whom they wish to recommend to their patients. I categorically recommend ASCH (American Society of Clinical Hypnosis) members as a number one choice and members of other highly reputable and ethical hypnosis societies as well. Again, to reiterate, hypnosis is a *process* that can be used beneficially or negatively depending upon the orientation or the skill of the operator. We remind our clients that hypnosis is a heightened state of awareness and that they will be aware of all varied and sundry stimuli that are present to them at the moment, but, that they will always be in control and that they can speak to us at any time during the hypnotic process if they wish. We further comment that, with the use of our relaxation technique, at least 90 percent of our subjects will not be aware that they are hypnotized, often actually denying that they have been hypnotized. We often use an example of one of our clients years ago whom we hypnotized for quitting smoking. He was an individual who had already lost two-thirds of his stomach from ulcer operations and was told by his doctor that he must quit. He had a very stressful job and smoked about three packs of cigarettes a day. I explained the hypnotic process to him, telling him that he would actually be in a state of heightened awareness but that all I required was that he relax during the process. Because of the quantity he smoked, I decided on a three-step process in which he would gradually wean himself over a three-week period. During the hypnosis process the basic thrust of my suggestion was that he would begin to lose the desire to smoke. After the hypnosis session, which was on a Friday, he left the office and was told to return the following week. When he returned he said, "When I left your office I knew I had not been hypnotized and I was quite discouraged because I knew I had to quit and I had not been able to. I lit up a cigarette and continued smoking while I worked throughout the day. On Monday morning when I awoke, for some reason, I wrote on the pack of cigarettes "8 a.m., first cigarette." I was curious to see how many I was smoking although I did not know why. Monday night when I went to bed I found I had smoked ten cigarettes instead of 60. Then I knew I had been hypnotized, whatever that meant."

This is a perfect example of exactly what we mean regarding the framework of the relaxation technique. It seems no matter how much we emphasize this aspect of the hypnotic process (that it is only a form of relaxation they will experience), the subjects bring their preconceived ideas from the movie versions and when they do not lose consciousness, they feel that they have not been hypnotized.

We wish to discuss briefly the function of hypnotic depth of trance. The literature is replete with references to depth, techniques for determining depth, and depth of trance is postulated as being important in the outcome of the hypnotic process. Some of the differences in the results in research projects are being considered due to differences in depth. It is generally conceded that the deeper the trance level, the more effective the hypnotic program for habit change. It is our opinion that depth is not that crucial and that there are other factors that override the depth of trance factor. Some years ago I wrote an article on hypnosis and charisma, suggesting that the element of charisma and rapport are actually more important than the depth of trance. I have found in my research that many of my subjects who only go under lightly receive as much benefit and sometimes more benefit that subjects who are deep-trance subjects.

INDUCTION PROCEDURE

We utilize the relaxation technique but would suggest that the therapist utilize any induction technique that he/she is comfortable with and he/she has found successful in his/her therapy. We will briefly discuss our technique and provide the rationale for it, beginning with an eye-closure technique by having the subject focus on some focal point, ideally the image of an eagle, which we will discuss later in terms of its metaphoric content. We stress the point of intense concentration and the eyes becoming tired, explain the normalcy of this during the induction procedure. We comment that the eyes will become tired—perfectly natural and perfectly normal, a function of eyestrain. Then we proceed with a body relaxation technique which we have modified from the Silva Mind Control relaxation technique. Begin with the scalp and have the subject concentrate on each portion of the body: scalp, forehead, cheeks, relax the muscles around the eyes, bring the relaxation through then neck and into the shoulder, upper arms, elbows, forearms, wrists, hands and fingers, chest, abdomen, hips, thighs, knees, calves, ankles, feet, and toes. In my public lectures I have often been asked if it would not be just as effective to begin with the feet and move toward the head. My reply to this is in the negative because by moving down through the body parts, once we get to the feet, we can further emphasize the importance of all the stress, strain, anxiety and tension flowing out of the bottom of the subject's feet. "You can feel this tension draining away and feel a wave of peace and tranquility begin to flow through your body as the tension drains away." Many of our subjects state emphatically that they can actually feel the stress drain away. As long as the individual feels stress, he/she obviously is not able to reach the same depth of relaxation as a subject who can allow the stress to drain away. At this point we begin a countdown technique. Generally from 80 to 0 and 60 to 0, depending on the subject and whether it's the first, second, or third visit. We comment that with each descending number the subject will be able to allow him- or herself to become even more relaxed. Then we use the visualization technique which again is determined by the subject and the problem, often using the following description: "I want you to visualize a beautiful hot summer day, a small Vermont lake, and there's a boat near shore, very safe, very secure. The boat has a soft mat on the bottom and you're lying on this mat in a swimsuit (if female) or trunks (if male). Looking up into the sky, you can see a beautiful bald eagle gliding effortlessly in the sky. You can imagine the determination in the eyes and the strength in the wings, the power in the talons, and the incredible freedom expressed in the movement of the eagle. You can feel your body absorb the wonderful radiant life-giving energy of the sun, you can feel the warmth, and you can feel the boat rocking gently, ever so gently, lulling you into a deeper, deeper state of relaxation." Before using the lake visualization, it might be wise to check to make sure that the client does not have any unusual fear of water. Another technique we frequently use is the visualization of a person standing at the end of a tunnel. We talk about the tunnel as being warm and safe and at the bottom will be a mat and we have the subject begin to glide gently into the tunnel like a feather shifting back and forth. At various points in the process we comment that he or she can see the light at the top of the tunnel getting darker and then when the client reaches the bottom, he or she can no longer see the light at the top of the tunnel; it is warm and safe—a return to the womb. Safe, warm, and secure. Another visualization would be the movement of walking across a wonderful field, describing the sun, and so on. He/she can hear the birds and the insects, smell the fresh grass, feel the gentle breeze and the warmth. He/she walks across a small bridge, feeling the warmth of the sun, smelling the freshness of the air, and then as the client moves forward he/she begins to ascend a small incline. He/she reaches the top and is standing in front of a beautiful temple with brilliant white marble columns, and begins to walk gently up the steps and enter the temple, basking in the glory of the beauty of the white marble, the pictures, the statuary, the frescoes, the gold, the incredible beauty and purity of the temple. The technique can be geared to a particular client and his or her problem. We will comment on some of this visualization and its impact on the therapeutic process momentarily. We have commented on the use of the eagle as a focal point in beginning the typical eyestrain technique. This particular visualization has various functions: (1) it signifies strength and power, (2) it epitomizes freedom, (3) the eagle itself has spiritual overtones, frequently becoming a symbol within the framework of organized religion. The symbol of the eagle is often seen in the Lutheran church and has resonances in Catholicism. When we suggest and visualize the eagle gliding effortlessly, silhouetted against the clear blue sky, we comment on the eagle breathing clean, fresh air, and that he is free to choose to glide, climb, and soar. The eagle becomes a symbol of freedom. This freedom then becomes important in our dialogue and our analogies and metaphors which we will discuss later. After we get to 0 in the countdown, then we begin the content of our program. This will be discussed in relationship to eight modalities which we utilize separately or in conjunction with each other depending on the nature of the problem.

MODALITY ONE: POSITIVE AFFIRMATIONS

The first modality comes under the heading of positive affirmation. The positive affirmation which we will focus on and use in every session is a modified version of that of Émile Coué: "Every day in every way, you are getting better, better and better. Every day in every way you are becoming more positive, more self-assured, more relaxed, more content. Every day in every way you are becoming better, better, and better. And as you become more confident you will be able to deal with the problems on the material level more effectively, creatively, productively and efficiently" (Coué 1923). A number of years ago I had a student who came to me in a depressed state. I had known him reasonably well and had tried to hypnotize him several times, as he had wished to experience the phenomenon of hypnosis. We were never able to achieve even a light hypnotic trance. He came in one day very depressed and asked if there was something I could do. His comment was that although he realized he was not hypnotizable, he had hoped that I would try it again, because he felt that hypnosis might be able to break the depression. I simply looked at him and told him emphatically that I could cure him in five minutes if he were willing to abide by my prescription, that it was very simple and because it was so simple I felt assured that he would *not* do it. He was eager enough to want help and assured me that he would religiously do what I suggested. I told him about Émile Coué's affirmation and suggested that he take a piece of string, tie ten knots in it, and, in the morning when he got up, say aloud, "Every day in every way I am getting better, better, and better" ten times. Then he was to repeat this procedure in the evening before he went to sleep. Within a week he returned with the depression totally abated, feeling great, and looking exceptionally well. As we read the works of Émile Coué (1923), and biographical references to Coué, we find that these positive affirmations were incredibly effective in healing hundreds of thousands of people in France. When Coué came to this country, the simplicity of his program was not in tune with the American scientific mind, and he was ridiculed and soon left the United States to continue his work in France. We firmly believe that these positive affirmations of Coué can and do have beneficial effects in the hypnotic process and in our work with clients.

MODALITY TWO: BODY AS A TEMPLE

After we finish, "Every day in every way you are getting better, better and better," we say, "Your body is a holy temple in which your spirit lives, your body is a holy temple in which your spirit resides. You are spiritual and physical. You are mind, body and spirit." This particular affirmation has been included in all my hypnotic work, even when I demonstrate hypnosis to audiences. This particular statement was made by an Indian swami who spent a semester at the University of Vermont and gave lectures in the religion department. I had occasion to meet with the swami for an hour after he had given a lecture to the author's class in medical sociology. The author discussed his use of hypnosis in his work with students and in therapy, and the swami's comment was: "Whenever you hypnotize anyone, always make the statement that the body is a holy temple in which the spirit lives, the body is a holy city in which the spirit resides." I have found from experience that this particular affirmation has incredible potential in raising self-esteem, and certainly is effective on the level of ego strength. It builds a foundation for self-esteem that transcends the other two levels. I have found that even atheists do not respond negatively to this statement, because the statement is not doctrinaire or religious, but rather emanates from a spiritual position. The spirit can be equated with the soul, the religious spirit, the life force, the inner essence— whatever the individual wants to call it, is perfectly fine, but he/she sees the relationship between mind, body and spirit, the tripartite division, not a duality as expressed in the American Weltanschauung.

The Western emphasis upon the dichotomy of mind and spirit has evidenced in the Cartesian system, which allows for self-esteem to be developed only on the material/situational level. Self-esteem, which exists only on this level, has no foundation to give it strength and substance. One time one of my clients commented in session (he was an atheist) that he could not get this statement out of his mind and that it seemed to have an incredible impact upon him. I might also mention that when he came in this particular day, his general demeanor was much happier and more content than when he had been hypnotized for the first time. "The body is a temple" is an incredibly powerful force in helping to develop self-esteem. It creates the unity of body, mind, and spirit. Julian Johnson refers to the mind as a servant and comments that the mind is a powerful servant but a bad master. He further suggests that the mind is like a computer. It is neutral, it cannot think, it only functions automatically. The mind is a function of habits. I frequently make use of the metaphor of the mind being similar to a phonograph in which the needle cuts the groove and the groove is a habit. The dialogue would run something like this: "You are made up of mind, body, and spirit. Your mind is a wonderful servant but a bad master. Your spirit is the master and you are a function of mind, body, and spirit working together." Too often in the West we think in terms of mind and body, and when we do this the body functions as a prison; the doors are closed, the spirit is locked inside, and the mind takes over and functions on its own. Smoking, depression, phobias/anxiety are all habits—they are grooves in the phonograph record. The mind cuts the groove and then merely operates in the groove since it has no real power of its own and merely utilizes energy. It can do nothing except what is programmed into it. When only materialistic concepts are programmed into the mind, then it can only function at the level of the material/situational. When we open the door of the body, the prison becomes a temple, the temple is free, and the spirit can become the master and direct the mind. When this happens, behavior can be changed—the spirit provides the strength. Consequently, the power and the strength, like the power of the eagle, lies within the self. You have made a choice to change your thinking, or to quit smoking, and so on. You have made the choice, and the power and the strength to bring about the change lie within yourself.

MODALITY THREE: DISASSOCIATION TECHNIQUE

A number of years ago when I was working closely with two colleagues in hypnosis research, I serendipitously discovered a technique to build self-esteem which I have called the disassociation technique. This particular day we were sitting around talking, and one colleague had commented on reading the works of Theodore Roszak, specifically *Where the Wasteland Ends* (1973). In this book, Roszak mentions the dualism of the 'up and down' concept derived from the work of Newton and his discovery of gravity. We consistently think in terms of up and down. Later in the conversation, he referenced one of the works of Carlos Casteñada, *The Eagle's Gift* (1981). In this book we encounter the concept of out-of-body experience, or astral travel, being used metaphorically. I suggested that we try something different, and they both answered in the affirmative. I began a brief induction technique, merely pointing to each, saying "sleep," and placing them into a light hypnotic trance immediately. Then, after an extremely short deepening technique, I utilized the following statement: "In the West, ever since Newton and his concept of gravity, we constantly think in terms of up and down. We go uptown and downtown. We go up to the office or down to our homes. We have created an up and down paradigm that has locked us into a simple duality. In India, however, instead of dealing with up and down they deal with in and out. In a moment I am going to begin speaking in German and then, at that point in time, your *consciousness* is free to float out of your body. You are free to explore other realms and universes of existence, other realities. You can go as far as you want or stay as close as you want. I remain as your guide. You are totally safe, and at the first word of English you will return to your body feeling stronger, more positive, the spirit bringing back a greater strength with it." At this point I merely began to count in German, to conjugate a few verbs, total nonsense. After about five minutes of speaking German, I then went into English. I then brought them out of the hypnotic trance and asked them what they had experienced. The response was staggering. One of them had travelled around Vermont, going to Rutland, then Burlington, around Church Street, observed people, and his observations of people on Church Street resembled some of the observations recorded by people on an LSD trip in which bodies and heads seem to flow and melt into each other. The other, by contrast, went to London to Picadilly Circus, and there observed the crowds as they passed by. They both commented that this was one of the most intense experiences they had ever participated in. The first had had an out-of-body experience once and immediately saw this as a true out-of-body experience. The other wanted to go through the experience again immediately. The first said he wished to experience it again but not for a day or two, because of its intensity. Shortly after this particular experience, I met the swami, mentioned under Modality Two, and discussed this particular phenomenon with him. His comment was, "This is what people call out-of-body or astral travel. It is a natural state, it is good, it is safe. It is all right to use it, and it will be beneficial in your therapy as long as you use the affirmation of the 'body as a holy temple'." Since then, I have utilized this experience effectively with many clients. The partic-

ular experience they have varies, and many client transcripts are included here (see Appendix A). The transcripts are their comments immediately following the out-of-body (disassociation) experience. In classic
psychology we can tell this a disassociation, and its positive value is
that it allows the mind to slow down, literally to stop, to become a
void, and, after a relatively short period of time, to experience literally
nothing. The very nature of this void itself seems to have incredibly
positive effects. We have had total personality changes resulting from
a single experience out-of-body, and in reading the transcripts it will
become evident that there have been increases in self-esteem as a result
of this technique. I want to suggest that ideally the hypnotist speak a
foreign language, a language unknown to the client. On several occasions I have used German with Jewish students who are familiar with
Yiddish. I have had several students clearly point out that when I would
use a German word that they were familiar with, they would snap back
into this reality. Then when I was using German words with which
they were not familiar, they would immediately flow out of their body
and into another realm of existence, and that the process was a continual in and out from this reality into another reality. This is referenced
in the transcripts. I have used a tape of a swami chanting in Sanskrit
with clients who are familiar with German. The difficulty with the tape
is that you are not the operator and have no control, that is, control in
involving the use of your own voice and its qualities. We do not typi-
cally recommend tapes. And we would strongly recommend that you
observe your client very closely and maintain a strong spiritual bond
during the process.

When I utilize the out-of-body technique with our clients, I do not
discuss this before the session. I have found through my work that if
this technique is discussed before it is utilized in the therapeutic session, the client is usually so 'psyched' up to experiencing the phenomena that he or she negates the possibility of it happening. One of my
clients, whom I tried to take through an out-of-body experience five
times, was unable to achieve the experience. Each time she looked forward to the experience with eager anticipation and then felt disappointed. Finally I was able to take her out but it was essential to hold
her wrist firmly but not too tightly throughout the session, and this
particular sense of security was sufficient to allow her to achieve the
experience. After the session I ask my clients what they experienced
when we began the foreign language. Did they listen? Did they experience a void? We usually let them describe whatever experience they
had. Almost inevitably, 90 percent of my clients do have some experience that is unusual. It may be just a feeling of a real void itself, which
is not possible under normal circumstances, or it could be the white
light which is very often visualized, or in one instance the Christ figure

presented himself. We do not necessarily discuss the out-of-body as an out-of-body or astral experience, but make the decision on the basis of the intellectual background of the client. If we are dealing with a client who is very conversative and does not believe in the astral state, I certainly do not use this concept; we merely call it, "a technique used to achieve a temporary form of disassociation so the mind is able to be still, and afterwards there is a sense of well-being as the result of the stilling of the mind."

MODALITY FOUR: WHITE LIGHT CONCEPT

Through most of our hypnosis sessions we utilize the concept of the white light. In the framework of spirituality, the white light is referred to as the God light, and one will find many references to the concept of the protection of the dual light. First you visualize a golden light around yourself, and this is the Christ light. Surrounding the golden light is a white light, and this is the God light. We find that the Renaissance painters were aware of the phenomenon of the golden light, which we are only beginning to understand. The concept of the golden halo around the paintings of Christ were probably the artist's rendition of the golden aura. Many people have commented that they see golden auras around some of the important religious teachers in India, especially the swamis. Since it is difficult to paint an aura, the concept of the golden halo came into being and was utilized to portray this purity. The golden light is then the Christ light, and again the halo was painted golden. You will find today that in many spiritualist services, the service centers mainly around the concept of the white light, the healing light. Today there are psychic healers whose main technique is the use of the white light. Silva Mind Control also teaches the use of the white light for protecting and healing.

We utilize the white light in terms of visualization. Frequently I start the technique using a small, seven-watt clear light bulb in a clear glass globe. This particular light is very white and is excellent as a focal point for the beginning of the eyestrain technique. Then the concept of the white light as a protection and a healing can be woven into the hypnotic dialogue. Frequently I will begin by saying, "Concentrate on the white light, see nothing but the white light. Think of nothing but the white light. Listen to the sound of my voice and relax and as you visualize that white light, see it as a healing light. Feel the white light flowing over and through your body. Visualize that white light. Use that white light to heal and protect." Sometimes at the end of the hypnotic process, I again will use the white light concept in the bringing out process. "See the white light, positive energy, flowing around and through the body. Feel this white light, the healing white light, the protecting white light, the soothing white light."

The concept of the white light is important; it is easy to utilize in terms of visualization and it gives the client a tool that he/she can use to help him- or herself. Within the framework of dialectic therapy, from a pragmatic perspective, we try to give our clients tools they can use to help themselves. Whether the white light is truly the God light is not important, but if the client believes in the power of the white light, he/she can use this to begin to help him- or herself. It is our opinion that when a client sees him- or herself as a pawn in the game of life he/she is placed at a decided disadvantage in terms of successful therapy. The hard-core determinism of Freud provides clients with little that they can use to help themselves. In the framework of the mechanistic model, the therapist must unravel the fabric of the past in order to find the knot that provides the basis for the neurosis. We cannot stress often enough that we are not concerned with the past in our therapeutic model but rather that we emphasize the goals. We begin with the present to help the client move into the future. We frequently tell our clients that there are many little techniques that they can use to help themselves; in fact that part of the therapy will be a determination of which techniques are most effective for each client, much as in the framework of Milton Erickson. So far, we have discussed four modalities which we utilize in the hypnotic process with all our clients. I should add that thus far none of our clients have resented or found any of these techniques unpleasant or undesirable.

Since writing this chapter I have become acquainted with the concept of the violet light or the light of St. Germain. The violet light is composed of light pink and light blue. The light pink rays are God's love rays or, in more scientific terms, they are composed of cosmic energy which penetrates all matter and operates at an extremely high frequency. The light blue rays are God's healing rays; thus, when we combine the two, we have a light violet ray. We now use the violet rays without referring to the composition of them but clients find the experience very relaxing. We suggest to the client that he or she is surrounded by light violet light and that it is penetrating the body and helping him or her to relax.

MODALITY FIVE: ENERGY

In our therapy we are constantly utilizing the concept of energy and energy transfer. Historically the work of Anton Mesmer in the 1700s can be identified as energy transfer. Mesmer called his particular process "animal magnetism." It is believed that Mesmer's work was actually preceded by Father Hehl in East Prussia in the 1600s. Following the work of Anton Mesmer we have references to energy made again by Baron von Reichenbach. Baron von Reichenbach talked about "ode energy" and identified the positive and negative polarities of energy and said that when people shake hands, the basic reason why a handshake is of short duration is because you have a positive/positive or negative/negative polarity coming together. We know implicitly that when dealing with magnetism in the sense of iron, that negative poles strongly repel and that positive/negative strongly attract. To illustrate, a number of years ago I had a student who was exceptionally sensitive to this particular phenomenon. He was not one to shake hands and was extremely uncomfortable if you were to place your right hand on his right shoulder. His discomfort was so intense that only with the greatest effort was he able to contain himself. More than likely he would hit you. On the other hand, if you placed your right hand on his left shoulder, he did not experience any discomfort. Recently, the aspect of energy and energy transfer has started to become more prevalent in the literature with more research work being done in the area of parapsychology. Following Baron von Reichenbach, Wilhelm Reich developed the concept of "orgone energy" and developed orgone energy boxes which we utilized to cure people with various illnesses including cancer. Wilhelm Reich died in prison in Maine as a result of a persecution for his work with orgone energy, since the AMA did not approve of his work. It is not important whether we call it animal magnetism, ode theory, or orgone energy; the concept of energy and energy transfer is accepted and even crucial in modern therapy.

I have been able to utilize animal magnetism with a number of individuals. You create an energy flow by forming a circuit: place the left hand above the head (three to six inches) and move the right hand over the body (three to six inches) to form a circuit. Individuals who are responsive to energy transfer will become strongly aware of the energy exchange and with their eyes tightly closed will be able to identify any part of the body over which the right hand is moving (three to six inches). Not all individuals are responsivle to energy transfer on a conscious level but all individuals can respond to energy. It is believed today that energy transfer is the basis of psychic healing. Psychic healers are able to extend the energy far beyond the normal, as evidenced by Kirlian photography. In our therapeutic process we utilize the concept of energy figuratively and it is our position that hypnosis, when it is conducted properly by a therapist, does actually contain components of energy transfer. The therapist is able to give energy to the client during the process, even though he is 20 feet away. In another example, I worked with a woman who had had spinal surgery and was having a great deal of pain and discomfort in that area. After the hypnotic session she said she felt a strong soothing warmth in her back directly over the area of surgery. The therapist had no idea which vertebra was operated on and was sitting ten feet away from the client during the hypnotic process.

In the hypnotic process we use the concept of energy, especially when we bring the subject out. I say: "You will feel positive energy flowing through the body; you will feel more and more positive energy flowing around and through the body; feel this energy as it surges through the body." I can actually feel energy being expended during this hypnotic process and it is my contention that when hypnosis is used properly, it contains an element of energy transfer and, therefore, the therapist must be physically and psychically "with it" if he/she is going to do the best job.

MODALITY SIX: REGRESSION

Regression is an important concept in the field of hypnotherapy. A few years ago a new journal came into being called *Hypnoanalysis*. Hypnoanalysis is akin to Freudian psychoanalysis and it should be noted that apparently Freud, although he studied under some of the leading hypnotists of his day, was not proficient in the use of hypnosis. It has been suggested that since Freud could not use hypnosis in regression, he developed psychoanalysis as a technique to replace hypnoanalysis.

Hypnoanalysis, or regression, is the technique used to take the client back in time to the various periods of his or her maturation process. A responsive client can be brought back systematically all the way to the birth process and the author has taken many individuals through the birth process so that they could actually describe in detail what was happening and how they felt. One time while regressing a student, the author hit the age of eight at a particular point in time, June fifteenth, and the subject immediately evidenced severe pain. It was clear that at that point in his life something had happened, possibly some accident, that created a very painful reaction. We did not explore this since one does not want to make the client feel pain, even during the hypnotic process, and so immediately he was taken back to another age. Regression is only used by the authors as a way of getting at some particular situation which has been experienced by the subject, and is of importance in the therapeutic process.

Several times I have taken clients back to help them locate or remember something of importance. To give an interesting example, a student came to me one day asking if I would regress him and help him find his lost knapsack, which contained all his notes for the semester. It seems that on Thursday night he had his knapsack and on Friday it was missing. He did remember going downtown and getting drunk on Thursday night and Friday he was awakened by a guard in the Health

Department lobby, where he was sleeping on the couch. He had no recollection of how he got there and the guard was totally at a loss to explain how he could have gotten into the Health Department, since the building was locked. We took him back and found that he had started out on Thursday night at eight, with a group of friends going downtown to a bar. We progressed until oneA.M., when they returned to the dorm. He and his friends entered one of the suites; he remembered eating a baloney sandwich and then taking off across the campus. We were able to trace his route up through the hospital parking lot. He remembered falling down and when he got up he no longer had his knapsack. Then he proceeded down to the Health Department, climbing the fire escape and finding the fire escape door on the second floor unlocked. He remembered nearly falling off the railing before getting into the building, wandering downstairs and going to sleep on the couch. The author suggested that he go to the "lost and found" at the hospital to see if some one had found his knapsack in the parking lot and had turned it in. He did this; the knapsack was there and apparently the recollection was accurate. We have followed this procedure several times in similar situations.

MODALITY SEVEN: REINCARNATION

Reincarnation regression is also a hypnotic modality that can be utilized by a competent hypnotist. Ostrander and Schroeder in *Psychic Discoveries Behind the Iron Curtain* (1970), comment that the Soviets have done a great deal of exploration research in the area of reincarnation regression. They comment that the Soviets state emphatically that only a very adept hypnotist can actually utilize reincarnation regression and, further, that this particular trance is identified with an EEG pattern of very high wakefulness. The author does not recommend reincarnation regression as a common practice but is firmly in agreement that reincarnation regression can be of extreme value in dealing with clients who seem resistant to the effectiveness of the usual modalities.

We do not purport to suggest that reincarnation should be accepted as a reality by the hypnotist or the client, but that its use can be extremely effective in therapy.

Another very interesting and amusing example relates to a friend of mine who wanted to go through a regression. We took him through the process and he began to relate a life in the 1800s as a gambler in the West. At one point I asked if he carried a gun and he said, no, only a walking stick. Then he went on to relate the fact that not only was he successful as a gambler but that he became a bridge builder with the money he had accrued during his card-playing career. He began to describe a public gathering at the opening of a bridge. Many people were walking across it and, due to a technical error, the bridge collapsed. He said that the crowd became extremely angry and hostile toward him and his comment was, "What in the hell are they mad at me for?" Then, in a rather loud explanation, "Son of a bitch! one of them has just cut off my head!" thus abruptly terminating the session. After the session, he mentioned that he did not carry a gun but that his walking stick came apart and at the end of it was a long pointed stiletto. He laughed at this because he said, "You asked whether I carried a gun but you didn't ask if I carried another form of protection." Then he commented on the fact that, as an infant, his mother said he would never sleep without something covering his neck. He mentioned that even today he cannot sleep unless his neck is protected and than even if he were sleeping in the nude on a hot summer's night he would have to have part of the sheet around his neck or he could not sleep. While this particular idiosyncracy would seem relatively unimportant, the example does show how the reincarnation/regression process can be used to explain behavior that previously had no reference point.

We do not advocate reincarnation/regression, nor do we suggest that anyone believe in reincarnation, but only point out that it is a modality that can be used to achieve a breakthrough when all other modalities fail. It is our belief that only the most gifted hypnotists should attempt reincarnation/regression and that they should be prepared for unusual consequences.

The following example is a case history in which reincarnation was used effectively, not in actually facilitating a breakthrough but in providing time, since the client was extremely suicidal and her reincarnation/regression, for her, provided the knowledge that proved to prevent suicide as a possible behavior. The woman in question was young, intelligent, and borderline anorexic. Her presenting complaint was of hearing voices and of deep depression. She had gone to several counselors but received no help. When she came to me, she was already mildly schizophrenic. One night her husband called and asked if they could come over as she was very depressed and suicidal. It became evident that she was in a very serious condition and I considered calling a psychiatrist friend of mine and having her admitted to the hospital. Before resorting to this, I talked to her husband and suggested I would do a reincarnation regression to see if we could unearth anything significant. Before proceeding, it is necessary to digress momentarily and discuss several factors that had occurred during some of the sessions. During one session I suggested she listen to music during the day but she said no, she couldn't—that during the summer she and her husband had gone to a Taj Mahal concert and that the star was looking at her throughout the concert, although there were several thousand people present. She also told me she especially liked the color black. We began the regression and she had great difficulty regressing and proceeded to give descriptions which resembled a travelogue before coming to describe a small black boy in Africa. He was 12 years old and was playing with bow and arrow up in a tree while watching some of the men build a type of platform for a dance celebration that was to occur soon. I then said, "You are now 13 years of age. What do you see and what are you doing?" She became agitated and, when pressed, said no, she was not 13 years of age because she had committed suicide while still 12. At this point she broke out of the trance in a cold sweat and in severe pain. She then proceeded to say that she would never commit suicide in this life and go through that pain again. At various sessions when she was particularly bad she would say; "If I could only commit suicide and end this pain, but I now know that no matter how bad things seem in this life, it is nothing compared to the pain in the afterlife." The regression did not do anything dramatic in terms of schizophrenia but it provided the time necessary to work with her. At this time, I sent her to a psychiatrist friend of mine and we both worked with her. She never had to be hospitalized. Although we cannot say that she is cured, she is marginally functional and not a ward of the state nor has she ever had to be given any antipsychotic drug.

MODALITY EIGHT: HABIT CHANGE

Habits are amenable to change and positive affirmations and metaphors can be extremely beneficial in hypnotherapy directed at habit change. All therapy should be directed toward change but we are particularly talking about explicit behaviors that one wants to change without therapy. In the case of smoking, one of the visualizations that we utilize is taking the individual into a beautiful temple and describing the incredible beauty in the white marble, the gold, the frescoes, the icons, all this beauty which is part of a Near-Eastern temple. We then comment,

Within this temple there is a brazier and there are leaves burning in it which are creating clouds of smoke. The smoke you see billowing up begins to flow over all the beauty in the temple, and as it flows over the gilt, the frescoes, the paintings, the icons, they begin to take on a dull smudged grey appearance. Then a caretaker comes in and puts out the fire. He throws the brazier outside. He opens all the windows in the temple and clean fresh air begins to flow through. This clean fresh air, as it flows through and over the surface of the inside of the temple, begins to slowly wash away the smudge and dirt of the smoke. Soon the inside of the temple begins to be restored to its original clear beauty. You have chosen to give up smoking and in the same fashion clean fresh air which you breathe in will slowly begin to wash away all the impurities in your lungs. Your lungs which now are a dirty, dull, grey color will slowly but surely begin to take on their original pink beautiful color. Your lungs will return to their original healthy state.

Similar to this, visualizations and metaphors can be used with other habits.

We find that hypnosis can be extremely beneficial for habit change. The point we wish to emphasize the most is that with the use of hypnotherapy to change habits, one should never work with the negative aspects of the habit but only the positive, in other words, in the case of smoking, the therapist must not make reference to the fact that smoking can cause emphysema or lung cancer but rather should emphasize the positive healthy state of the lung and that clean fresh air will bring the lung back to its healthy condition.

We never use hypnosis to eliminate an old habit but rather we discuss and develop the idea of the client forming a new habit. In the case of smoking, the client will develop the habit of breathing clean fresh air and he/she will feel good about this. We point out that he/she has made the choice; he/she is free to make the choice; this choice will benefit the client and his/her close loved ones; and further, this choice will benefit all of humanity because we are all part of a greater whole. We always emphasize the fact that in therapy one can never actually eliminate a habit without replacing it with a new habit. Our emphasis in therapy therefore is on the development of a new habit. This new habit can be interjected by the therapist or the client can help in the discussion of what he or she wants in a new habit to replace the old.

MODALITY NINE: THE UTILIZATION OF RELAXATION TECHNIQUES

Under this section we would include such techniques as TM (transcendental meditation), Silva Mind Control, ultra-depth hypnosis relaxation, and others. We will not discuss the techniques but merely point out that "sound meditation" as developed by Schultz in Germany in the 1930s is an excellent form of self-relaxation. One might want to study books on meditation, possibly go through Silva Mind Control oneself, or study ultra-depth under the workshops given by Walter Sechort, so one can teach one's clients some of the various techniques which they can use effectively to help themselves. We do not particularly advocate traditional self-hypnosis and I absolutely refuse to teach a client self-hypnosis, per se. He will teach clients meditation, various forms of yoga meditation techniques, possibly ultra-depth, but will not teach traditional self-hypnosis. We would strongly recommend that every hypnotherapist study some of the various relaxation techniques and use whatever technique he/she finds particularly beneficial for his/herself since he/she will then be more effective in teaching these to clients.

CONCLUSION

These hypnotic modalities have been discussed rather briefly but provide the basis for a hypnotist to help the client. It is our position that the positive affirmations, the body as a temple, the out-of-body, and the white light, and the energy should all be used or can all be used by the hypnotherapist for the development of self-esteem. These provide the basis for the development of self-esteem on level three, the ego as an epoché reduction, or ego strength. We very clearly point out to our clients that when they develop a spiritual base line for positive self-esteem they are then in the driver's seat and can deal with adversity. Just recently, for example, I worked with a client on weight control. I commented that rarely does one find obesity or overweight problems that do not also have other problems as a base. The client confirmed this in her case and the author then proceeded to discuss the role of self-esteem. I emphasized the fact that her goal would be the development of self-esteem and that when self-esteem is increased, the need for compensatory mechanism, in this instance over-eating and carrying extra weight, and/or other neurotic tendencies will of themselves disappear. The client mentioned that she had been seeing another psychologist and asked if it would be beneficial for the author to get in touch with the other therapist so as to get a background fill-in, which would facilitate his therapeutic focus. I rather bluntly pointed out that I frankly did not care what the background was, that I was concerned with starting at point B, that I found the past of no real consequence in helping the client to overcome neurotic tendencies or to deal effectively with the overweight problem.

We believe sincerely that the focus of all therapy, except possibly cigarette smoking (which may be a habit in and of itself), should be the development of good self-esteem, in that when self-esteem is bettered, the symptoms disappear. We clearly point out to our clients that when they develop good self-esteem, they are in the driver's seat and can make the decisions and follow through with the choices that they wish to make.

Appendix A: Astral Projection Transcriptions

Case 1, Middle-aged Male, College Graduate

Subject saw purple, a bright almost liquid brilliant type of purple, very pleasing. It was also interspersed with flashs of white. Then he saw red lips, as in the lipstick ads, just lips, a continuous flow of red lips. Then two major fears popped into his mind, fears that we had never discussed previously and that seemingly were completely unrelated to the total process. The fear of flying: "I have never flown in an airplane since 1962," then "there was a fear of maintaining my support level. My sales level, i.e., a fear of my sales dropping which, of course, are always possible in the area of sales. These two fears interspersed themselves during this process." He had no sensation of being in the chair until I began to speak English and said he would be coming back, up to that time, he had a sensation of not being here although my voice kept him in touch with this reality.

Case 2, Middle-aged Male, College Graduate

Subject made comment that nothing too dramatic happened; that he was in and out of touch with my voice but felt very good. He then related that the first movement out was in relationship to seeing the colors red and black swirling together. He then lost contact with all feeling of the body except that his hand functioned to maintain the contact with this reality, that is, he had a sensation of his fingers touching the chair and this remained as a source of security. Although his hand remained in contact with the chair, his body lost all sensation and it appeared as if both the chair and his body or his consciousness were floating, with the only contact being through a touch of the hand to the chair. He saw little else except the reference to the color, the sensation of no body, and the need to maintain contact with this reality, vis-à-vis the chair. However, he stressed over and over that he had an incredible sensation of peacefulness: commenting, "I know it is trite, but I feel so peaceful." And over and over, "I feel so peaceful, I did not have a thought in my head, I know I need to buy paint, rollers, but I really can't focus on it, I don't have a thought in my head, I feel so peaceful."

Case 3, Tim, Age 20

Tim: Just as soon as you started talking in that language—German—it was, I recognized it, like right out I didn't feel like my body so I just sort of felt like, spiritual like, out in like a whole huge vastness. It reminded me of the time like when I was just a little kid, and when I had a bad experience from penicillin because I am allergic to it and I sort of had that feeling of being overpowered you know, just like everything was all around me so I just let the feeling come. I wasn't scared about it or anything like that and I sort of felt the same, no recurring fear of that feeling of stuff like. Then all of a sudden I just let the feeling, like, just be there. Well, you know, there is nothing to fear really. I kept listening to that, all of a sudden I was on top of that feeling, I felt like I was just like, it was the first time I was on top of it and it was like right below me, like that, and it just started, then it just went right away. All of a sudden I was just drifing in and out of like, sort of like, dreams. Like I had about three or four like, different American dreams, they weren't German, like that and like a couple of times I remember like my eyes almost started to open. They sort of drifted back, I am trying to remember what my dreams were and I can't remember what they were. There were four, one was not finding something, I can't remember, God, what was it all about?

Steffenhagen: Did you see any colors?

Tim: In my dreams?

Steff: Yes, or as you were going out.

Tim: No, it was just like in the beginning, it was like a lot of darkness, and there was just a lot of stuff. You know, it was just like that, a whole vastness of being in outer space. All of a sudden I was on top of it. I wasn't a part of it anymore. It was just like a huge bomb and I was just sort of lying right on it and all of a sudden, I was just like felt it flowing just right way, just like that, I don't know why that I started like sort of dreams, I just had three or four different types of dreams or like dreams or like thought patterns or something that was going on for sure between me and other people and stuff like that. I don't know, maybe I was thinking of of something that happened today or something like that but I can't remember what they are now. But, I remember it happening like about three or four times that I had like you know, it was like a dream, then all of a sudden it was just like I remember and kept listening to you, then all of a sudden you said that we were going to come back.

Steff: How do you feel now?

Tim: Good.

Steff: Pleasant experience?

Tim: Ah, I feel like being an initial part of it, sort of like bewilderment, then I was just sort of trying to understand what was going on, and then that wasn't happening, so I just let the words just take their place and then like when I couldn't understand, when I was trying to understand when I was feeling all that, sort of like that helplessness type stuff like that and when I didn't try to understand, that's when I got over that, I didn't try to understand, I just said "Oh!" Like that and all of a sudden there was a bunch of people, like, I remember hearing a bunch of people talking, at first, I couldn't understand them. I said, "What the hell's the matter," I couldn't understand them for a minute, all of a sudden they began making sense and I didn't understand them again. Then they didn't make sense and that's the last I heard of them. [It is important to note that there was some talking going on in the outer office, at that time and his mind zeroed in on the English and he came back before I brought him back through the use of the technique.]

Case 4, Jim, Age 21

Jim: With my eyes closed and you're talking to me in a relaxation thing, if you put me, like, usually in a boat and I'm sitting on the water, I can see all these things, trees and water and blue sky. Instead, I saw absolutely nothing but, uh, a color I'd never seen before. It was not black, and it was not dark, and it was no color like the sky, no color like this room with all these blues and browns . . . and all this very confused color that I've never seen before. Very, very strange, and it seemed . . . I can't . . . it's . . . it's coming together of some kind of a, well, not smoke, but the way smoke kind of billows in a very beautiful, very funny color, not black and not dark, but no shape, absolutely none at all. And I was thinking of some very . . . at one point your voice sounded very, very very funny, and things, instead of coming together, going this way, went that way, and then your voice . . . I don't know what you were saying—numbers, or something, because I once took German for three days and it was like the same word over and over again, but your voice changed in tone or, it was maybe harsher, I don't know, and it went the other way, the same color though. It was just the strangest thing. I could see, uh, what was it I saw? Instead of this rounded, it was a box and again it was like things coming out of it, and I started to think again, and it's so hard to describe. And it was black again, it was no longer this new color, I don't know how to describe that color: it was not a dark color either, kind of, but it was like nothing I'd ever seen before, it was neat. And it's really . . . my whole body, I could feel nothing, absolutely nothing at all, until you started speaking English, I could feel my hands were numb . . . but only when you started speaking in English. That was really something. But I was upset when you started speaking English again, because the whole thing ended just like that. That was crazy.

Steff: Any similarities at all to an LSD trip?

Jim: Yes, at the beginning when you started it, I had no idea of its being another language, and as soon as I did the chair went this way—went sideways—and I could feel my bottom going up and all of a sudden—also when you were telling me the difference between up and down, and when you said up it seemed like my whole body went up, and then down, and then it stopped, but when you started speaking in German, the whole—like on tripping which you never get—the whole seat was going like this, coming back down, and then this way, that way, and I didn't see anything except this neat color which is weird, whatever you call it, I don't even know how to describe it. And usually when I close my eyes and it's dark I see squares, which is strange because in tripping things are never square, things are always there's no—like, I can look at a building and the sides will look like wiggling, and in that way it was like tripping, but this color, I've never seen a color like that one before. What a color, I can't even describe it—it was not black. That was really weird.

Steff: Great, see why I'm interested in exploring this?

Jim: I have more energy now than I had when you woke me up. I don't know why. It's just like now, I came in here real tight, I only had three hours' sleep last night and I really came in yawning, and now I'm really so much more awake, my eyes don't feel so heavy, or as tight and stuff, which is usually what happens whenever you do it, I come out feeling really like I just got up you know, and I'm ready for a whole new day. It's different—it was fun . . . I saw a rocket ship with someone in it with a funny helmet on his back, in that color, that one funny color. Now how I would see that there was a ship with a guy in it I don't know because everything was the same color that I can't describe, but yeah, a rocket ship. The ship coming up from the bottom like a jet, and then it went away quickly and got into that, where it wasn't happening . . . there was something else that reminds me that I also saw . . . oh, something you said before reminds me that there was something else . . . in another one I didn't see things like that.

Steff: Okay, let me just read a little bit more of . . .

Jim: Oh, there's something about . . . for just a few seconds . . . it was like . . . I couldn't feel it but I could see fright of some sort, like when your voice changed, I remember it changing drastically. There was like a funny feeling, but usually if I feel fright I feel it right here, but I didn't feel it. The thing went like—woosh—very funny. I don't know if this was before the rocket ship. I don't know why but I saw a rocket ship but it wasn't like a rocket ship we know at all, because it was this tiny thing, but there was this huge man in it.

Steff: Oh!

Jim: I did see a few bars, not a prism, a discrete prism, but just a few bars, but other than that I didn't see anything. Coming back there was this, well, it was quicker than going out. The coming back was this thing all of a sudden and it was back, my sight was the way it usually is, and I could feel myself again and there was a definite difference in wherever I was. It was changed, a different place, a different time, a different thing.

Steff: Then this final point as stated by another subject: "I awoke with an incredibly smooth, warm energy flowing in a complete pattern through and around me. I experienced a beautiful trip which revitalized me and made my day incredibly more enjoyable." Isn't that something?

Jim: Yeah, very similar . . . The last time that I tripped—when I've tripped and it's good and It's visual, everything is rounded and good and moves in that way instead of seeing things as a square they do level off, and the way this was, so therefore it was exactly what I look for in a good trip because it was that flowing and that breathing. And then if it's a colorful trip, I just get off on the colors changing: these colors didn't change, this was a brand new color. So that in that way, that's right, it was, ah, more like ah—it was a trip. At least it brought me to that part of the trip which is fantastic and everything, you know, breathes and stuff, flows and which I haven't seen or haven't done that in so long until just now.

Steff: Notice that I couldn't use those same terms if someone hasn't tripped, and yet, even though he's never tripped, we get the same results.

Jim: I didn't—I can't—smell.

Steff: What about at the beginning.

Jim: The smell, no. The smell at the beginning was from, was in your mouth, maybe. Hum, and then there was this other odor, which was right around when I think I saw that rocket, I don't know, but I saw that. The whole time, almost the whole time when you were speaking in German there was another odor; it wasn't the odor in this room, it wasn't in your mouth either because when you brought me back I could smell that again and then I could feel my body at the same time again. What was the smell? How can I describe it? It was not displeasing at all, but it was just a different smell than the thing was before. That's really making a lot of sense.

Steff: Well, maybe it was a smell you've never smelled before.

Jim: That could be, because maybe it was the smell of that color, which I'd never seen before. That might be it because I can't—it wasn't anything I could say was sweet, like a flower, or a sour odor, not a damp odor, and not a chalky or dry or dusty odor and not minty or anything like that. I couldn't feel that smell because I couldn't feel anything, but I couldn't see the smell either. There was a smell, there was an odor, and that's all I can tell you about it.

Steff: Oh!

Jim: My eyes would be fluttering and I'd want to open them or I'd feel, if he doesn't make me come out, I'm going to come out, but in this no way! No way that I'd get out without your bringing me back out, maybe because you can't feel your body at all. It's just that you don't have control, though you don't have control over what you're seeing, you're in no position to do something you're not told to do, and in that sense, no way I would open my eyes, no way I would do anything because I just wouldn't know to do it.

Steff: You'd just stay there and groove.

Jim: Yeah, that was so different from any other time, just completely different, much nicer. The others felt good, but that was far superior. A little trip in the middle of the day.

Steff: I think the really important thing here, which sounds weird, but I feel very strongly that I am your guru, your guide, and it's more than a physical guide, it's a spiritual guide.

Jim: Okay, I've had dreams in my life that were just like fantasies beyond my wildest dreams, but not like that, nothing like that, I just wouldn't dream something that bizarre, well, not bizarre, but different. In dreams I'm like flying in my dreams, floating in my dreams even tripping in my dreams, I think, but not like that.

Steff: You know there's fantastic dimension to this, and when everybody has the same . . .

Jim: Speed! It's the speed in which you just go from here to there you know, like a supersonic thing to another world, and all of a sudden just to become part of it and leave as quickly, actually quicker, than you got there. It's too much.

Case 5, Tom, Age 20

Tom: I could key into some of the words you were saying because I know some German and know their meaning and that gave me a focal point and I was kind of taken away from that space. I was in and snapped back to what you were saying and interpreting that and when I couldn't understand what you were saying I was able to get back into that space really comfortably and you were kind of background figure but still there. My focus was here rather than with you. There is a real interesting transition on the going out. There was a dichotomy, a part of me was going out and another part of me was going to stay right here and not move and a kind of dialogue between the two reassuring this body that I will go out awhile and be back. Sort of like it's my turn to play, it's my turn. I will go out awhile, then I will be back and it took awhile to get that worked through. I got out and kept my eyes flashing back on this to make sure everything was ok, kind of just checking it out but the place I went to—there was no gravity. There was no physical reality of coming back or going out. Mostly I was off the ground—just walking through the space kind of a dusky space to a bright sunshiny space and a kind of a back and forth. Then I got to looking at it spatially, where I was in relation to this spot and I went around one spot that was very bright and positive and behind me it was less positive and darker. But it was ok about that dark space except that I felt I had stuffed some things back there that shouldn't be there. Kind of a sadness but it was ok. Just before you started counting me out there was a real excitement about jumping off a cliff and a rocky cliff and I took a swan dive off it and rolled in the air. That was just as you were counting me out. I wanted to get into it more. I don't know where I would fall or whether I could propel myself. I couldn't quite get that down, could go with the flow of gravity down but couldn't pick it up and go back up or out as much as I wanted to.

Steff: Share your thoughts? Was the space angular or curvilinear?

Tom: The space was more curved and flowing. A lot of trees in there. I enjoyed that.

Case 6, Dennis, Age 20

Dennis: I experienced basically the same thing as a dream technique under hypnosis, no actual dream only fleeting images. A train of thoughts went through my head, raced through my head, I can't even tell you, there were so many of them.

Steff: See any colors?

Dennis: No identifiable ones, very deep dark and deep.

Steff: See any white?

Dennis: I saw a priest who was white, very comforting. I saw a few people getting shot, very uncomfortable. I saw someone peeking around a corner at me, it was very disturbing. My left toe was very uncomfortable, my left hand seemed tingling, I changed positions [he didn't] I feel good now.

Steff: How do you feel about yourself now?

Dennis: Fine! Good!

Steff: Did you feel your body?

Dennis: Most of the time I felt apart from my body—I felt parts of it at times, like my hand and toe.

Case 7, Peter, Age 23

Peter: I saw orange-red. A black cat's face with sharp pointed teeth which came at me, it wasn't pleasant but it didn't scare me. I then saw white. I felt my hands were sources of energy receptors. I felt my body was very light and almost as though it was going to levitate. I didn't want to come back. It was a super pleasant experience. I felt my body twitch.

Observations: His hands were very cold. A lot of body twitching. Heavy breathing suddenly turned to barely observable breathing just before coming out.

Case 8, Steve, Age 20

Steve: That was weird, because the last time I told you there were a lot of images. This time it was . . . I was . . . It may have something to do with the part I was at today. I was at this incredibly long table with chairs going down both sides of it, lots of chairs, a very long table and that was it. The rest was kind of relaxing and peaceful. I had body pulsations which was kind of neat because I hadn't felt that before. My eyes go like this (he showed movement).

Steff: So you felt your body this time?

Steve: Yeah, I was very conscious of that. I also saw my eyes, the first time I've ever seen my eyes. You know, I was looking at myself. I was about two feet above my body and couldn't go any further. Just before you started to say it's time to come back, I started looking at myself. You always do that. You always take it away too soon. it's time to come back and I say no it's not. (Both laugh.) You didn't uh, you were counting weren't you.?

Steff: A little bit. When you were looking at yourself, where was it from?

Steve: Right here, right next to me, much more. I would have been out here I am sure. It was strange.

Steff: Any other sensations at all?

Steve: No colors, that was what I missed, no colors. A lot of circular movements. A feeling of visual movements. My head was like this (made a movement of his head being on its side). Did I even turn my head?

Steff: No.

Steve: Are you sure? That's interesting because I did. I went like this. I felt myself going back. I rolled over here and then came back again. There was something a little strange this time.

Steff: What?

Steve: I don't know. It was strange though. I ended up getting a little tense. Whatever was around me was pulsating. It wasn't just skin. No color out there. Just a blue eye. My own eye. The first time I have ever seen my own eye before. I have seen the third eye before, that image you get of the third eye but I was definitely looking at myself. I was right next to me. Not very far away. Yeah, you look all right man.

Case 8, Pat, Age 20

Pat: It was really strange. I would zoom in and out. Strange, little stories were going on, strange, my heart started pounding away. It was weird. That was really amazing. I would concentrate, then lose track then something else would come into my head, the last one, I don't know what happened, something made me jump. I don't know what it was that scared the hell out of me. My heart was going a mile a minute.

Steff: So what were the stories?

Pat: They were pretty pointless stories. Nothing cosmic at all, like I was dreaming them, I think it was the deepest I have ever been under. I was super relaxed until that happened. That was good. It was excellent. I felt a little better like about half way through I was relaxed so much like when you first started your incantations (laugh) but it was like I was picking energy, really strange, like I was getting a tingling feeling like I was getting off on something but then it was like stories.

Steff: Did you see anything?

Pat: I saw a car accident and I think that was when I popped out of it. It wasn't a very big accident, a little Pinto.

Steff: Any idea where?

Pat: No, some parking lot. It was weird. I was walking along and the bumper came off the Pinto. It was weird. I had a few other things happen. Maybe I had things on my mind but that was actually like I saw it when it hit it was like I was there.

Steff: Maybe you were.

Pat: That is what it felt like, like I was there. I got really confused like I couldn't get my bearings. It scared me. Then I heard your voice again and I tried to relax. My heart was flying like a dream like you are walking along and stumble and then you will be asleep and put your foot out and keep your balance like when you are falling. That was really good.

Steff: OK?

Pat: When you were talking about getting out of our consciousness, that was about what I was doing. I wasn't really perceiving things differently but like I was cruising around observing but not playing an active role, random things could come in at timed sequences, dumb little things.

Steff: Car accident, like you were there, then when you came back you jerked.

Pat: Did I jerk? I wasn't aware of it. At the beginning I got a real tingling feeling, then no body sensation until I returned.

Steff: Very structured.

Case 9, Mark, Age 21

Mark: Incredible rush. There was a period of about, I don't know, I don't know it was really short but something let go and I just had this incredible sensation of moving at an incredible rate of speed almost like a feeling of something when I am sitting on a train and it goes rushing by a train station. Just sort of looking and seeing another train go zipping by real fast having that incredible rush and then you wouldn't let the rush continue and sort of pulled me back into a really deep relaxed state. But, I felt kind of in this room. Still in that one instance I feel like I lost all sense of reality and then throughout the rest of the experience I was wavering around the perimeter of my body but not making a clean breakaway. It was like I felt a surging upward and flowing back down. Sometimes when I was conscious of you talking in German for a brief moment I felt I had a visual experience of something rushing by me and it was like a very blurred light image, nothing, nothing but this quick whirring.

Steff: What color?

Mark: At one point I felt like an ebbing circle right up here in my forehead between my eyes. It was mostly a feeling of not feeling my body, or not feeling where my body ended and where the chair began and just being in tune with this energy force, energy field that was me and not feeling it confined in my skin. It was just sort of pulsing and I didn't know whether to take that as being out of my body or what. I was grooving on whatever it was.

Case 10, John, Age 24

Steff: What did you think of that?

John: I was as removed from my body as I have yet encountered: I was really; I was just conscious thought rather than my body, when you started talking to me I had a hard time at first to figure out how far away from me you were. I was just pretty high on the hypnosis. The words you were rapping to me, ah, made no sense to me whatsoever, at first several times throughout, I thought you were counting uh! but then uh! then it sounded like phrases or stories or something, it really didn't make sense, then again at times, it sounded like you were counting, you know, uh! say it sounded like you were going up a scale you know, seven something, eight something, nine something or something like that, that was my impression. I have no idea what it was you were saying it sounded like German to me, I don't know anything about German but that's what it sounded like uh, it's frustrating at times, uh! those were my first thoughts.

Steff: What about the consciousness in your body?

John: Like I said, my physical body was a separate entity. I realized it was there, there was no fear of being away from it and yet my existence was a mental state of mind, like I said, there was no fear or up-tightness, I knew my body was sitting in the chair and I knew you were sitting next to me talking to me and yet my thoughts and my energy were contained at a separate space from my body.

Steff: What was it like? out there?

John: I talked to you one time about how I was thinking about you know, that transcendental meditation might be a good thing and I don't know if I told you or not but a couple of years ago, while trying to relax in bed one day, I just started concentrating and I started spacing out and at that point in tme, I had the same sensation that my thoughts were a separate reality away from my body. That's pretty much the way I felt this time, you know, its's a very comfortable place, it was fully aware that it was a part of a whole entity, as a body, but the body part wasn't important it was just that existence was just mental at that point in time.

Steff: Any colors or anything?

John: No, I don't think there were any colors. There wasn't visual thought whatsoever, it was totally auditory as far as I was hearing the words but I wasn't trying to picture what they meant or what they were or anything else as far as I can recall, I had no mental or physical visions of any kind of colors or anything else. Does that deviate off course?

Steff: Yeah, to some extent. A little, it's uh, was it just the sound of my voice or any other sounds out there?

John: Uh. I was just listening to your voice not knowing what to make of it, it sounded very alien, sounded very different and I wasn't seeking to make an analysis of what you were saying. I had no desire, ability, necessity to try and translate or get into what you were saying. I heard you and that was about it, I was questioning myself saying; you know, is he counting, what's he rapping to me about, you know, it sounded. . . .

Steff: I bet it was comfortable out there?

John: My state of mind was comfortable but after a while uh! the words started to a distraction from not knowing what they were, causing the distraction, I guess.

Steff: Did you hear anything else except my words?

John: Uh! I heard the refrigerator kick in once, and I heard some people out in the hall and I didn't pay any attention to it, but it wasn't important or in any kind of sense.

Steff: How did you feel about the whole experience?

John: Uh! I thought that this particular occasion I was as deep as I have ever been, probably deeper, that was when you were explaining the in and out. I don't think that the words you said to me, whatever it was that you had said you know, that you are flying around you know, I mean uh! I didn't get a message from you, it didn't take me anywhere. I was out in space and I heard what you were saying, but you're out in space.

Steff: The problem I think today was the loud talking in the hall.

John: Like I said, I was just floating around. Different thoughts kept going through my mind but it was definitely different from the first time, your voice was confusing and frustrating, the second time around your voice was, just couldn't get any higher, who can make any sense of it but I wasn't looking for it to make any sense. I don't know why I woke up when I did, uh! but nevertheless I did.

Steff: It was the noise, it came banging on the door.

John: I heard the keys come into the lock and I was disappointed in myself that I woke up when I did.

Steff: Well, I wouldn't have kept you under much longer anyway.

John: I don't mean that it was frustrating or it was bad vibes, just that I thought that I was in such a relaxed state of mind that it wouldn't have bothered me. There was no negative vibes or I'm not bumming out or anything, it's just a distraction in my thoughts and was very contrary to where I was at. It was just relaxing, and I was just cruising around.

Steff: Any colors?

John: A sensation of brightness, but no sensation of color.

Steff: Just brightness then?

John: Yeah, uh, uh.

Steff: Like soothing?

John: Like the light, you know. Like the sun or something, you know. I was in a bright star that was shining and it was very relaxing, but I looked for a yellow, and a red but there was none there.

Steff: Why did you look for yellows and reds?

John: Ah! I looked you know, I don't know. I just did. Looked for the brightness of the sun. But then again, I suppose there are no actual reds or yellows, just energy, just light. I was looking for others and didn't find any. I remembered it from the last time, I said do I, no I don't. A girl flashed in my mind, you know, and I don't know why, I mean, uh! while I was in Connecticut I picked up a girl who was hitchhiking who was the younger sister of a girl who goes to school here and went out with a guy I know, but somewhere along the line she popped into my mind, there's no attraction to her or anything else I have no idea why she popped into my mind, but she did. Because I was just around. I was definitely more relaxed than the first time, until the distraction at the end.

Steff: As I said, I wouldn't have let you go too much longer, it's really annoying when you put a sign up and somebody interrupts.

John: It was no fault of yours or mine, I don't know what on the part of that guy's stupidity or whatever, are there any secretaries around?

Steff: No, I think she went out to lunch.

John: So maybe because there's no one around, he just figured he'd be nosey and check out what's going on.

Steff: No, he said he was checking out the building, to see if all the locks were intact, oh well.

Case 11, Dale, Age 21

Dale: I want to think on it, because I don't think of the words for what it was like; it was like something below me, but not in the sense of being below me, so you know what I mean? Another thing that was more . . . I kept going to a different place that was neater than where I was, but where I was saying super, if you can follow that. And I kept getting touches of something. The time—I don't know when it was—but one time I thought, OK, we're going to do this; what are we going to do next? I was anticipating again. I said, God don't do that, and then I got back down and there was a time when I felt like my whole head just went like this (twisting motion). It didn't go anywhere, but . . . I guess it did, but I just kind of felt like my neck went like that, kind of forward and up, and it was like "up there" rather than down here somewhere. I don't know what happened, I guess it came back into line probably somewhere along the line. It just kept going . . . and then I'd come back, like that. And, as you say, with more practice, I get to see whatever it was that was there. I'd get more and more of it each time.

Steff: Was there any form out there?

Dale: The only thing I saw was . . . I saw a baby's face—I don't know where that came from, or what it was doing. And then I saw a baby at a table, with a bottle in its mouth, in a baby's chair. And, uh, the rest of the time I was just kind of floating around. Some different . . . uh, some colors, but mostly just changes in light, dark to light, and things like that, not really . . . it was kind of really animated. And the only weird sensation I had was when you started counting me back, and it was somebody having a vacuum, that's it, it was like someone having a vacuum cleaner.

Steff: Sucking you back?

Dale: I don't know what it was, I really had no idea what it was. All of a sudden I just felt like I was being pulled, and I was like, I was trying to like run, but I couldn't do anything. I was trying like a son-of-a-bitch! All of a sudden I realized I was in a really black place, really dark, and I don't know it was empty. It was like being, I kind of had the feeling of being in outer space but I didn't really see a whole bunch of stars or anything, it was dark but light, but I could see, so it wasn't dark. But then, there was no way I could stop from being . . . I was looking this way and it was just great. And then you said, you hit five, and I just had a sensation boom, I'm here. My whole body became rigid, and I felt my arms were . . . not stiff, but . . . I felt "I'm" here and I just went, Oh shit, I'm here. Shit, I had been so happy. It's weird, because I had no idea I was there. I had no idea I was there until I had to come back.

Steff: Did you have any sensation of form at all out there? Like, any sensation about your body, any sensation about anything about you as a form.

Dale: I had no sensation of me as a form until I was coming back. And then, I didn't see myself as me but I was myself as a body, I guess. I was a body and I was trying to find something to hang on to, snatch onto something (laughter). Until, until the, I was just, the only time I was aware of having any form really was when I felt my head coming . . . like that. Other than that, it was just a lot of light, and real shapeless images, spaceless.

Steff: Any similarity to an LSD trip?

Dale: Uh, yeah, the bit about being—I guess it would be "spaced"—it didn't seem like that when I was there, but I knew where I was when I started coming back because it was just like being up in the sky and coming back down to here. And I was just the same, not the sensation of being pulled back, but all of a sudden realizing where I was . . . God, I didn't like that. I was really mad at you, really was angry. I didn't think you were going to do it: I said, if I can find something to hold . . . but there was nothing. There was light and there were things, but there was nothing I could see or grab and I couldn't run fast enough. It was just like a vacuum cleaner, just like a piece of dirt in a vacuum cleaner—you're not going to be able to do anything about it. Is that the same sensation a lot of people have when they go through this thing?

Steff: Everybody has a similar but different experience, however there is a common denominator in every one who does it.

Dale: There's nothing to it. All you're doing is saying, I guess it's counting in German? Is that what you're doing?

Steff: Partly.

Dale: I really don't know what you're doing; I didn't make any sense of what you're doing anyway (laughter). All of a sudden, I was just—

Steff: You were there.

Dale: Yeah.

Steff: You're the sixth one I've done, and everyone had done the same thing. You're the second who saw a baby. One person saw a ship with a space man in it.

Case 12, Barry, Age 22 (had been hypnotized many times)

Barry: These are my observations of the hypnotic induction technique utilizing the counting of numbers in German, and the suggestion of going "out" rather than up or down. The induction began with the progressive relaxation exercise that we commonly use. At this point I had the usual feeling of being very relaxed and tranquil. I believe the suggestion was given to go out, and the counting began. I would like to make the point that it is difficult to recall the induction process, due to the (deepness) of the trance and rapidity with which the effects took place. From this point on I had partial amnesia of the experience. I cannot recall any further suggestions or comments made by the operator. I did experience a total loss of my general reality orientation, more so than with any previous induction technique. What does stand out in my memory, was the very unusual and unique feeling of my mind flowing with ideas and visualizations It was truly unique in the sense that I did not "will" any specific pictures in my mind or any ideas, they flowed uncontrollably. It was specifically pleased with the vividness and clarity of the visualizations and the creativity of my imagination. The experience was extremely enjoyable and pleasant, but was also frustrating due to the amnesia. I feel that the key to the success of the technique is in the counting. This had the effect of completely disorienting my touch with the outside world.

Case 13, Mike, Age 22

Mike: Well, when I concentrate I get a buzzing in my head—like when my ear is shot off—it just came when you said my consciousness would go out— it stopped and it came back when you started speaking English.
Steff: Any colors?
Mike: Near the end—slow reds and yellows like they were swirling together and traveling backwards, like when you were saying a word—it was like it was being said in my mind.
Steff: How do you feel now?
Mike: Relaxed—not much different—no real difference. I kept getting pictures of other things—I tried to concentrate on what you were saying.
Steff: Any white?
Mike: No.
Steff: Any black?
Mike: I think so—very soothing colors—colors were flowing very slowly and off into the distance.
Steff: Any body feeling?
Mike: One foot felt slightly asleep. I couldn't move anything, getting really relaxed. I feel much more relaxed no anxiety. I feel much better. It was almost like dark, reds and yellows, golds, dark but not preventing my seeing, dark

images. Almost like a total calm peace with myself—at the end. Then, I kept hearing myself say trust—trust him.

Case 14, Chris, Age 22

Chris: I got to the point where I was simply relaxed . . . It was more relaxing as time went on. It was the best right before you said in ten seconds you will awake—I will count from one to ten and at that point I felt at the deepest stage. My mind was completely blank except for the sound of your voice. I was unaware of any of my bodily functions. I was very high—like when I meditate I strive for that point where there is no incoming stimulus and my mind is at a blank stage.

Steff: Experience anything, color?

Chris: Yes, some. There was black. I have my eyes closed—I see a light shade— someone turned the light on. I would come and go. I was super relaxed. It was a good feeling. I am feeling like I just came off a high or something. I feel great.

Case 15, Mark, Age 22 (had been hypnotized many times)

Mark: Throughout the first part of the induction; during the standard procedure I found myself going a lot deeper than I have ever gone before. I haven't been hypnotized for a while now. It was a standard count but when you entered into the second part when you started telling me that we would no longer be dealing with the opposition of up and down but with the opposition between in and out. The first thing I remember when that started to happen I started to have experiences like a hypnogogic—is that correct? Experiences or just before I go to sleep I have quite a bit of flash recurring images but not focusing on any one thing. I got the feeling I was traveling along a road ah— two of the things I remember especially was a row of a couple hundred coffee cups with incredibly rounded glistening edges. This was all during the very first part when you were explaining in and out and I was getting at a place— along the road was a fence blocking the path and from then on things go much more abstract. It wasn't a matter any more of being able to formulate specific images that have reference to objects in this world that I could say I just started projection patterns of extreme colors—beautiful colors on this fence and the fence itself disappeared and I seemed to be free floating—a weightless feeling something I have never felt before. With the standard procedure I always feel heavy. But, this was very weightless . . . Not to have to worry about . . . gravity seemed to play no part in it and I couldn't say I was in a trance—it was something entirely different and if I did project any, the colors were especially purple, purple—bright and prominent and I really enjoyed looking at it and the only time in fact I can remember sharp geometric shapes. A point where two triangles—purple triangles merged were from the right and left fields of my vision merged together and immediately lost the sharp angles—they merged and became a circle and that is the only time I can remember any geometric angles. Geometric angles and edges to a surface were pretty much absent. Seems as though I was dealing more in a kind of flow thing. The analogy I can give is of watching wisps of smoke and how they curl around each other and flow back out but all the time the colors were very vivid and I was never sure of a point of reference. I was never sure if I was sitting in a chair and I was never sure where I was in relation to what I was seeing. That was part of it more than anything else which is something in regular hypnotic techniques I always feel as though I am feeling very heavy and in a deep trance but there is always a point of reference for my thoughts, my projections and my fantasies or my dreams or whatever relates to me in a place either answering questions or having a dream but in this case it seemed relatively absent. I never heard your voice again. I mean I really couldn't hear what you were saying— if you did say anything to me at all until about the count of two when you wanted me to—you said return back in which is very interesting because in regular hypnosis the only time I feel that is when I am going to sleep. Sometimes I have slept when I was very tired. I want to hear your voice but this time I felt a heightened state of around it. I could say it was heightened state of around. I definitely was within this process. I think I would say it was a matter of going to sleep or having a dream. It was very different from that. There is no clear story line, no characters, no points of reference to anything outside of itself. It almost appears as though it was beautiful chaos which I don't have to be striving to bring some order to. I seem to be able to relax within it rather than having to formulate images.

Steff: Did you want to come back?

Mark: I think I did. I don't know how difficult it was to get me back. I remember my body twitching and feeling the weight of my body all of a sudden and it seemed an incredible bulk but that passed very quickly and I feel very good now. What struck me especially was the fact that in the beginning it seemed as though it was a journey rather than a static position. In regular hypnosis you almost feel like a piston. You are in one position. You are constantly moving up or down in that position in that place whereas in this there are no referential points and movement was always out—a journey kind of thing and once that passed there was no problem. I didn't try to say I am moving this way or that way or worrying about coming up or going down. I just seemed to be part of a continual flow.

Appendix B:
Self-Esteem Tests

SELF-ESTEEM SUBTEST I   Steffenhagen/Burns
MATERIAL/SITUATIONAL (REVISED 1983)   (SEI)

ANSWER KEY: (X) Indicates high score of five (5).

Directions: Please read the questions carefully and check the correct box for each question which best indicates the way you feel *most of the time*. Try not to leave any blanks.

1. I seek new challenges.
   (X) Strongly Agree   ( ) Agree   ( ) Neutral   ( ) Disagree   ( ) Strongly Disagree
2. When things go wrong I become very discouraged.
   ( ) Very Often   ( ) Often   ( ) Sometimes   ( ) Rarely   (X) Almost Never
3. When faced with a decision I prefer many choices as opposed to a few.
   (X) Strongly Agree   ( ) Agree   ( ) Neutral   ( ) Disagree   ( ) Strongly Disagree
4. I feel I am as competent as the average person.
   (X) Strongly Agree   ( ) Agree   ( ) Neutral   ( ) Disagree   ( ) Strongly Disagree
5. When I contribute to group discussions I believe my contributions are as valuable as those of others.
   (X) Strongly Agree   ( ) Agree   ( ) Neutral   ( ) Disagree   ( ) Strongly Disagree
6. I am willing to take control of a situation when asked to.
   (X) Very Often   ( ) Often   ( ) Sometimes   ( ) Rarely   ( ) Almost Never
7. I am likely to postpone uncomfortable tasks.
   ( ) Strongly Agree   ( ) Agree   ( ) Neutral   ( ) Disagree   (X) Strongly Disagree

Self-Esteem Test I first appeared in *Hypnotic Techniques for Increasing Self-Esteem* (New York: Irvington Publishers, 1983), p. 212. (Reprinted by permission) Self-Esteem Tests II and III are reprinted by permission from R. A. Steffenhagen and Jeff D. Burns.

8. I prefer to compromise rather than maintain my position.
   ( ) Very Often   ( ) Often   ( ) Sometimes   ( ) Rarely   (X) Almost Never
9. I am intimidated by aggressive people.
   ( ) Very Often   ( ) Often   ( ) Sometimes   ( ) Rarely   (X) Almost Never
10. It is important to me to work at maintaining good physical condition.
    (X) Strongly Agree   ( ) Agree   ( ) Neutral   ( ) Disagree   ( ) Strongly Disagree
11. I would rather have a job I enjoyed than one which paid more, but I didn't enjoy.
    (X) Strongly Agree   ( ) Agree   ( ) Neutral   ( ) Disagree   ( ) Strongly Disagree
12. I like to participate in physical activities with others, even if I am mediocre.
    (X) Strongly Agree   ( ) Agree   ( ) Neutral   ( ) Disagree   ( ) Strongly Disagree
13. I do not like to look in a mirror.
    ( ) Strongly Agree   ( ) Agree   ( ) Neutral   ( ) Disagree   (X) Strongly Disagree
14. Other people think I am physically attractive.
    (X) Strongly Agree   ( ) Agree   ( ) Neutral   ( ) Disagree   ( ) Strongly Disagree
15. Doing menial work makes me feel inferior.
    ( ) Very Often   ( ) Often   ( ) Sometimes   ( ) Rarely   (X) Almost Never
16. At times I enjoy being totally alone.
    (X) Strongly Agree   ( ) Agree   ( ) Neutral   ( ) Disagree   ( ) Strongly Disagree
17. I will support the value system of my profession, even if my own values are dissimilar.
    (X) Very Often   ( ) Often   ( ) Sometimes   ( ) Rarely   ( ) Almost Never
18. I sometimes enjoy wearing clothing which differentiates me from others.
    (X) Strongly Agree   ( ) Agree   ( ) Neutral   ( ) Disagree   ( ) Strongly Disagree
19. I can enjoy being alone in a social situation as much as if I were with my peer group.
    (X) Strongly Agree   ( ) Agree   ( ) Neutral   ( ) Disagree   ( ) Strongly Disagree
20. My inhibitions can keep me from having a good time.
    ( ) Very Often   ( ) Often   ( ) Sometimes   ( ) Rarely   (X) Almost Never
21. The idea of moving to another part of the country frightens me.
    ( ) Strongly Agree   ( ) Agree   ( ) Neutral   ( ) Disagree   (X) Strongly Disagree
22. I tend to be self-confident.
    (X) Strongly Agree   ( ) Agree   ( ) Neutral   ( ) Disagree   ( ) Strongly Disagree
23. People respect me for my lifestyle.
    (X) Strongly Agree   ( ) Agree   ( ) Neutral   ( ) Disagree   ( ) Strongly Disagree
24. I may avoid doing things because of what others would say.
    ( ) Very Often   ( ) Often   ( ) Sometimes   ( ) Rarely   (X) Almost Never
25. I am willing to acquiesce (give in) rather than "cause a scene" in a social situation.
    ( ) Strongly Agree   ( ) Agree   ( ) Neutral   ( ) Disagree   (X) Strongly Disagree
26. I would rather watch social and sports events than participate in them.
    ( ) Strongly Agree   ( ) Agree   ( ) Neutral   ( ) Disagree   (X) Strongly Disagree
27. I take the initiative to meet people in a social situation.
    (X) Very Often   ( ) Often   ( ) Sometimes   ( ) Rarely   ( ) Almost Never

SELF-ESTEEM SUBTEST II   Steffenhagen/Burns
TRANSCENDENTAL/CONSTRUCT   (SEI)

Directions: Please read the questions carefully and check the correct box for each question which best indicates the way you feel *most of the time.* Try not to leave any blanks.

28. Physical appearance can prevent one's ability to succeed.
    ( ) Strongly Agree ( ) Agree ( ) Neutral ( ) Disagree (X) Strongly Disagree
29. I would like to change all aspects of my physical appearance.
    ( ) Strongly Agree ( ) Agree ( ) Neutral ( ) Disagree (X) Strongly Disagree
30. Physical appearance is secondary to peace of mind.
    (X) Strongly Agree ( ) Agree ( ) Neutral ( ) Disagree ( ) Strongly Disagree
31. I would never engage in an unhealthy activity solely as a result of peer pressure.
    (X) Strongly Agree ( ) Agree ( ) Neutral ( ) Disagree ( ) Strongly Disagree
32. The only way I could change an unhealthy habit is if I had others' support to do so.
    ( ) Strongly Agree ( ) Agree ( ) Neutral ( ) Disagree (X) Strongly Disagree
33. If I felt a need to lose or gain weight I would attempt to do so.
    (X) Very Often ( ) Often ( ) Sometimes ( ) Rarely ( ) Almost Never
34. I seem to complain about my health more than the average person.
    ( ) Strongly Agree ( ) Agree ( ) Neutral ( ) Disagree (X) Strongly Disagree
35. The only reason to maintain personal hygiene is to avoid embarrassment.
    ( ) Strongly Agree ( ) Agree ( ) Neutral ( ) Disagree (X) Strongly Disagree
36. I need support from others to adhere to a physical self-improvement regime.
    ( ) Strongly Agree ( ) Agree ( ) Neutral ( ) Disagree (X) Strongly Disagree
37. It is important to pursue intellectual interests to lead a fulfilled life.
    (X) Strongly Agree ( ) Agree ( ) Neutral ( ) Disagree ( ) Strongly Disagree
38. My friends' successes can accentuate my failures.
    ( ) Very Often ( ) Often ( ) Sometimes ( ) Rarely (X) Almost Never
39. If I try hard enough I am able to acquire a general understanding of almost anything I want.
    (X) Strongly Agree ( ) Agree ( ) Neutral ( ) Disagree ( ) Strongly Disagree
40. I usually get all the encouragement I need to do what I want.
    (X) Strongly Agree ( ) Agree ( ) Neutral ( ) Disagree ( ) Strongly Disagree
41. In the long run criticism is always healthy.
    (X) Strongly Agree ( ) Agree ( ) Neutral ( ) Disagree ( ) Strongly Disagree
42. I will explore possibilities that others find useless.
    (X) Strongly Agree ( ) Agree ( ) Neutral ( ) Disagree ( ) Strongly Disagree
43. I am hesitant to bring up a new idea when I feel it is unsupported.
    ( ) Strongly Agree ( ) Agree ( ) Neutral ( ) Disagree (X) Strongly Disagree
44. In a social group I let others make the decisions without me.
    ( ) Strongly Agree ( ) Agree ( ) Neutral ( ) Disagree (X) Strongly Disagree
45. I am willing to change my opinion if and when convinced by others that I am wrong.
    (X) Strongly Agree ( ) Agree ( ) Neutral ( ) Disagree ( ) Strongly Disagree

46. Success, whether it be personal, material, or vocational, cannot be fully achieved if the individual is dissatisfied with him/herself.
    (X) Strongly Agree   ( ) Agree   ( ) Neutral   ( ) Disagree   ( ) Strongly Disagree
47. Inner peace is an essential element of success.
    (X) Strongly Agree   ( ) Agree   ( ) Neutral   ( ) Disagree   ( ) Strongly Disagree
48. Even when things are going bad I can remain optimistic about my life in general.
    (X) Strongly Agree   ( ) Agree   ( ) Neutral   ( ) Disagree   ( ) Strongly Disagree
49. People give me compliments they do not mean and I do not deserve.
    ( ) Very Often   ( ) Often   ( ) Sometimes   ( ) Rarely   (X) Almost Never
50. I believe there is more to my existence than living day to day.
    (X) Strongly Agree   ( ) Agree   ( ) Neutral   ( ) Disagree   ( ) Strongly Disagree
51. Others are usually bragging when they speak of their accomplishments.
    ( ) Strongly Agree   ( ) Agree   ( ) Neutral   ( ) Disagree   (X) Strongly Disagree
52. I am rarely happy when I am alone.
    ( ) Strongly Agree   ( ) Agree   ( ) Neutral   ( ) Disagree   (X) Strongly Disagree
53. Without the opinion of others I would not be able to understand my true feelings.
    ( ) Strongly Agree   ( ) Agree   ( ) Neutral   ( ) Disagree   (X) Strongly Disagree
54. I brag about my accomplishments.
    ( ) Very Often   ( ) Often   ( ) Sometimes   ( ) Rarely   (X) Almost Never

SELF-ESTEEM SUBTEST III
SELF-AWARENESS/INTEGRATION

Steffenhagen/Burns
(SEI)

Directions: Please read the questions carefully and check the correct box for each question which best indicates the way you feel *most honestly* or *most of the time.* Try not to leave any blanks.

55. My goals are clearly established and unambiguous.
    (X) Strongly Agree   ( ) Agree   ( ) Neutral   ( ) Disagree   ( ) Strongly Disagree
56. Right now, in my life, I can identify both short and long range goals.
    (X) Strongly Agree   ( ) Agree   ( ) Neutral   ( ) Disagree   ( ) Strongly Disagree
57. I understand the reasons for my "moods."
    (X) Very Often   ( ) Often   ( ) Sometimes   ( ) Rarely   ( ) Almost Never
58. I get a good feeling when I accomplish a goal.
    (X) Very Often   ( ) Often   ( ) Sometimes   ( ) Rarely   ( ) Almost Never
59. I look for new ways to do things that others find impossible.
    (X) Very Often   ( ) Often   ( ) Sometimes   ( ) Rarely   ( ) Almost Never
60. In situations where personal failure has occurred, much can always be learned, new ideas established, and positive benefits ensue.
    (X) Strongly Agree   ( ) Agree   ( ) Neutral   ( ) Disagree   ( ) Strongly Disagree
61. I never give up even when I define a situation as clearly hopeless.
    ( ) Strongly Agree   ( ) Agree   ( ) Neutral   ( ) Disagree   (X) Strongly Disagree
62. I would work hard for a "better" future reward rather than accept a "lesser" reward now.
    (X) Very Often   ( ) Often   ( ) Sometimes   ( ) Rarely   ( ) Almost Never
63. I am not the person I should be.
    ( ) Strongly Agree   ( ) Agree   ( ) Neutral   ( ) Disagree   (X) Strongly Disagree
64. I sometimes find myself interrupting others while they are speaking.
    (X) Strongly Agree   ( ) Agree   ( ) Neutral   ( ) Disagree   ( ) Strongly Disagree
65. Laws are made to be broken, as long as you don't get caught.
    ( ) Strongly Agree   ( ) Agree   ( ) Neutral   ( ) Disagree   (X) Strongly Disagree
66. Selfish people get the most out of life.
    ( ) Strongly Agree   ( ) Agree   ( ) Neutral   ( ) Disagree   (X) Strongly Disagree
67. Because I deserve the credit for my own ideas, it would be unwise to collaborate with others even if this would increase the speed and likelihood of a significant discovery.
    ( ) Strongly Agree   ( ) Agree   ( ) Neutral   ( ) Disagree   (X) Strongly Disagree
68. Things I find "funny" others find inappropriate.
    ( ) Very Often   ( ) Often   ( ) Sometimes   ( ) Rarely   (X) Almost Never
69. I am easily hurt by things that others say.
    ( ) Strongly Agree   ( ) Agree   ( ) Neutral   ( ) Disagree   (X) Strongly Disagree
70. I find it hard to develop a sense of trust in any relationship.
    ( ) Very Often   ( ) Often   ( ) Sometimes   ( ) Rarely   (X) Almost Never
71. If I hurt someone's feelings unintentionally, I will try to make verbal amends rather than "let it slide."
    (X) Very Often   ( ) Often   ( ) Sometimes   ( ) Rarely   ( ) Almost Never

72. When I am the mediator in an argument between two people, I am objective and impartial even though one may be a friend while the other is not.
(X) Very Often   ( ) Often   ( ) Sometimes   ( ) Rarely   ( ) Almost Never

73. When I have a problem that creates undue tension, I try to relax and gain a feeling of tranquility so I can revaluate things.
(X) Very Often   ( ) Often   ( ) Sometimes   ( ) Rarely   ( ) Almost Never

74. I take the time alone to find the source of my personal and social conflicts.
(X) Very Often   ( ) Often   ( ) Sometimes   ( ) Rarely   ( ) Almost Never

75. When I determine "something is wrong" in my relationship with another, I tend to procrastinate and "let it slide" in hopes it will go away.
( ) Very Often   ( ) Often   ( ) Sometimes   ( ) Rarely   (X) Almost Never

76. There are times when it is better to "get a point across" to someone indirectly rather than directly.
(X) Strongly Agree   ( ) Agree   ( ) Neutral   ( ) Disagree   ( ) Strongly Disagree

77. The truly enjoyable things in life cost money.
( ) Strongly Agree   ( ) Agree   ( ) Neutral   ( ) Disagree   (X) Strongly Disagree

78. I control my temper well and display emotions appropriate to the situation.
(X) Very Often   ( ) Often   ( ) Sometimes   ( ) Rarely   ( ) Almost Never

79. Life is what you make of it.
(X) Strongly Agree   ( ) Agree   ( ) Neutral   ( ) Disagree   ( ) Strongly Disagree

80. I am probably more "defensive" than the average person.
( ) Strongly Agree   ( ) Agree   ( ) Neutral   ( ) Disagree   (X) Strongly Disagree

81. I am quick to provide a witty "comeback" to someone who has insulted me, and when I don't it is because I feel it is unnecessary.
(X) Very Often   ( ) Often   ( ) Sometimes   ( ) Rarely   ( ) Almost Never

Appendix C:
Mapping Strategies

Self-esteem subtest I (material/situational)

Component	Element	Question Numbers
Physical or self-image	Flexibility	1-3
	Status	4-6
	Courage	7-9
Mental or self-concept	Flexibility	10-12
	Status	13-15
	Courage	16-18
Social or social concept	Flexibility	19-21
	Status	22-24
	Courage	25-27

Self-esteem subtest II (transcendental/construct)

Component	Element	Question Numbers
Body construct	Success	28-30
	Encouragement	31-33
	Support	34-36
Mind construct	Success	37-39
	Encouragement	40-42
	Support	43-45
Spirit construct	Success	46-48
	Encouragement	49-51
	Support	52-54

Self-esteem subtest III (reality orientation/integration)

Component	Element	Question Numbers
Social interest	Perception	55-57
	Creativity	58-60
	Adaptation	61-63
Goal orientation	Perception	64-66
	Creativity	67-69
	Adaptation	70-72
Degree of activity	Perception	73-75
	Creativity	76-78
	Adaptation	79-81

Bibliography

Ansbacher, H. L., and Ansbacher, R. R. *The individual psychology of Alfred Adler*. New York: Harper Torchbooks, 1956.

Barnes, H. E. *Social institutions*. New York: Prentice-Hall, 1946.

Barron, F. An ego-strength scale which predicts response to psychotherapy. *Journal of Consulting Psychology*, 1953, 17, 327-333.

Becker, H. *The outsiders*. New York: Free Press, 1963.

Bierstedt, R. Nominal and real definitions in sociological theory, in Gross L. *Symposium on sociological theory*. Evanston, IL: Row Peterson and Co. 1959.

Birx, J. H. *Pierre Teilhard de Chardin: Philosophy of evolution*. Springfield, IL: Charles C. Thomas, 1972.

Branden, N. *The psychology of self-esteem*. New York: Bantam Books, 1969.

Brownfain, J. J. "Stability of the self-concept as a dimension of personality." *Journal of Abnormal and Social Psychology*, 1952, 47, 597-606.

Cassirer, E. *An essay on man*. New York: Doubleday Anchor Books, 1944.

Castenada, C. *The eagle's gift*. New York: Pocket Books, 1981.

Chambliss, W. and Seidman, R. *Law, order and power*. Reading, MA: Addison-Wesley, 1971.

Cohen, A. K. *Delinquent Boys*. New York: The Free Press, 1955.

Cooley, C. H. *Social organization*. New York: Scribner's, 1909.

Corsini, R., ed. *Current psychotherapies*. Itasca, IL: Peacock, 1973.

Corsini, R., ed. *Handbook of innovative psychotherapies*. New York: John Wiley and Sons, 1981.

Coué E. *How to practice suggestion and autosuggestion*. U. S.: American Library Service, 1923.

Davis, K. E. "Near and dear: friendship and love compared." *Psychology Today*. February, 1985.

De Chardin, P. T. *Human energy*. New York: Harcourt Brace Jovanovich Inc., 1962.

Farber, M. *The foundations of phenomenology*. Cambridge, MA: Harvard University Press, 1943.

Fromm, E. *Escape from freedom*. New York: Holt, Rinehart and Winston, 1941.

James, W. *Principles of Psychology*. Vol. 1. New York: Henry Holt, 1890.

Johnson, J. P. *The path of the masters*. Beas: Panjab, Sawan Service League, 1939.

Kardiner, A. *The individual and his society*. New York: Columbia University Press, 1939.

Kennedy, M. C. "Beyond incrimination: Some neglected facets of the theory of punishment." *Catalyst*, Summer 1970, 5, 1-37.

Klagsbrun, F. *Too young to die*. New York: Pocket Books, 1981.

Laughlin, H. P. *The ego and its defenses*. New York: Appleton-Century-Crofts, 1970.

Lettieri, D. J., et al. NIDA Research Monograph 30, *Theories on Drug Abuse*. U. S. Publication, 1980.

Lewin, K. *Resolving social conflicts*. New York: Harper & Row, 1948.

Marx, M. H. *Theories in contemporary psychology*. New York: Macmillan, 1964.

McCann, H. "Self-esteem and social deviance theory," in *Hypnotic techniques for increasing self-esteem*. New York: Irvington Publishers Inc., 1983.

Mead, G. H. *Mind, self and society*. Chicago, IL: Chicago University Press, 1934.

Menninger, K. *Whatever became of sin*. New York: Hawthorn Books Inc., 1973.

Merton, R. K. "Social structure and anomie." *American Sociological Review*, 1938, 3, 672-682.

Lindesmith, A. R. and Gagnon, J. H., "Anomie and drug addiction." Chapter in *Anomie and deviant behavior*, ed. by M. B. Clinard, New York: The Free Press, 1964.

Parsons, T., ed. *Max Weber: The theory of social and economic organization*. New York: Oxford University Press, 1947.

Parsons, T. "Max Weber's sociological analysis of capitalism and modern institutions," in Barnes, H. E., ed., *An introduction to the history of sociology*, Chapter XIII. Chicago, IL: University of Chicago Press, 1947.

Ostrander, S. and Schroeder, L. *Psychic discoveries behind the iron curtain*. New York: Bantam Books, 1970.

Robinson, J. P. and Shaver, P. R. *Measures of social psychological attitudes*. Ann Arbor, MI: Institute for Social Research, 1973.

Roszak, T. *Where the wasteland ends*. New York: Anchor Books, 1973.

Seeman, M. "On the meaning of alienation." *American Sociological Review*, 24: 783-791, 1958.

Sellin, T. *Culture conflict and crime* [Report of the Subcommittee on Delinquency of the Committee on Personality and Culture, Bulletin 41]. New York: Social Science Research Council, 1938.

Snyder, C. "Inebriety, alcoholism and anomie." Chapter in *Anomie and Deviant Behavior*, ed by M. B. Clinard. New York: The Free Press, 1964.

Sperry, R. W. *Science and moral priority: merging mind, brain, and human values*. New York. Columbia University Press, 1983.

Steffenhagen, R. A. "An Adlerian approach toward a self-esteem theory of deviance." *Journal of Alcohol and Drug Education*, 1978, 24: 1-13.

Steffenhagen, R. A. *Hypnotic techniques for increasing self-esteem*. New York: Irvington Publishers Inc., 1983.

Steffenhagen, R. A. and Flynn, J., "Self-esteem and anorexia." Chapter in *Hypnotic techniques for increasing self-esteem*, ed. by R. A. Steffenhagen. New York: Irvington Publishers, 1983.

Steffenhagen, R. A. and Burns, Jeff D. *The social dynamics of self-esteem: theory to therapy*. New York: Praeger, 1987.

Sutherland, E. H. *Principles of criminology*. Philadelphia, PA: J. B. Lippincott, 1947.

Szasz, T. S. *The myth of mental illness*. New York: Harper & Row, 1961.

Taylor, S., Wallon, P. and Young, J. *The new criminology: for a social theory of deviance*. New York: Harper & Row, 1973.

Wilson, C. *The occult*. New York: Vintage Books, 1973.

Wood, G. *The myth of neurosis: overcoming the illness excuse*. New York: Harper & Row, 1986.

Index

About the Author

R. A. STEFFENHAGEN taught at Rochester Institute of Technology from 1955 to 1966, when he went to the University of Vermont, from which institution he retired as full professor in 1988. He has a very diverse background, all of which has contributed to his theoretical work. He is a social psychiatrist with a strong background in phenomenology and demography, and is a clinical psychologist.

He has extensive experience in drug research, has published numerous articles, and has presented papers at national and international conventions. His articles have appeared in the *International Journal of Social Psychiatry, International Journal of the Addictions, Journal of Individual Psychology, Drug Education, American Journal of Psychiatry, Drug Forum, Deviant Behavior,* and *The Indian Journal of Clinical Hypnosis.*

He has been able to apply knowledge from his empirical research to the development of self-esteem theory of deviance and, in turn, to apply this theory to the development of the current self-esteem therapy. He belongs to the American Psychological Society and American Society of Clinical Hypnosis.

He has appeared in *American Men of Science, Who's Who Among Human Service Professionals, Men of Achievement, Distinguished Americans,* and *Two Thousand Notable Americans.*